NEVER A BYSTANDER
Indian Railways in Transition

NEVER A BYSTANDER
Indian Railways in Transition

SUDHEER KUMAR

STERLING PUBLISHERS (P) LTD.
Regd. Office: A1/256 Safdarjung Enclave, New Delhi-110029.
Cin: U22110DL1964PTC211907
Mobile: +91 82877 98380/+91 120-6251823
e-mail: mail@sterlingpublishers.in
www.sterlingpublishers.in

Never a Bystander: Indian Railways in Transition
©2022, Sudheer Kumar
ISBN 978 81 954046 6 7

All rights are reserved.
No part of this publication may be reproduced, stored in a retrieval system or transmitted, in any form or by any means, mechanical, photocopying, recording or otherwise, without the prior written permission of the original publisher.

Edited by: Sanjiv Sarin

Printed in India

Printed and Published by Sterling Publishers Pvt. Ltd., Plot No. 13, Ecotech-III, Greater Noida-201306, U P, India

*Dedicated to the Indian Railways,
which has made me what I am.*

Contents

	Foreword by R. Rajeshwar Upadhyaya	ix
	Foreword by Philip C. Zerrillo	xiii
	Journey of a Thousand Miles ... A Journey I Cherished	xv
1.	Seeds for the Future: Formative Years	1
2.	Challenging Assumptions: Mahakumbh at Allahabad	12
3.	Not Only Heat and Dust: A Decade at Kanpur	14
4.	Fatal but Not Fatalistic: Small Things Make a Big Difference – Firozabad Rail Tragedy	29
5.	Resourcefulness: The Uses of Adversity – Tap Changer, the Heart of the Locomotive	35
6.	Hardiness and Grit: When You Stand Alone – Unprecedented Rains in 40 Years	39
7.	Enabling Learning Agility: Chicago for Simulator	43
8.	Quiet Leadership: The Relentless Way – A Policy Revamp	47
9.	Decisiveness Matters: ARNO Convertor for 50 Years	54
10.	Silo-Bridging: The Heart of Collaboration – Cadre Restructuring Forgotten	57
11.	Last Man Standing: Who Really Matters? Baroda House	62
12.	Where There Is a Will, There Is a Highway: 25 KV Overhead Wires at 7.2 m	64
13.	North Star: The Best Is Often Elsewhere Too – Leadership Development at HEC Business School Paris	71

14.	Mining Insights from the Gemba: The Astonishing Kalka Hills – 1:40 Grade	75
15.	Collaboration Tales: Future Focused Solution Oriented – Nabinagar Power Plant	80
16.	A World Record, Quietly: Carbon Credits	85
17.	First Mover Disadvantage: Not Really – Escalators and Windmills	90
18.	Audacity, Courage and Hope: Madhepura Public – Private Partnership	94
19.	Unintended Consequences: Benefits in Retrospect – Dankuni for Chittaranjan, West Bengal	114
20.	Cutting the Nose, Spiting the Face: Kanchrapara, West Bengal	118
21.	No Deal Is Also a Deal: Tokyo, Japan	121
22.	Acres of Diamonds: Transforming Coal – Dhanbad, the Coal Capital of India	125
23.	Actions Change Destiny: Varanasi and Diesel Sheds	160
24.	Stakeholder Mismanagement: Some Lessons from Train Sets	166
25.	Pygmalion at Play: Empowering People – A Patiala Story	170
26.	Change Architecture I: Inside-Out Transformation – An Indian Story	172
27.	Change Architecture II: Driving Culture of Empowerment	188
28.	Clarion Call: Building Consensus for Major Reforms – Parivartan Sangoshthi	197
29.	The Future Is, Unforgivingly, Now! Private Passenger Trains	207
30.	Brief and Intimate Biographies: Some Alchemist Personalities	214
31.	Other Aspects	241
	Acknowledgements	266

Foreword

Chaotic is a word synonymous with India and the Indian Railways – India's own microcosm. There is a method in the madness says one Shakespearean character. But as you dig deeper you will also notice a madness in the method. The Indian Railways is no single story, no single thing. It is an epic. The size, complexity, nuancing diversity and all the conflicts and opportunities of the Indian epic Mahabharata are here. It is a concretised version of the Mahabharata in full flood – connecting every part of India; connecting every Indian with an array of feelings ranging from joy to anguish to romance; but always nostalgia. We know platforms, stations, train tracks, trains, booking counters, crowds, the feared ticket collector, the wayward ticketless traveller, the crazy-eyed unkempt drifter; the train engine – giant and powerful, inspiring every child with awe and admiration – we know all of this organically in a deeply intimate, deeply cellular way.

What lies behind this magic? What comprises the innards of this stupendous majesty? What happens on the inside? Behind the scene? How does the catering value chain work? The signalling system? On deep, lilac nights, foggy and cold, we have occasionally peered through the window to see a man holding an aged lantern swinging it from side to side – green, luminous, cutting through the dark silence ... who is he? What is his story? Are they everywhere – on all the train-tracks holding a green or red lantern? Or guarding a crossing? And dozens of people like him – nameless, faceless, untouchable, untouched?

The Indian Railways has a soul. It touches you and transforms you in ways you have not noticed. It caters for the nation like no other single entity does. Every day, abundant, relentless, ubiquitous, detached, maternal. Yes, very maternal. The view from the inside is most fascinating as provided by Sudheer Kumar's deeply personal experience flowing into a narrative that engages, instructs, inspires, informs.

Behind the romance of the trains is a science and fact-based, evidence-based mechanism – the one that fathoms operational excellence, supply chain, design thinking and innovation, transformation and change management, crisis management, dissonant stakeholders, strategic thinking, visionary leadership, emotional intelligence, etc. So extensive is the array of themes that the book morphs itself into various *avatars* – transformation at Dhanbad, unprecedented in the Indian Railways; the Public Private Partnership at Madhepura; a decade at Kanpur; and a fascinating array of stories for all readers, including the ones about fracturing out of suboptimal traditional practices – stories of India and Indian Railways in transience.

The book by Sudheer Kumar, rightly titled, *Never a Bystander*, is a remarkable and a memorable addition to the growing corpus of writings on the Indian Railways. His book stands out for a variety of reasons – its racy reading style; the core-content of change and transformation as cases for understanding how things happen at the ground level and how often Western models of management fall short when it comes to dealing with the complexity of the Indian landscape. It is extensive and spans 37 years of Sudheer's experience and all this captured with such candidness as to engross readers from all walks.

The book's appeal to the corporate professional, the senior executive, the probationer, and the general readers is obvious. Sudheer's writing style is intimate but not subjective; it's direct but not un-empathic; it's exhaustive without being exhausting. Its inside out narrative does justice to the readers in that it provides them with a binocular to understand the inner workings of the Railways.

The last four chapters of the book narrate how the transformation journey of the Indian Railways was begun in earnest with participation from all stakeholders. And documents ever so sincerely the transformation agenda of the Indian Railways in this coming decade. It's a textbook example of driving change, even, sometimes against asphyxiating resistance. It is a document of trials, tribulations and triumphs. It is absolutely worth the time invested in reading.

From the beginning, Sudheer Kumar has demonstrated a restless energy that strives to do more and be more. All the narrative comprises a human side and an enterprise side. Since it's drawn from the personal experiences of Sudheer, the two sides sit next to each other, thus giving a holistic perspective.

I met Sudheer Kumar in the context of driving *'emotionally intelligent leadership'* at the Indian Railways. Our meeting at the Rail Bhavan, Delhi and the synergistic energies of the forward looking,

Foreword

utterly humane and exceptional, Chairman Railway Board, Ashwani Lohani, was fortunate. It brought me in touch with the core of the Indian Railways and its admirable people who run this piece of magic with such dexterity and commitment. In the various exchanges that followed, Sudheer Kumar's musings and reflections formed nebulously, at first. Then became crystal clear. A book was born!

The heterogeneity, the expanse, the complexity of the Indian Railways is truly baffling and a portion of that has been astutely captured in this book. An ace professional with deep and reflective experience, Sudheer Kumar brings 31 chapters of delightful engagement. What you will experience is *relentless leadership, quietly.*

R. Rajeshwar Upadhyaya
Visiting Faculty, Leadership and Change Management,
Emotional Intelligence,
Indian School of Business, Hyderabad;
Dean, Academy of Applied Emotional Intelligence;
Polymath and Mythologist Leadership and CEO Coach;
Master Trainer MHS Emotional Intelligence

Foreword

Make an effort with tenacity to make real impact that works and don't just create an impression with deception.

–Ernest Agyemang Yeboah

This book is, at one level, chronicles the professional career of Sudheer Kumar, but the larger story is one of how tenacity, integrity, insight and perseverance can impact the lives of more than a billion people. In my professional career, I have met few people with the strategic brilliance of Sudheer Kumar, and I dare say there are even fewer who have the insight, discipline, drive and persistence to execute their brilliant creations.

This book follows the journey of how a determined young man from a small town rose through the ranks of the world's largest employer to make tremendous contributions to his organisation, society, the people of India, and the resiliency of a nation. Today, onlookers have started to notice many recent changes and improvements in the Indian Railways operations – modernised stations, clean and hygienic commissaries that can be viewed 24/7, GPS tracking of trains and their arrival times, schedules that can be viewed and tickets that can be purchased online at any time by the general public. For employees, the opportunity to view their progress and performance in real-time, diagnose potential safety failures, and perform their tasks with less cumbersome obstacles to overcome have been a welcome relief. The impact of Sudheer's journey shows how some small but important steps can create a huge momentum in an organisation. This book provides the background and reasoning behind many of these changes and their impact.

While small changes can have a large impact and inspire the workforce and management to reach for greater results, the crowning achievements in this book are nothing short of revolutionary. Whether it was reforming of the organisational structure, offering a differentiated passenger experience through privatised rolling stock, or convincing global manufacturers to 'Make in India', one begins to see the impact that an individual can have in this life.

Having met the person and read this story, I would recommend this book for young people to read as they begin their professional journey. A brilliant but humble person, Sudheer mixes anecdotes, industry wisdom and common sense as he tells the story of his journey on the rails of India. The story is both inspiring and a guide to how to conduct one's self.

Philip C. Zerrillo, PhD,
Former Deputy Dean, Indian School of Business, Hyderabad
Professor of Marketing Thammasat University, Bangkok
Author and Public Board Member

Journey of a Thousand Miles ... A Journey I Cherished

Sahawar is a town and a tehsil (township) in the Kasganj district of the Indian state of Uttar Pradesh. It is 100 km away from the cities Bareilly, Mathura, Agra and Aligarh, and is almost 250 km from the national capital, New Delhi, and state capital, Lucknow. The town has a population of about 24,000. The name of the railway station is Sahawar Town (SWRT). It is a part of the Izzatnagar Division of North Eastern Railway. This railway station has recently been connected to the single line electrified network of Indian Railways (IR). The station has just one platform for the 12 trains that halt here.

This is the small township where I started my primary education. I used to live with my maternal grandparents. There was a beautiful Radha Krishna temple on one side and a primary school on the other side of our house. It was quite a beautiful place. Every day, I attended the evening *aarti* (a ceremony in which lights are lit and offered to God) at the temple which was like heaven on earth. The *prasad* (offering) that was distributed after the aarti attracted everyone in the vicinity.

The school was run by an old saintly person. It had a thatched roof and an earthen floor. We sat on the floor. I loved going to school because of my affection for *Guruji* (teacher). There was only one teacher in the school which had about 30 students. The school was very neat and clean. The strict discipline demanded that students compulsorily wore the school uniform and were always punctual. My grandmother used to iron my uniform using an old charcoal fired press. Although the town had electricity, we used a kerosene lamp for studying as electric supply was very erratic.

My grandfather was a doctor and had a small clinic in Sahawar. After school, I always went to his clinic and keenly observed him attending to patients. My grandfather owned a mango orchard. Sometimes we visited the orchard. After his sudden death due to cardiac arrest in 1969, I shifted to my parents' place in Mirganj and was admitted to the sixth standard in Dr Rajendra Prasad Inter College.

Mirganj is a small town in the Bareilly district of Uttar Pradesh. It has a population of about 13,000. I studied here for three years and passed the eighth standard. Mirganj town, which is in the ambit of Moradabad Division of Northern Railway, has a railway station named Nagaria Sadat (NRS). It is situated on a double line electrified route between Moradabad and Bareilly. This station has one platform for six trains that stop there. Mirganj is about 31 km from Bareilly.

Thereafter, I had to relocate and get admitted to Parker Inter College, a Christian school in Moradabad, for my education up to the tenth grade. This was the best school in Moradabad district in Uttar Pradesh. Moradabad, situated on the banks of Ramganga river, was founded by Rustam Khan, the governor under the Mughal Emperor Shah Jahan. The city was named after Prince Murad Baksh, the youngest son of Emperor Shahjahan. Moradabad is 167 km from New Delhi and 344 km from Lucknow.

The city is known as Pital Nagri (Brass City) for its famous brass handicraft industry. It has a population of about 8.9 lakh. The slogan, 'Man is the noblest deed of God' written on the top of the school building inspired me a lot, and I remember it very fondly even today. I passed the 10th grade examination from Uttar Pradesh Board with first division. Overall, 56 students got first division in a batch of about 250 in Parker Inter College. It was one of the best schools I ever studied in. It had a big playground, very large science laboratories, separate for the 10th and 12th grade students.

I went to yet another school, Kundan Model Inter College, for my 11th and 12th grade, in Amroha, a small district in Uttar Pradesh, about 130 km from New Delhi. This school was run by the Sugar Mill (Kundan Sugar Mill) in the town. Amroha has a population of about 2 lakhs. It is famous for mangoes, handloom weaving, carpet manufacturing and pottery making.

The unique thing about this school was that the school management published an annual magazine with a photograph of the 'Best Boy' on the front page. This student was always a graduating student of the school. Basant Singh, the school principal himself selected the best boy based on the performance of the students all through their stay in the school till the 12th grade. Basant Singh was a terror for the students as he lived on the school campus and stood at the gate of the school very often, to ensure that not only the students but also the teachers were punctual.

Yet, he was very kind to the needy students and provided free books and stationery to them. I studied here only for two years, for 11th and 12th, but was selected for the front page of the magazine: 'Best Boy of 1976'. I was the topper in 11th standard. Basant Singh expected me to be the topper of the school even in the 12th standard Board examination. I lived up to his expectations.

Two of us from this school (my friend Vijay and I) were selected by Pantnagar University to pursue Bachelor of Technology course. I got into this university by a lucky chance. I had arranged with Harsh Wardhan Lal for depositing of my 12th grade marksheet with the Registrar, Pantnagar University. Harsh was three years senior to me and had completed BSc from Hindu Degree College, Moradabad. I had come to know him through a common acquaintance, and he became my guide. He was the topper of Rohilkhand University, Bareilly. He was very strong in Physics and Maths. Physics was one of my favourite subjects. I used to meet him to seek guidance and solutions to complex problems in Physics. He was always a great help. His father was a Naturopath of repute in Uttar Pradesh and used to work in Gorakhpur. Very often, he would tell me: 'Wrong living, wrong eating, and wrong thinking' were the root cause of all health-related problems. Naturopathy works on this simple principle.

As soon as I got my marksheet, I requested Harsh to deposit it as he was going to Pantnagar to submit his own certificates. Vijay also gave him his marksheets. I handed him mine, properly sealed in an envelope. Within three weeks, Harsh and Vijay got admission letters from the University. Vijay got admission to BTech (Civil) while Harsh got BTech (Electrical). Vijay had studied with me in 11th and 12th standard. He came from a farmer's family. His father had a big farmland and many orchards.

I did not get any call letter from the University. I waited for another 15 days and then decided to pursue BSc in Physics. But I was quite sad. I had applied only for Electrical Engineering while Harsh and Vijay had applied for all the four disciplines of engineering. In fact, I had obtained higher percentage of marks than Vijay, yet did not get the offer of admission. Quite often, I thought that I too would have got the offer of admission if I had also opted for Civil Engineering. But then, I was not interested in pursuing any other discipline. I had therefore applied only for Electrical Engineering.

Both Harsh and Vijay went to join the University in the first week of July 1976. My mother was quite sad and emotional. My career was taking a turn she was not happy about. Initially, I wanted to study Biology and become a doctor, but my father convinced me not to pursue medicine as medical education took longer and required quite an expense. He had limited means to support.

After seeing me anxious, my father decided to go to Pantnagar and meet the Registrar to find out the reason why I had not got admission. The admission process was still in progress. He carried all my marksheets and other papers. On meeting the Registrar, he came to know that my marksheet had not been deposited. It was quite surprising. But then, on receipt of the marksheet from my father, and looking at the percentage, the Registrar assured him of my admission to Electrical Engineering and handed over the admission letter.

Late in the evening, he came home along with my admission letter. The environment at home suddenly changed. My mother, a God-fearing lady, went to the temple to offer obeisance in gratitude. After two days, I left for Pantnagar. Harsh and Vijay had already joined the University. The first thing I did was to meet them. By then they had come to know the process of admission. Both of them had been accommodated in one room in the Tagore Bhawan Hostel. It was a triple occupancy accommodation. When I reached there, I decided to join them as there was a vacancy in their room. We were united again. I had no bitterness as to why my marksheet had not been deposited with the right officials.

What we later discovered was that the envelope containing my marksheets was dropped in a box kept in the Registrar's office. The admission committee could not link it to my application form. Harsh and Vijay's marksheets were handed over without an envelope and were therefore visible and considered. What a chance!

Pantnagar is a town and a university campus in Udham Singh Nagar district in the Indian state of Uttarakhand. It is 70 km from Nainital. The town is home to the first Agricultural University of India, which was inaugurated by the first Prime Minister of India, Jawahar Lal Nehru, on November 17, 1960, as Uttar Pradesh Agriculture University (UPAU).

Keeping in view the contributions of Pt Govind Ballabh Pant, the Chief Minister of Uttar Pradesh, the University was rechristened Govind Ballabh Pant University of Agriculture and Technology (GBPUA&T).

The University is regarded as the harbinger of Green Revolution in India. 'The prosperity and development of our villages is the prosperity of our nation' is the motto of the University. After independence, development of the rural sector was considered as the primary concern of the Government of India and that is the reason why this University was established. The University has been set up in collaboration with the University of Illinois USA, on the pattern of Land Grant Agriculture Universities of United States, the contract of which was signed in 1959. The University is spread over an area of more than 12,000 acres which makes it the second largest university in the world in terms of contiguous area, the largest being the 'University of the South', Sewanee, USA which has a 13,000 acres campus.

Land Grant institutions in USA are covered by Morrill Acts of 1862 and 1890, signed by Abraham Lincoln, wherein federally controlled land is granted to the institutions, and they in turn can sell the land to raise funds to establish themselves.

I graduated in Electrical Engineering with a Gold Medal. Harsh had fallen out of the competition in the first trimester itself. My own journey was very fulfilling and rewarding. My Cumulative Grade Point Average (CGPA) of 4.972 out of 5.000 remained the highest for the next few decades that I know of. My entire stay at Pantnagar was in Tagore and Patel Bhawan hostels. This had been the most memorable stay due to the favourable climate, food, playground, pattern of education, competencies of professors and the excellent library. Books by American authors were available through the course at a token rental of ₹2 per book. The library was fully air conditioned.

Being the topper of my University, I was offered direct admission by the Indian Institute of Sciences (IISc) Bangalore (now Bengaluru) to pursue MTech in Power Electronics in June 1981. However, a last-minute decision by my family changed the course of my career.

It was a happenstance that while pursuing my MTech at Indian Institute of Technology (IIT) Delhi, I had taken the Combined Engineering Service Examination, conducted by Union Public Service Commission (UPSC), Delhi in August 1981. UPSC is a statutory body and directly reports to the President of India. It was formed on October 1, 1926. The Commission is mandated by the Indian Constitution to appoint candidates for the services of the Union of India and All India Services.

Joining IIT Delhi for pursuing my Masters was also a matter of chance. I had already been admitted to IISc in 1981. The academic session at IISc was to begin in the first week of August 1981 but for some reasons, it got delayed by a fortnight and so I appeared in the entrance exam for Masters at IIT, Delhi on July 29, 1981. The result was declared the next day and I qualified for an admission to MTech. *This was a big turning point in my life.* I joined IIT, Delhi on July 31, 1981.

The Engineering Services Examination was scheduled to start from Saturday, August 8, 1981. Since most of the students at IIT Delhi were taking this exam, I also decided to do so, especially since the examination centre was UPSC, Delhi, which was very conveniently located. I could only prepare for a week. Before coming to Delhi, I had no intention of taking the exam as it would have been impossible for me to do so if I had continued with my earlier plans of joining IISc, Bengaluru. There was no way I could have travelled from Bengaluru to Delhi to take this examination after joining IISc in the first week of August 1981.

I was selected by UPSC and was allotted Railways, the most sought-after service in those days.

Most of my postings over the past 37 years have been unpredictable. However, each assignment brought a new challenge. I have always tried to give a hundred percent of my effort and changed the way the things were being done. I have always tried to question the status quo. My innate desire to learn at each stage of my career, and to do well has continued to guide me all these years. Often, there were departures from the routine in not only accomplishing an assignment but also in thinking through the new processes.

For instance, in the very first posting after the completion of my probation period in May 1985, I handed over approximately ₹10,000 in cash to the supervisors who reported to me, in order to fully empower them to purchase various electrical items. I was completely unmindful of the fact that the Government cash needed to be handled in a much more professional manner than I had done.

A new Area Control Office was being set up at Old Delhi railway station for the Bikaner Division of Northern Railway. This was supposed to improve operational efficiency of the Bikaner Division with one Local Area Control Office for better coordination with the Delhi Division. A lot of cash is required whenever such construction work is done. I thought of distributing this cash amongst supervisors doing the work to give them flexibility to buy whenever and whatever they needed from the market. Consequently, I lost more than two months salary as some of the supervisors could not give details of the expenditure amounting to ₹2,500–3,000. This was a lot of money in 1985. My salary was around ₹1,300 per month. This had to be recouped by seeking help from my parents. It never occurred to me that money given to my own men without keeping a record will not get accounted for when the need to settle the accounts would arise. It was the first lesson of my professional life.

This however did not change my firm belief of trusting my own people in whatever domain and positions I have worked, and probably this has been my greatest strength as well. Trust creates a personal bond between you and your colleagues. Another instinct was to be professionally honest, irrespective of the consequences because that is what would define me as an individual.

I remember that for many years, Electrical discipline had been advocating superiority of Train Sets for passenger travel to reduce journey time and to provide better comfort to passengers while Mechanical discipline had been harping on the merit of locomotive-hauled passenger operations. These two disciplines were adversaries. In August 2016, the Ministry of Railways decided to redistribute work between Mechanical and Electrical disciplines to improve coordination and fast-track decision making, and to reduce disputes.

Pursuant to the new order, electric and diesel locomotives and 25 KV electric traction systems were to be looked after by Member Traction as one unified Traction System, and all Coaches and Electrical Multiple units, Wagons and Train Sets were to be looked after by Member Rolling Stock, as one unified Rolling Stock System.

Prior to the redistribution of work between Members, diesel locos were looked after by the Mechanical wing and Train Sets were looked after by the Electrical wing. Redistribution reduced day-to-day disputes on how much to electrify and how much to run diesel locomotive on Railways. Once this was done, the professional views of each of these wings swapped. It was most certainly unfair. My professional views remained unaltered. My own department did not like my unchanging and original professional stand. I had always believed in calling a spade a spade. After all, it was a matter of professional propriety.

Train Set is a type of train where coaches are self-propelled and such a train does not require any locomotive to haul it. Axles of such coaches are fitted with traction motors to drive them. Their rate of picking up speed is faster than that of locomotives. Technical superiority of Train Set over loco hauled trains is well established and remains so.

Forthrightness gives you the courage of conviction to face the realities without being mired into departmental affinity and remaining in denial by hiding behind a falsehood. This also turned out to be my strength which I have cherished much. But, in the process, you develop enemies within and outside the department. My view has been – so be it.

I remember an event when I was working on the Madhepura project for setting up a new factory in Bihar. A lot of arguments were being put forth in favour of Railways itself doing the maintenance of the locomotives which this factory produced, harping on 'maintenance has been our core competence'.

If something is our core competence, we should be the best in that field. I am afraid we are not. Not for anyone's folly, but the system that does not promote excellence due to siloed working.

Reforms for changing such a work culture are in the offing. The Union Cabinet has already approved a single service for Railways in December 2019 as against the eight services that we have today.

We were finding it utterly difficult to maintain ABB locomotives procured in 1996, just after the warranty of five years was over in 2001, since our technicians and supervisors did not have the required skill-set to maintain high-end technology. I had stuck to my point of view that we must go for a comprehensive solution and look at buying the performance rather than buying the product, and today we have the Madhepura model where the supply and maintenance of locomotives is being done by Alstom. All of us find it as the best course of action today. If I had also been in denial and maintained that we were the best, the Madhepura project would not have succeeded.

I have always believed that I must live the life of my people who work day-in and day-out and keep the wheels of Indian Railways moving. Unless we do that, it would be impossible to change the course of the organisation and make such changes a part of the culture, once practised over a long period of time. I have always respected the self-esteem of one and all, whatever might have been their position in the pecking order.

My first-hand experience with railway accidents convinced me that unless one accepts one's failures, it's not possible to take any corrective action. This gave me the courage not only to face the superiors, but also to guide my staff to accept their share of responsibility and move on. Root cause analysis for any abnormal work will give you the right direction and insights to improve, but if you hide this reality for short-lived gain by not accepting the responsibility, the ultimate responsibility will still be yours. The problem will follow you like a shadow.

When I landed at Dhanbad, I asked my safety officer to log all unusual incidents that lead to safety implications. The statistics of the Division became the worst and we were being criticised. I did not relent. Eventually, it paid rich dividends. In the next financial year our safety record was the best in the whole of East Central Railway (ECR) and we were awarded the safety shield. Truth always prevails.

Working in operations in the two initial years of my career really paid rich dividends. I attribute this to the changed attitude of the staff working under me. This is very vital for an organisation which runs 24x7x365, where truthful reporting enables the top management to take a particular course of action, whereas hiding the facts will change the course of action.

During my entire career, new designs evolved with active collaboration of the people who were maintaining the rolling stock.

A new maintenance philosophy evolved from my desire to improve the asset reliability. New predictive maintenance techniques were established. All this has now become part of a standard protocol in Railways. This is very satisfying. Old design rolling stock was phased out much before the Codal (i.e., as laid in Railways code of practice) life, which improved Railways operation. All this was done though it was not exactly in line with the laid down policies. But everybody supported it as the passion to perform was extremely high and the intent was right.

New maintenance and operating regimes were put in place. This has helped the organisation in an unprecedented manner. New practices have become the new culture of maintenance of rolling stock.

Training of drivers has been systematically improved with the induction of simulators. The international exposure that I got has been one of the main driving forces to evolve new practices in Railways. Partnership with the OEMs of technologies and setting up a locomotive factory with private sector investment to produce state-of-the-art locomotives and to create benchmarks for the organisation to upgrade itself have been a hugely satisfying endeavour.

A new power plant has been set up at Nabinagar to generate electricity for the traction requirement of Railways. Procurement of major sub-systems based on the concept of Life Cycle Cost (LCC) has become a new normal for Indian Railways, which has systematically helped in enhancing the production of locomotives in Railways own factories.

Manufacturing electric locomotives without any labour unrest in a factory which had been manufacturing diesel locomotives since inception has been a transformative reality. What a smooth transition took place at Varanasi! The Diesel Locomotive Works (DLW) at Varanasi now manufactures electric locomotives.

There can be no other higher priority for a transport organisation like Railways than safety. This triggered a huge infrastructure development on Dhanbad Division where I worked as Divisional Railway Manager. During my two years of tenure in this Division, the capacity of freight traffic catapulted from a stagnant level of about 82 million tonnes to 100 million tonnes.

Then came the big opportunity of transforming the Indian Railways, focussing on process, structure and cultural reforms in order to improve service delivery – something that had not been attempted over the last 4–5 decades. The field units were handsomely empowered to have complete autonomy in their area of influence not only to improve rail operations but also to improve safety, punctuality and cleanliness at stations. This also led to improved healthcare and employee satisfaction. Human resource development has been one of the key areas for improvement and hence adequate empowerment and delegation to various Centralised Training Institutes were undertaken in mission mode.

The recent initiative of opening the Rail sector to private investment to run passenger trains is in the pipeline. I will be delighted to see it succeed.

This book attempts to bring out my journey in detail. Individuals, no matter how competent or charismatic, never have all the resources needed to overcome tradition and inertia and bring change, especially in a huge organisation like the Indian Railways. Collaboration with people at all levels has been my guiding mantra all through this journey.

Control over emotions and senses, being level-headed and tranquil under all circumstances, and concern for all has always been with me through thick-and-thin. Determination and enthusiasm in whatever I have done, and the pleasure of the journey of doing has been hugely motivating.

Things which are not in our control, happen in a flash like an earthquake without giving any warning or inkling, but what can be done to manage the adversity is fully within your control, provided you are able to keep a balance, and are in complete command of the situation without being carried away by emotions that paralyse you. Adversity may turn into an opportunity.

I have tried to bring out these facts in this book, but with no intent of casting even an iota of aspersion against anybody. I did want to express freely for the sake of clarifying the dynamics of the organisation. What is right and what is wrong can be inferred by the reader. Descriptions, however, have to be taken with a pinch of salt. I would like to apologise upfront, in the beginning itself, if someone is hurt from my actions. These are, after all, my personal experiences and personal views.

Sudheer Kumar
Former Additional Member Indian Railway Board

Seeds for the Future: Formative Years

Although, I had joined IIT Delhi, foregoing my place at IISc Bengaluru, I did not like the overall environment at IIT for inexplicable reasons. I stayed at IIT Delhi for around three months. I got an offer of appointment from Bharat Heavy Electrical Engineering (BHEL) for a posting at Haridwar in September 1981. I had 15 days to decide on the offer. I decided to join this Public Sector Undertaking (PSU) mainly due to a fascination for the place, being at the foothills of the Himalayas and at the banks of river Ganges. I quit IIT and joined BHEL on September 28, 1981.

BHEL is a Government of India undertaking, established in 1964, with the bulk of its manufacture being power plant equipment. It also manufactures electric locomotives. BHEL has 17 manufacturing plants all over India. It has the capacity to produce power plant equipment of 20,000 Mega Watts per annum; and its annual revenues are $3 billion (₹22,000 crore).

Haridwar is an ancient city and an important Hindu pilgrimage centre in the north Indian state of Uttarakhand where river Ganges exits the Himalayan foothills. *Har Ki Pauri* (the steps at the bank of the river), the largest of the sacred *ghats*, hosts *Ganga Aarti* (earthenware lamps with wicks soaked in ghee are lit) every evening in which tiny flickering lamps are floated off the steps of the ghat. It is one of the most serene places I have seen in my life. In fact, this is what fascinated me to join BHEL. If my offer of appointment had been for any other plants of BHEL, I would not have quit IIT.

My roll number for Engineering Services examination was 1,000 (one thousand). All my batchmates knew it because it was easy to remember. Everyone was very keen to know my result, after all they had high expectations from me. My classmate, Vijay, had secured admission to MTech (Civil) at IIT Roorkee. The distance between Haridwar and Roorkee was 32 km. It would take 45 minutes by car to reach Roorkee. Every Sunday I went to Roorkee and had lunch with Vijay. IIT Roorkee was famous for Civil Engineering. Sunday lunch used to be very special and would remind me of the specialty food at Pantnagar. Vijay and I had studied together right from the 11th standard. We were also roommates at Pantnagar in the first year.

Sometime in March or April 1982, when I reached Roorkee like any other Sunday, Vijay congratulated me for my selection in the UPSC exam and took me to a book shop that had the newspaper which had published the result of Engineering Services. I had secured the eighth rank. Recruitment by Railways was therefore assured. It took almost a year to get the appointment letter due to inordinate delay in police verification. I got my offer of appointment from the Ministry of Railways in May 1983. I resigned from BHEL and got the three-year bond transferred to Railways. All this took time and finally I reported for training on June 22, 1983, at the Central Railway Headquarter at Bombay VT. I took an oath that was administered by the Assistant Senior Deputy General Manager. My batchmates had joined long back in March–April 1983. I had no idea whatsoever that the date of joining had a significant impact on the career growth, especially for assignments as General Manager and beyond. In Railways, the career is decided by the date of joining and the date of birth, as if a computer does the selection irrespective of your personal competencies, merit and contributions.

For two years of our training, which we call 'probation', we went around the whole country doing *Bharat darshan* and, in the process, learnt a lot at different Railway establishments. We had an all-India Card Pass A with the endorsement 'Anywhere to Anywhere'. The high point of the training was the Foundation Course at Staff College, Baroda (Vadodara) where officers from all services meet and stay together for four months. This creates a good bond between different services.

It was during this period that I got a call for attending the convocation at Pantnagar. I was to be conferred my degree and awarded the Gold Medal. I was not able to go as it clashed with the final exams of the Foundation Course at Staff College. I could not attend such an important event of my life. Sometime later, I went to the college take my degree and the medal. I collected the medal from the State Bank of India. As if all this was pre-ordained!

After two years of Railways training, we were posted to our allotted Zones. I was allotted Northern Railway. I reached Baroda House, the Headquarter of Northern Railway in Delhi, in May 1985.

I met C.P. Gupta, Chief Electrical Engineer (CEE), Northern Railway, for my first posting. He asked me if I had any preference. I opted for Electric Loco Shed, Kanpur. I had a love for complex

Seeds for the Future: Formative Years

Working night shift worsened my situation as I did not have a proper place to stay. I used to share a twin bedroom in the guest house. I had just one bed allotted to me. The experience of working in the night, and not being able to sleep in the day, was extremely frustrating. Many times, I would feel like quitting the job. I had grand plans to get into research after my graduation. This used to haunt me quite often. After three months, I got a full room allotted in the guest house, thanks to N. Venkatesan, DRM Allahabad. Slowly, I started learning and enjoying the job and understanding the technical aspects of a locomotive. Locomotive technology is one of the most complex technology in Railways and takes a long time to grasp. You need to know electrical, electronics, mechanical and control system quite well to fully understand a locomotive. Even with this knowledge, you need a teacher to guide you initially.

Venkatesan was a very caring and a very hard-working person and had the longest tenure of four years as DRM Allahabad. Subsequently, he became Member, Indian Railway Board.

Time passed. One evening all officers had assembled in the Officers Club to bid farewell to Pradeep Bhatnagar, the Chief Area Manager, Kanpur, who had been transferred and posted as Senior Divisional Operating Superintendent, Allahabad. The function was over at around 11 p.m. This was on January 25, 1986. While leaving the Club, R.N. Lal, the Senior Divisional Electrical Engineer who was also my boss, asked me to go to Tundla the next day and take charge as Assistant Electrical Engineer (Operations). The officer concerned was proceeding for an induction training at Staff College Vadodara. This post was very crucial for the operations of the Allahabad Division as it dealt with the drivers and running of trains. It was a 24x7 job, so it could not be kept vacant.

I had no time to prepare, but I had the entire room to myself in the guest house so I could keep my belongings there safely before going to Tundla. I had just started feeling a little comfortable and confident, despite working the night shift. The thought of the difficulty of getting to know people at a new place crossed my mind. I had never been to Tundla. I was anxious about my assignment. Next day was January 26, the Republic Day of India, a public holiday, which is celebrated across the nation. The Constitution of India had come into effect on this day in 1950.

I packed my belongings in a sack, kept them in the room, gave the keys to the caretaker and proceeded to Tundla. I took an early morning train from Kanpur and reached Tundla at around 12.30 p.m. S.P.S. Yadav, the Loco Foreman, Tundla, came to receive me at the station and guided me to the guest house. Yadav was a very disciplined, well-dressed and a soft-spoken person. The first impression I had of him was good.

An independent room was reserved for me in the guest house. There was a good recreation room there and a badminton court as well. Yadav put me at complete ease. He informed me that the officers were busy playing a cricket match. He arranged for my lunch and deputed an attendant who would take care of my daily chores. Except for my clothes, I had nothing else with me in the guest house.

In the evening, I met V.K. Aggarwal, Assistant Electrical Engineer (Operation) who was proceeding for the induction training, essential for further promotion.

For me, it appeared to be a welcome change. After my brief interaction with the supervisors and V.K. Aggarwal, I realised that I had come to the right place. My apprehensions were over. Tundla is considered as a godforsaken place. It is 415 km from the Divisional Headquarter at Allahabad and therefore Divisional officers visited Tundla infrequently.

Tundla is a town in the Firozabad district of Uttar Pradesh and is famous for a Catholic Church built in 1860. It has a rich heritage of British rule. It has a population of around 50,000. It is 24 km form Agra, 17 km from Firozabad and 210 km from Union Capital, New Delhi, on the Delhi–Kanpur section of North Central Railway.

It is an important junction for tourists coming to visit Taj Mahal at Agra, a UNESCO World Heritage site. Taj Mahal was commissioned by Shah Jahan in 1631, in memory of his wife Mumtaz Mahal who died on June 17 that year. Construction of Taj Mahal was completed in 1648. It is one of the wonders of the world.

After two months of my temporary posting, my regular posting orders as Assistant Electrical Engineer (Operations), Tundla were issued. My duty was to ensure availability of drivers, pay attention to locomotives and find the root cause of failure, coordinate with traffic department, and ensure safety in train running. The work environment was somewhat tense, as relations between the administration and the running staff (the drivers) were not very congenial. I learnt that the running staff had once threatened to resort to work-to-rule if the working conditions in the running room and lobby did not improve. Running room is a place where drivers take rest after working a train at the outstation. Normally they stay there for six hours and take meals.

Lobby is the place where drivers report for duty and wait for their turn to take charge of a train. Drivers are supposed to work for a maximum of ten hours from sign on to sign off. They also have to wait for one to two hours at the lobby to pick up their allotted train and therefore their duty hours quite often cross ten hours; this was resented. After all the job of a driver is quite strenuous. They would therefore stop the train and ask for relief even at stations where there was no crew changing point. This created serious problems for the administration. This is the work-to-rule regimen It generally happens when the relations are not cordial between staff and administration.

Running room and lobby must provide a clean and peaceful atmosphere with all the required facilities like toilet, clean water, food, tea, good furniture and linen.

Sensing the mood, I decided to look after the personal grievances of drivers and therefore made it a point to visit the lobby every day before going to my chamber at the control office. I made sure that I also visit the running room every week. These visits made me easily approachable to drivers and other supervisors and listen to them. It was very useful. Every day I used to meet three or four drivers who used to be called from the line to see me as they would have either failed to comply with the instructions or caused detention of trains or failed to troubleshoot a fault in the locomotive. Drivers were supposed to inform the Control Office within 15 minutes of any unusual occurrence while driving a train.

For the initial few days, I found that Bimlesh, my Technical Assistant, would guide me to question the drivers more on routine matters than on technical aspects of the failure. I was not very happy about this exercise. There was no personal touch in this. I did not find any positive outcome of this exercise. Everyone used to be scolded in abundance for some reason or the other. There was no place to understand the problems of the person who had been asked to meet me. It was simply not benefiting anyone – neither the driver nor the administration. Yet that was the work culture.

Bimlesh was the guide to the officer posted there and also a link between the officer and the outside world. He had been working for a very long time. He had good technical knowledge and was a good-natured person. He would help me in my personal matters also. He had good institutional memory. Even so, the drivers were not getting any substantial benefit out of his competencies. A change was required.

Troubleshooting a failed locomotive was very difficult for drivers. Sometimes even expert supervisors found it difficult to pin down a fault. Expecting the drivers to identify the faults was like asking for the moon. I wanted that drivers who came to see me go back a little more educated. That way, they may not repeat the same mistake. It would give them more confidence in handling the locomotives.

I therefore decided to put up a black board in my chamber to explain the circuit diagram and remove any doubts in their minds. It was an unusual action. I was convinced that this was the way forward. To cite a few teaching lessons that helped the drivers:

- ICDJ – Impossibility to close circuit breaker (DJ) in locomotive
- TWAC – Tripping without apparent cause in locomotive
- Tripping in operation C in locomotive
- Leakage test in air-braked trains
- Protection of train in case of emergency by putting detonators
- Function of relays Q118 and Q44 in locomotive

Once the practice of teaching started, the drivers started feeling quite satisfied and my regular visits to the crew booking point started evoking extremely good response. I was able to see changed behaviour amongst the drivers. The charge sheets issued dropped to insignificant numbers from the usual average of about 300–400 in a year. This was seen as a big welcome change by the staff.

The hostility which the Running Staff had with the administration almost vanished in about 6–8 months and the environment became very congenial. My only guidance to my staff was – tell the truth, accept your mistakes, and improve operations and safety. Train operation is our bread-and-butter was made loud and clear. We all had good intentions. But being in denial and hiding problems would not serve anyone. Thus, I gained full support of my staff. My words resonated with the people. Human beings are emotional creatures, we neglect this fact at our own peril.

A mini loco shed is called an 'out pit'. This is a place with a small covered shed with a pit to undertake under-gear examination to ensure safety. Small defects can be rectified, and locomotives properly cleaned. This was located right in front of my residence. I used to go to the out pit every day before going to the lobby, and thereafter I would go to office. This was my fixed routine. This allowed me to meet everyone every day and be informed of what was current with all the issues. I used to listen to their difficulties; some used to get resolved without much effort.

The Section Controllers who were responsible for controlling the movement of trains also started seeking my advice. The Section Controllers reported to Traffic Officers. A camaraderie evolved. Whenever there was a malfunction in a locomotive, I was requested by the Chief Controller to come to the Section Control Board to plan the movement of trains. I was thoroughly enjoying this type of work. I was directly responsible for locomotive operations and maintenance in my allotted section between Kanpur and Ghaziabad.

Seeds for the Future: Formative Years

Section Control Board is a place in the Control Office where a geographical portion of the railway line on a Division is controlled centrally. All movements of freight and passenger trains of that section are decided from this place by the person designated as Section Controller. The Controller works for six hours only as it is a high concentration job. He plots a time-distance graph on a big, printed sheet like a graph paper kept in front of him on a realtime basis. Stations are marked (from one end to another) in ascending order on Y-axis (distance) while time is plotted on X-axis. The slope of this graph (distance divided by the time) gives the speed of the train. Each movement of all the trains running on the section is plotted on this graph. The steeper the line graph of a train, the higher the speed. Every train is uniquely numbered. This graph is preserved for any investigation and future reference and to identify reasons for delays.

The style of functioning that I adopted came to the notice of the DRM Allahabad as well, and within 6–8 months the DRM started talking to me regularly. He would talk to me every day between 6.00 and 6.30 a.m.

I made it a point to attend each accident. I used to do it to ensure that drivers were not harassed unnecessarily in case of an accident or derailment. I would generally be the first person the DRM spoke to at the site of the accident, to ascertain the facts. I never hid anything even if it was to my detriment.

Professional honesty paid rich dividends as the system was showing signs of improvement. Once you accept your problem, the answer is easy.

One of the ways to improve line capacity (line capacity – number of trains that could be run in 24 hours) on Indian Railways has been to run heavier, longer and faster trains. In that pursuit, long haul-operation was one of the noblest ideas generated in mid-1980s. The intent was to couple two freight trains together, carrying almost 8,000 tonnes of freight, with two locomotives, one at the head and the other at the centre of the train (thus locomotive power was distributed) to run non-stop except for an operational halt to change the driver. This train would be 1.2 km long and used to be worked with change of crew at Kanpur and Tundla between Mughalsarai and Ghaziabad. This would cover 700 km in 11–12 hours. An average speed of about 60 kmph was superb. The average speed of freight trains had generally been 22–24 kmph. At least one long-haul train loaded with coal ran every day towards Delhi.

Quite frequently, I was asked by the DRM to go to Mughalsarai and get a particular train formed and escort right up to Ghaziabad. Travelling in a locomotive is called 'footplate' inspection in railway parlance. Whenever there was a difficulty at Mughalsarai, I was the troubleshooter. Footplating for 11–12 hours at a stretch was quite arduous. However, the pleasure of accomplishment used to motivate me to do it. The train would stop only at Kanpur and Tundla over the 700 km run. There were no loop lines at stations that could accommodate a 1.2 km long train. G.S. Chauhan, Loco Inspector, used to accompany me at Mughalsarai and travel with me up to Ghaziabad. He would also offer me home-made rotis (bread) in the locomotive. Very frugal food and a cup of tea was all that was available on such a long journey. Commitment and passion to successfully run such a train kept us going despite all the odds.

The long-haul operation got stabilised with rudimentary communication system between the drivers of the front and the middle locomotives. For this communication, wiring used to be done from one end to the other end of the train to use magneto telephone to enable the driver and the guard to speak to each other. This 1.2 km long wire between the two points was hung all along the wagons. The rear locomotive used to be controlled based on the current drawn by the front locomotive and the notch position (a locomotive has 32 notches to increase or decrease the voltage) of the front locomotive. The driver of the rear locomotive took one or two notches less than the front locomotive to avoid any unusual train forces. Drivers also communicated through whistle codes to understand the notch positions.

There was no other way to control the train. It was a Herculean task; nevertheless, the skills of the inspectors and drivers made this operation a success. It was a superb performance by any standard. The train ran like the Rajdhani Express, ahead of even Mail Express trains. It became the defining success story of that time. Perseverance and commitment can make you deliver anything you think of.

Even after three decades, long-haul operation continues, of course with only one technological intervention: Very High Frequency (VHF) communication between the two drivers. A Locotrol is a new technology that allows a coordinated control between the front and the rear locomotive through radio frequency communication without the need for a driver in the rear locomotive. The operation of the second locomotive is controlled by the front locomotive wherever Locotrols have been provided on the locomotives. We do not require the rear locomotive to be manned by a driver in the Locotrol operated system. Locotrols have however not been widely proliferated on Indian Railways even now. The protocols established in the mid-1980s are still valid, and a majority of long-haul train operations continue on the same pattern wherein two locomotives are manned, but instead of wired communication using magneto telephone, a VHF handset is available with the drivers and guard to communicate and control the train.

I completed a little more than two years of my tenure at Tundla before being promoted and posted at Allahabad.

As I reflect on my formative years of working in the Railways, I firmly believe that our people are our most important resource, and therefore you must live their life to understand them better, to improve overall efficiency. Give your 100 per cent, all the time, every time, and do it with devotion and a feeling of joy. You are bound to succeed. Enjoy the journey. You will cherish it in times to come. If you are satisfied with the output and the outcome, you have succeeded. You measure your success yourself.

2

Challenging Assumptions: Mahakumbh at Allahabad

My next posting was in the construction wing of Traction and Power Supply at Allahabad in March 1988. Preparations were in full swing for the forthcoming Purna Kumbh Mela which was to be held in Allahabad in 1989.

Allahabad is a city in the Indian state of Uttar Pradesh. The city is the judicial capital of the State in which Allahabad High Court is the highest judicial body. It has a population of about 12 lakhs. The city lies close to *Triveni Sangam*, the confluence of three rivers – the Ganges, the Yamuna and the Saraswati. The Mahabharata mentions a bathing pilgrimage at Prayag as a means of atonement for the past mistakes and sins. Allahabad is also known as the city of Prime Ministers as 7 (Jawahar Lal Nehru, Lal Bahadur Shastri, Indira Gandhi, Rajiv Gandhi, Gulzarilal Nanda, Vishwanath Pratap Singh and Chandra Shekhar) out of the 15 Prime Ministers since India's independence in 1947 have had connections with Allahabad.

Purna Kumbh Mela, a holy festival of Hindus is celebrated every 12 years at Triveni Sangam. This mela is held in rotation at Prayagraj, Haridwar, Nashik and Ujjain every 12 years. *Ardh Kumbh* is celebrated every 6 years. *Maha Kumbh* is celebrated only at Prayagraj every 144 years.

I was not happy with my posting in Construction. I wanted to work in Operations. As a part of my new assignment, I was responsible for the construction of six additional Traction Sub-Stations (TSS) between Kanpur and Mughalsarai. This was to ensure running of electric trains without restrictions. Due to inadequate traction power capacity, the number of electric trains used to be limited in a section. Traction power supply tripped whenever the number of trains went beyond a limit due to overloading.

As the Division was preparing for Purna Kumbh at Allahabad in 1989, quite a few power supply related works were planned at Allahabad station. But TSS was one of the most important work. I frequently visited these six TSS locations. After full understanding, I realised that none of the sites could be considered ready for this work as land had to be acquired from the villagers. It was next to impossible to acquire any site and complete even one TSS before Kumbh Mela. At most places, the land near the track was agriculture land.

Rasulabad is a town under Fatehpur Dehat district of Uttar Pradesh. It has a population of about 8,000. The Government has proposed an International Airport near Rasulabad to handle domestic and international traffic. Rasulabad is 100 km from Kanpur and 100 km from Allahabad.

Though Railway land was available at Rasulabad, the size of the plot was small. Research Design and Standards Organisation's (RDSO) standard TSS layout could not be accommodated in the small land parcel. I decided to make the best attempt to have a new TSS constructed to a non-standard design. I met Sushil Chandra, the head of design of Power Supply in Railway Electrification (RE) organisation on this matter to seek his guidance. He used to stay in our residential complex and was quite open to new ideas. I met him quite often during morning walks. RE organisation is responsible for undertaking large railway electrification projects in Railways, and therefore their word was final in RE design.

After a lot of persuasion with Sushil Chandra in RE, RDSO and Divisional and Headquarter officers, it was agreed that a non-standard TSS may be constructed at Rasulabad. The thrust of the argument was to circumvent adverse reaction on RE by Traffic Department. They were happy running diesel locomotives. Diesel locomotives were however not so powerful and therefore trains lost time on the run and caused loss of line capacity. It was our bounden duty to provide a solution to the overloading problem on electrified routes. It was a challenge which each electrical engineer was to accept and do their bit. My persuasion with Sushil Chandra worked as it was a matter of prestige for the electrical discipline. As Sushil Chandra was an authority on Power Supply. RDSO and Divisional and Headquarter officers also agreed once I got a go ahead from Sushil Chandra. He approved the drawing for a non-standard TSS. It was quite unusual. This gave me an opportunity to execute some of the work in the Division. Other important work relating to Allahabad Yard remodelling, vital for the Kumbh Mela, was also completed. Work related to this TSS therefore picked up momentum.

It was established that a Traction Sub-Station can be built under mitigating circumstances on a land parcel which may not measure up to RDSO design.

Since I did not enjoy the job fully, I requested CEE to transfer me out of Allahabad. In February 1989 I was transferred to the Kanpur Shed, a place I had initially aspired to work. But I had not liked this place due to chaos and confusion in the work environment.

3

Not Only Heat and Dust: A Decade at Kanpur

I arrived at Kanpur amidst staff agitation due to the unfortunate death of Maiku Lal, a staff of the Shed. He was run over while crossing the railway track near Electric Loco Shed. There was a long pending demand of a foot overbridge (FOB) across the railway tracks. This was not being agreed to. R.N. Lal was in-charge of the Shed; he was there while I was posted there the first time in 1985. He asked me to prepare an estimate for the sanction of this FOB. It took me three weeks to collaborate with various departments and prepare a proposal costing ₹30 lakh. It was a big proposal at the time. Today this FOB may cost about ₹5 crore.

General Manager Northern Railway visited Kanpur on the occasion of the inaugural run of Shatabdi Express from New Delhi to Kanpur. Shri Madhavrao Scindia was the Minister of Railways. The function was well conducted. R.N. Lal was instrumental in organising the function. The proposal for the FOB was discussed with the GM and he agreed to it. This was my first success. It was later sent to the Headquarter (HQ) for sanction.

From now on, R.N. Lal started depending on me for materials planning, handling staff matters, coordination with the Division and any innovation that I would consider for improving the reliability of locomotives. It was not so in my earlier posting in 1985. The environment in the Shed was not really enthusing due to lack of cleanliness, criss-cross workflow, poor and inadequate toilets, lack of uniform for staff and lack of critical materials. R.N. Lal was a very competent and compassionate officer. But he was not able to pay full attention as the pressure of loco related work was quite demanding. I engaged myself in ensuring materials supply, listening to staff grievances, and resolving them to the extent that I could. I would always empathise with the staff. As Divisional Electrical Engineer, I naturally did not have full control over the functioning of the Shed. But I was happy contributing to improving the system even with limited control. R.N. Lal had completed a long tenure at Kanpur and got transferred to RDSO Lucknow. V.K. Aggarwal replaced him.

Within a month of Aggarwal's taking over, I was promoted to Junior Administrative Grade and posted as Senior Divisional Electrical Engineer of Traction Machine Repair Shed (TMS) at Kanpur, in December 1990. TMS was responsible for the repairs to various electrical machines used in locomotives of the entire Railways. However, the officer who had to hand over charge to me in December 1990 did not do so for at least two weeks. I took charge on January 9, 1991. It was a critically vital installation for high level of reliability and availability of locomotives. The work culture was like that in a workshop. There was only one shift in 24 hours. I was used to a live wire kind of environment.

Time Office is a place where staff members mark their daily attendance. And for doing so there is a standard protocol of picking up a 'token' from this office and depositing the same with the supervisor in-charge. The supervisors, in turn, recorded these tokens and sent them to the Time Office as a mark of daily attendance. Each staff was allotted a number which was written or engraved on a circular metal token. This token was safely put on a board in the section inside the shed and given back to the staff at the close of the shift. This was again deposited by the staff with the Time Office. This protocol was followed each day.

A new Time Office building, a staff canteen and a recreation room had been constructed, but they had not been commissioned. There were two recognised labour unions representing the staff – Northern Railway Men's Union (NRMU) and Uttar Railway Mazdoor Union (URMU). They were at loggerheads with each other. The new Time Office building was not getting operationalised as one union wanted to shift to the new location while the other was opposed to it. It was pending for more than a year. While on the one hand there was a pressure to give a higher output in the last quarter of the financial year, on the other, the staff unions were agitating due to inadequate facilities. It was a catch-22 situation. TMS had nearly 500 staff members and all of them were working in one shift. It was a fairly large number.

Since failure of the machines was high, it was always a daunting task to meet the requirements of the two Electric Loco Sheds of Northern Railway – Kanpur and Ghaziabad – in addition to other sheds of Indian Railways. In the month of January, the pressure of work was always high.

Normally, the unions used pressure tactics whenever the demand for output was high. The annual inspection by the GM was also due.

An agitation to commission a new Time Office started. I always engaged with the staff whenever there was a problem. I had learnt this early in my career at Tundla and Allahabad.

I met both the unions. After a marathon meeting, I decided to let the staff decide the place they would like to choose for their attendance. They had to, after all, use this place to pick up and drop tokens daily. They would also use the new canteen and recreation room. The deal was struck. I suggested that two tender boxes with a hole in the centre be kept at the entrance gate marked 'New' and 'Old'. A date was decided to give the option to staff to drop their tokens in either of these boxes in the morning.

Obviously, whichever box had a higher number of tokens, would be the option that would be implemented. In case of a tie, I would have the final say. Counting would be done in the presence of union representatives in my chamber. A team was formed to complete this exercise. This decision was taken with the consent of both the unions and no sooner was this deal finalised, than a notice to this effect was put out for the information of all concerned. Time was of essence.

On the fixed date, the tokens were dropped, and the counting done. The new time office building became operational, as most of staff had chosen that option. This resolved the issue, hanging in balance for more than one year. Everyone was happy.

If you are honest in your purpose, you will be able to resolve any issue.

Think out-of-the-box. Respect sentiments of the people. Be fair. Don't have ego. You shall succeed.

Hitachi Traction Motor: First Armature Rewound

Within three months of my joining as in-charge of Traction Machines Shed, there was a spate of failures of Traction Motors (TMs) of WAP 1 locomotives employed to run Rajdhani trains. Around 60 new TMs failed in quick succession over 2-3 months, leading to a lot of dislocation of train operations in the Allahabad Division. All these TMs were sent by the Ghaziabad shed to us for repair. They were expecting the motors to be repaired and returned within 2-3 weeks. Our shed got choked. I did not have material to undertake such major repairs in such a short time.

Within a month of the receipt of these TMs, there was a coordination meeting at Chittaranjan Locomotive Works (CLW) where pan India officers of Railways were to meet. This was a big event. This meeting was to decide upon the action plan for improving the reliability of electric locomotives. Jagdish Upadhyay was the General Manager of CLW. He was later appointed as Member, Railway Board.

CLW was founded on January 26, 1950, to manufacture railway locomotives. It started manufacturing diesel shunting locos, 1,500 volt Direct Current (DC) locomotives, 25 KV Alternating Current (AC) and 1,500 volt DC dual voltage locomotives and later, the 25 KV state-of-the-art 3-phase locomotives. Today, it is the largest locomotive manufacturer in the world, with a capacity of manufacturing 430 locomotives per year. It also manufactures TMs used in locomotives.

Jagdish Upadhyay was regarded as an institution in the Electrical Department. He was one of the best locomotive engineers of his time. No one could go against his decision. He would be unquestionably right.

TAO659 type of TMS (575 KW rating) used to be provided in passenger locomotives built by CLW. These locos were called WAP 1 class ('W'- broad gauge, 'A'- alternating current, 'P'- passenger and '1'- series) and used to be deployed to work in the prestigious Rajdhani and Shatabdi trains. This loco was rated at 3,800 HP. These locos were first built in the 1980s. The manufacture of WAP 1 locos continued till the more powerful WAP 4 class of locomotive was manufactured that was provided with a better designed Hitachi TM (630 KW rating) in 1994. This loco was rated at 5,000 HP. About 64 locos of WAP 1 class were built by CLW and thereafter discontinued.

This design of TAO659 was taken from Alstom France and was not very reliable, especially for high-speed train operation at 130 kmph. CLW modified the design of the Stator of this TM. The TM has a fixed part called 'Stator' and a rotating part called 'Armature'. The Stator was designed with two coils. In between the two coils, there were rectangular springs made of steel alloy. These springs provided flexibility for relative movement of coils at higher temperature.

This design was modified by CLW and springs were replaced by fixed spacers. These springs used to lose their shape and cause failure. Using fixed spacers turned out to be worse than using springs.

It was a burning issue, and therefore I was asked by the Headquarters (HQ) to attend this meeting at CLW. I had already received 60 failed traction motors from the Ghaziabad shed. All these motors had failed while working mostly in Rajdhani trains, causing chaos. One Divisional Electrical Engineer from Ghaziabad shed, Sunil Mathur, accompanied me to CLW. No senior officer from the Headquarters wanted to accompany me. No one wanted to confront the GM. The design of fixed spacers was evolved by CLW under the guidance of Jagdish Upadhyay.

Normally, this coordination meeting continues for two days. This time the first day was engaged in issues relating to assistance of material required from CLW and other technical matters relating to the reliability of new locomotives manufactured by CLW.

Since the TM failure was a very sensitive matter, it was not discussed on the first day.

However, the next morning, Chandurkar, the Chief Electrical Engineer (TM) at CLW initiated the discussion on failure of the newly-designed Traction Motors which had failed in large numbers in NR. Punctuality of Rajdhani trains had been badly affected and the matter had reached the highest level in Railway Board. It had led to stabling of newly-built WAP 1 locomotives.

I was asked to present my observations on this matter in front of Jagdish Upadhyay. I was not informed about this in advance. It was a little perplexing to give an immediate response. But I had done my homework on the failed TMs.

No one else wanted to explain the reasons for failure. Fear of facing the wrath of Jagdish Upadhyay was writ large on everyone's face. I decided to explain the phenomenon of failure of these 60 TMs honestly and professionally. I had myself examined each failed TM in detail. The bolts holding the coils and fixing them with the frame of the stator had become loose. The coils had been damaged due to rubbing of armatures. The bolts were getting opened at very low torque, much lower than they were supposed to.

I gave my observations and personal views as to what could have led to the spate of failures, drawing analogy from the design of another type of TMs, Hitachi make HS 15250. When the matter was explained, there was pin drop silence. No sooner my explanation was over, than Jagdish Upadhyay complimented me for the courage I had displayed, the depth with which I had analysed failures and my explanation to the large gathering present in the hall. It was quite educative to all of them.

He said that the design was well-conceived but was not well-implemented by CLW. The ball was in Chandurkar's court.

This made my day. It gave me tremendous professional satisfaction. A decision to discontinue the manufacture of the new design of these TMs motors was taken right on the spot. This was my first encounter with Jagdish Upadhyay. He later became Member, Railway Board. During lunch, everyone complimented me.

I returned with great satisfaction. It motivated me to think out-of-the-box and look at the failed armatures of Hitachi TMs too. Mahesh Pant, the Senior Electrical Engineer looking after TMs manufacture at

CLW, had shown me the failed armatures of Hitachi motors at CLW. He had even tried to strip the failed coils of this armature using the force of an overhead crane but had failed. Failed armatures were lying on the shop floor at CLW. These armatures had piled up in big numbers in my shed as well. These used to be condemned and thrown, considering them as beyond repair.

The Original Equipment Manufacturer (OEM) of these traction motors – Hitachi, Japan – had not recommended any repair on these armatures. Railways had entered into a Transfer of Technology (TOT) agreement with Hitachi Japan for the manufacture of these motors at CLW. TOT was later given to BHEL also.

At TMS Kanpur, we tried a number of processes using various chemicals to soften the coils, and finally with the help of some very skilled staff and supervisors, we were able to lay down a new method of stripping, cleaning and rewinding these armatures. A Hitachi armature was successfully rewound. A new armature cost 8 lakh at that time. This was brought to the notice of the Railway Board.

Jagdish Upadhyay had taken over as Member, Railway Board. After learning that the Hitachi armature has been rewound by TMS Kanpur, he decided to visit my shed. After seeing the first ever rewound armature, he patted my back and asked RDSO to lay down new process sheets for rewinding of Hitachi armatures. He also wrote to Hitachi Japan about the need and success of such repair. This had not been recommended by Hitachi while transferring technology to CLW. It was yet another morale booster for me. Sethuraman, the Executive Director RDSO, stayed with me at Kanpur for a day to fully appreciate the way this armature was rewound. A procedure was laid down by RDSO for rewinding this armature.

This was a high point in my career. A new beginning was made for the repair of Hitachi armatures in 1991-92. A letter was written by Jagdish Upadhyay to Raj Kumar, the General Manager of Northern Railway, commending the innovative efforts put in by TMS Kanpur wherein he mentioned: *'Even Hitachi had not envisaged repair to these armatures, as the vacuum level at which these are impregnated, will not allow their dismantling.'* This was therefore a new beginning in some sense.

I guess, Indian Railways have so far repaired around 2,500 armatures, at the rate of 75–80 armature winds per annum, saving about ₹200 crore over the last 30 years (my estimate).

I was given the General Manager's award at the Railways annual function on April 16, 1992 as a token of appreciation and recognition of my work.

Union Unrest in Kanpur

In January 1993, an agitation took place in the Kanpur Shed. This Shed was adjacent to my Traction Machine Shed. V.K. Aggarwal was in-charge here. P.K. Wahi was DRM Allahabad. He asked me to go to the Shed and try to resolve the issues raised by the Unions. The DRM informed me that there was a tool-down strike.

In the midst of the *gherao* (protest) by the unions, I reached the Shed and tried to pacify the agitating staff. The staff knew me well as I had worked there for almost two years and had looked after their grievances. My credibility also came in handy. My conduct and performance in the TMS were also known to the staff. I heard them patiently and assured them of action to be taken to address their grievances. The matter was resolved, and the staff got engaged in their daily work.

The staff was agitating since they were being marked absent for arriving 15–30 minutes late. There was a practice of permitting 30 minutes late arrivals only thrice over a period of one month. If they came late on more than three occasions, their casual leave account was deducted by a half-day leave. General shift in the Shed started at 8 a.m. It was winter season. This practice had been discontinued by V.K. Aggarwal. Within a fortnight of this incident, V.K. Aggarwal proceeded on a foreign training. I was asked to look after both the Sheds – the Electric Loco Shed and the Traction Machines Shed.

Orders were issued for me to look after the Loco Shed temporarily. I however continued for six-and-a-half years as in-charge of the Loco Shed. It was the longest tenure ever of any officer there. R.N. Lal had also stayed there for a very long time, but less than my tenure. I looked after both the Sheds – the Electric Loco Shed and the Traction Machine Shed – for some time. B.B. Singh was subsequently posted to take charge of the TMS.

My major thrust was to streamline the work-flow – to clearly identify the crane area and the non-crane area, remove all the scrap piled for decades, shift toilets from the entrance to a far end and construct a separate toilet block, improve recreation rooms, renovate staff canteen and provide fresh potable water supply through an independent bore-well for the Shed.

Removal of scrap and establishing a clean and pleasing work environment along with well-lit notice boards made of glass changed the way the staff used to behave. Initially, most of the officers and supervisors thought that the glass notice boards would be broken by notorious elements every now and then and shifting of toilets may lead to agitation. All of them were wrong. The work culture improved. Workers felt pride in the place of their work. It was indeed clean and pleasing.

It was time to persuade the staff and supervisors to accept their mistakes and find the root cause, to improve the reliability of the locomotives. It was really difficult to market this idea. No matter how much I would assure – *accept your mistake and no one will be punished* – no one believed it. There were no takers due to mistrust between the administration and staff on this front. B. Ghoshal was my technical supervisor. He was a cool and calm person. His technical knowledge was simply outstanding. I regularly asked him to instil confidence amongst supervisors and staff, but no one would believe me.

The behaviour of the supervisors and technicians, in general, was quite unique. They accepted their mistakes only when they saw a failure with their own eyes and realised that there is no way someone else would have tinkered with the locomotive. Otherwise, they simply disowned everything even when it was obvious. The standard response was that someone else had done it. Very intriguing indeed!

One day, an overhauled locomotive failed in New Delhi on its first run. To identify the root cause, I ensured that the locomotive was padlocked and brought from New Delhi to Kanpur without anyone meddling with it. The lock was opened in the presence of officers and supervisors to ensure unbiased investigations.

The loco was checked by the concerned staff and supervisors, and the root cause and the staff responsible were conclusively identified. This was a fit case which no one could dispute. No disciplinary action was however taken against anyone. This was the beginning of a new era where people started accepting their mistakes. This was like *walking the talk*, and therefore it established a *faith* in the administration that despite a fault having been established and the concerned technician and supervisor identified, no one would be taken to task. It took two years to establish the new culture – *don't be in denial, accept your mistake and you will not be punished*. From then onwards, the performance of the Shed improved beyond expectations as the most difficult part of identifying the root cause became a very simple affair. Everyone used to accept their failure. Accepting a mistake would automatically fetch a pardon. The person accepting his mistake felt proud of his conduct.

My next three years as in-charge of the Shed were extremely fulfilling and rewarding. Unions were calm and quiet. The staff was very happy. Performance was at its best.

It was a *Ram Rajya* in true sense.

Ram Rajya is a system where the society operates on principles of equality, transparency, cleanliness, no fear, public-friendly administration, and good relations amongst all. Mahatma Gandhi wanted to develop such a utopian society and that is why he talked about Ram Rajya.

Sitaram Shukla: An Unforgettable Experience

He was a fair, well-built person with a high energy level. He was a very friendly human being. He was one of the most versatile technicians I had in the Shed. He was a member of the Territorial Army (TA). TA personnel are generally very disciplined. Every year he went to attend a month-long camp organised by the TA unit.

The TA is the second line of defence after the regular Indian Army; it is not a profession, occupation or a source of employment. It is only meant for those who are already in mainstay civilian professions. TA personnel usually serve in uniform for a few days every year so that they can bear arms for national defence in times of dire need or national emergencies.

Sitaram Shukla used to work in the Progress Planning and Inspection Office (PPIO) section of the shed. The duty of PPIO is to ensure that locomotives are called to the shed for inspection in advance and placed at nominated places inside the shed well before the start of shift at 8 a.m. every day. This ensured smooth working.

This work required lot of shunting operation for the movement of locomotives from one place to another. The Shed did not have proper shunting staff. Shunting staff belonged to the Traffic Department. There had been a perennial shortage of such staff. As a matter of practice, the shed staff used to perform shunting simply because it was within the boundary walls of the Shed. The job of Shed staff was to set the points on the track and give hand signals to the driver for movement of the locomotive as per the plans of PPIO in-charge. The locomotive used for shunting was driven only by regular trained only. These drivers worked in eight-hour shifts.

Whenever Shukla was on duty, everyone felt comfortable because he was a perfect planner and loved doing his work. The staff also applauded him for his dedication and devotion to duty. He was also proficient in driving locomotives. But he only drove in an emergency.

For certain reasons, Shukla started absenting himself. His family was in distress as he was not getting regular salary due to long absenteeism. The Shed staff used to contribute voluntarily on the day of payment of salary and arrange a handsome amount of money for his family. I also used to contribute.

Despite repeated counselling by colleagues, his family relations did not improve. He had started living with another lady. Shukla's children had boycotted him and prohibited his entry into his own home. These stories were known to people in the Shed and that is why they came to my notice as well. I spent time in the Shed for at least 9–10 hours every day. The Shed's environment is like that of a family. You therefore know many people personally. In fact, I used to know about 30–40 per cent of the staff and 100 per cent of the supervisors by name. I had around 98 supervisors.

On the fateful day, while Shukla was driving a locomotive, suddenly the locomotive went out of control and entered the building of the PPIO, breaking the brick wall. It was a major accident and led to agitation. Some staff members were always inside this room where the locomotive entered. This was a record room. All the locomotive data used to be preserved here. The data used to be updated on real-time basis. This room therefore always had four or five persons. A major tragedy was averted as most of the people working inside the room had gone to attend to the call of nature in the morning hours.

Unions started demanding posting of regular shunting staff from the Traffic Department. Engagement of the Shed's technician was to be discontinued forthwith.

The intent of the union was to not let administration take any disciplinary action against Sitaram Shukla. Since he was a sincere and hardworking employee, I decided to exonerate him as no one was injured in the accident. The building had been badly damaged, so it was repaired. The incident happened since there was no well-designed dead-end provided in front of the building. A standard design of dead-end was to be erected in front of the building. Besides, there was a technical fault in the shunting locomotive. One diode in the circuit had failed which led to a sudden progression of notches and the locomotive picked up speed. Sitaram was not able to control it. This was clearly brought out by Supriya Sen, Assistant Electrical Engineer of the shed. Supriya Sen did a one-man enquiry. Sen was a very cool and calm person, an extraordinarily brilliant officer, and an expert in troubleshooting. I had full faith in his competence. I decided to let Sitaram off. As soon as Sitaram Shukla was let off, normalcy was restored.

Time passed. We came to know from his colleagues that his family relations continued to be stressed. His unauthorised absences became even longer. He was not getting regular salary and did not get bonus which is generally disbursed before Deepavali (the festival of lights in India) festival, as he had not been working for a long time and had exhausted all his leave. His absence was treated as leave-without-pay. His children were really disturbed and impoverished.

After 3–4 months of unauthorised absence, Shukla reported for duty very early in the morning on yet another fateful day. He was taken on duty by the Supervisor concerned and was deputed for shunting duty. After long absence, the staff was generally taken on duty in the day shift starting 8 a.m., after he had met the concerned officer. This was to ascertain reasons for absence and to decide if any medical examination or intervention was needed.

Ashfaque Ahmad was in-charge of PPIO. He had taken Shukla on duty pending approval from the officer concerned, which in any case was to be obtained in the day. Ashfaque was a tall, well-built, and an extremely motivated Supervisor. His performance was superb, and therefore no officer used to question his decisions. Probably that is the reason Shukla was taken on duty so early in the morning by him.

As luck would have it, during the shunting, he somehow got in between the Central Buffer Couplers (CBC) of two locomotives and got badly injured. CBC is the part of a locomotive which is used to connect two rolling stocks for hauling a train. The weight of this component is about 500 kg. It can withstand a compressive force of about 200 tonnes. It is a massive sub-assembly of a locomotive.

The incident happened at around 5.15 a.m. Ashfaque informed me in a choking and trembling voice on the phone – '*Sir galti ho gai maf kar deejiya*' (I have made a mistake, kindly pardon me). When I asked him what happened, he narrated the incident. He was worried because he had taken Shukla on duty without following the standard practice and Shukla had met with an accident.

I thought it would be possible to save Shukla's life. My driver Aijaz used to stay 2 km away from my residence. My Jeep used to be parked in the Shed. Aijaz used to go to the Shed and bring it to my residence every day. All this would have taken at least 45 minutes. Rather than calling my driver, I decided to reach the Shed in my own car. I considered it that urgent. The Shed was about 7–8 km from my residence. There was a level crossing gate on the way, about a km from the Shed, but luckily the gate was open. I reached the shed by 6 a.m.

Dr Som Pal, the railway doctor, used to stay near the Shed and was in-charge of the dispensary attached to the Shed. He was a very cooperative and popular doctor amongst the staff. He came to the Shed and attended to Sitaram Shukla. By 6.45 a.m. we had shifted Shukla to the Railway Hospital in the hope that he would revive. Unfortunately, he passed away.

The day shift in the Shed starts at 8 a.m. A big agitation began as soon as the staff started assembling in the Shed at around 8.45 a.m. Shukla's family was contacted and called at the Railway Hospital. His wife was paid the requisite ex-gratia of ₹15,000 in the hospital itself by 11.25 a.m. Doctors decided to have his post-mortem conducted in the Civil Hospital, Kanpur. That is the law of the land. His body was sent to Civil Hospital duly escorted by Ramendra, my Divisional Electrical Engineer. In fact, Ramendra was proceeding on leave that day. He was going to Lucknow to meet his parents. After coming to know about the incident, he came rushing to the hospital. His residence was within walking distance of the Railway Hospital.

Ramendra, a tall and good looking individual, was one of the most dedicated and devoted officers I had in my team. His first posting after completion of his probation period, was with me. He was simply a genius. His mother-in-law was the Chief Medical Officer of Civil Hospital, Kanpur. This helped us in getting the post-mortem done quickly. The post-mortem report indicated death due to rupture of lungs and multiple fractures in the rib cage.

The agitation took an ugly turn, and the staff blocked the movement of traffic on the Delhi–Howrah route in Juhi yard that was in front of the Loco Shed. Staff and the local people sat on a *dharna* (sit-in strike) on the tracks blocking all train movements. They were demanding deployment of shunting staff, compassionate appointment to the ward of the deceased and all other compensation as admissible to staff dying on duty.

While we were trying to handle the post-mortem, all operations in the Allahabad Division had come to a grinding halt. It was chaos at its worst.

M.N. Chopra was my DRM, who asked me to amicably resolve the issue and have operations restored. Chopra had unquestionable trust in me. He had exceptional leadership qualities. He always motivated me and removed any difficulty that we faced. He never lost his temper. He was a good cricket player and a very soft-spoken person. He would neither feel stressed nor create any stress for anyone else.

The civil administration and the local police had been informed about the law-and-order situation. After Sitaram's body was despatched for post-mortem, I decided to reach the site of the dharna myself, without any police escort or any other officer. Some of the officers were busy looking after the Shed where the staff was agitating. Other officers were engaged in getting the post-mortem done.

I reached the site all alone with my vehicle driver and one supervisor and decided to address the people gathered there. Some of my well-wishers advised me to take Railway Protection Force (RPF) with me, but I refused. They felt that there was a lot of ballast all around the rail line and anything might happen, because the behaviour of the mob cannot be predicted. They may even start throwing stones at me in rage. I may even be made hostage till demands were fulfilled. In fact, nothing of this sort crossed my mind. I was sure, I would be able to handle the crisis.

My thoughts and strength were – *they are my men, and I have always taken care of them.*

The moment the mob saw me arrive, they started shouting slogans like *Inqilab Zindabad, Rail Prashashan Murdabad* (long live revolution, death to railway administration).

My driver Aijaz and my supervisor Rakesh Srivastava became worried. I asked them to be patient. Aijaz was a well-built, disciplined and a no- nonsense, very dependable person. Rakesh was an equally strong and honest person who used to handle the transport and general section of the shed. Whenever any staff member fell sick or there was an emergency, they approached Rakesh for assistance of a vehicle, and he helped them. I had clearly instructed Rakesh that under emergency situations even my official vehicle could be used without seeking my permission. This was an open secret. The staff knew it.

Police force was available in large numbers at the site for quite some time. The Deputy Superintendent of Police asked me – 'What should we do?' I requested him to wait. In my assessment there were more than 1,000 people, most of them being the Shed staff. The staff strength of my shed was 1,100. People from surrounding colonies had also collected there.

I put two drivers' boxes, one over the other, with the assistance of Aijaz and Rakesh in order to create a raised platform so that I could address the people. These were the boxes used by drivers to carry their provisions while they were on duty. I asked everyone to come closer to me so that I could speak with them.

I told them about the payment of ex-gratia already made to Sitaram Shukla's wife. I publicly promised to get the post-mortem conducted early. I said that I would do my best to get his son appointed on compassionate grounds within 15 days and ensure all payments. This made an emotional connection. I was able to sense the mood of the mob changing. I also appealed to them to clear the track as a large number of trains had been detained and passengers were suffering.

A majority of the people present belonged to my Shed. I knew quite a few of them by name. Senior Supervisors of the shed were also amongst them. The staff was more than convinced that the administration had no role whatsoever in the incident which led to Sitaram Shukla's death. They also got a clear communication from me that whatever best could be done would be done by me. Quite a few knew the circumstances Shukla had been passing through, on the personal and family front.

After the address, I asked all of them to go to the Shed, complete their work and allow the traffic to be restored, which was otherwise causing lot of hardship to passengers. I also made it clear that no disciplinary action would be taken if the allotted work was completed by them.

I asked a few Supervisors by name, like D.N. Prasad and T.R. Anand, to take everyone back to the Shed. The staff members had not caused any damage to Railway property. That was the best part. Both the Supervisors, Prasad and Anand, were generally respected by the staff. Within 10–15 minutes the blockade, which had been there for around three hours, was removed. The police force went back. I went to the post-mortem house.

People were guessing what could have led to this accident. The suicide angle was being murmured. I, however, did not believe in them and wanted to give the benefit of doubt to the deceased. This was to ensure that his family got full compensation and benefits as admissible.

I was sure that Shukla died on duty, and it would be considered like any other unusual incident. Ashfaque also got mental relief, the moment we decided to regularise Shukla's duty.

By 3.15 p.m., we were able to get the body back. After post-mortem we hurriedly decided to cremate the body keeping in view that the sun would set soon. His family had resolved to do the last rites quickly. His relatives had arrived from Lucknow and nearby places.

The electronic and print media at the post-mortem house got into a scuffle with the Shed's Unions. Print and electronic media were trying to project that the incident happened due to the negligence of the administration. The Unions, who were agitating against the administration in the morning and sitting on dharna, changed their stance and were in favour of the administration as the facts were in front of them. The matter was resolved by the supervisors and the officers present there by narrating past incidents related to his family and the compassion that the Shed's administration had shown towards Sitaram Shukla in the past.

Cremation was properly done at 5 p.m., well before sunset. I came back home at 7 p.m. after completing all the formalities. The situation that had arisen as a fallout of the unfortunate death of Sitaram Shukla was amicably resolved. This was Saturday, October 18, 1997. The next day being a Sunday, all other paper formalities were done on Monday, October 20, 1997.

The appointment of his son was not without another twist. His son, Arun Kumar Shukla, submitted papers related to his educational background. The certificate pertaining to 10th grade turned out to be in the name of another person when the welfare inspector went to Hindi Sahitya Sammelan, Allahabad, to get the certificate verified. The school principal seized that document and asked the candidate to be produced, failing which the school would file a First Information Report (FIR) against the son with the police. As soon as this was told to Shukla's family, they all came along with both the Unions to seek pardon and save the family from any further trauma.

The Unions wanted me to help the family again. I persuaded all concerned to return all the papers which the family had filed for compassionate appointment and seek fresh application along with certificates of educational qualification till the 8th standard. Sitaram's wife was asked to furnish a fresh application.

An educational qualification of 10th standard would have fetched him a Class C job while qualification of 8th standard would get him only Class D job. This was enough of a setback and punishment to the family.

A Class D job was offered in about three-and-a-half months, on February 9, 1998, due to complications that got created due to non-verification of the 10th grade certificate and re-processing of the case a second time. Precious time was lost in settling the complications that arose because of the false certificate.

Railways administration had a stated policy for a long time wherein, in case of the death of an employee while in active service, as a token of compassion to the family, an employment is offered to the spouse of the deceased employee. The spouse has a choice to exercise the option either to take up the employment herself or to give her consent in favour of her son or unmarried daughter, provided the son/daughter give an undertaking that he/she would look after the mother. Such an employment is called as compassionate appointment. The grade of employment depends on the educational qualification of the candidate being offered such an appointment. Compassionate appointment to Sitaram Shukla's son brought closure to this tragedy. I was quite relieved as the family could get some money for subsistence.

Fatal but Not Fatalistic: Small Things Make a Big Difference – Firozabad Rail Tragedy

Firozabad is a city near Agra in the Indian state of Uttar Pradesh. It is the centre for India's glassmaking industry and is known for the quality of bangles and glassware produced. It is 37 km from Agra and 230 km from Delhi. It is on the Kanpur–Delhi route of North Central Railway. It has a population of about 6 lakhs.

The Firozabad accident was one of the worst rail disasters involving the loss of more than 350 lives. On August 20, 1995, at 2.55 a.m., the 2801 Purushottam Express (Puri to New Delhi) collided with the rear of the 4023 Kalindi Express (Kanpur to Bhiwani). Kalindi Express was stuck between two signals – starter and advance starter of the Firozabad station. A *nilgai* (blue bull) had been run over by Kalindi Express, and as a result the vacuum brake pipe of the train had been damaged, causing brake application. It was, therefore, not able to run. It was a dark, cloudy night with frequent rains in the section.

The gravity of the accident was such that the then Prime Minister, Shri P.V. Narasimha Rao, made a suo-moto statement in Lok Sabha on Monday, August 20, 1995, indicating human error as the prima-facie reason.

An ex-gratia payment of ₹5,000 for the dead, ₹2,000 for grievously injured, and ₹500 to passengers with minor injuries was announced by the Minister of State for Defence, Shri Mallikarjun.

The site of the accident was very difficult to approach. There was a high embankment of about 25–30 m on either side. Very near the site of the accident, the railway line went over a big, open drain, about 20–25 m wide. The size of the drain was big enough to accommodate a railway coach lengthwise. It had a terrible stench. The smell of garlic that had spread all around was making the site almost unapproachable. A consignment of garlic had been loaded in Kalindi Express. Since the five rear coaches of Kalindi Express and eight front coaches along with the locomotive of Purushottam Express had been completely damaged, the garlic had scattered at the site. Frequent rains followed by bright sunshine was making relief and restoration work a Herculean task. The bad smell of garlic and the stench emanating from the drain was aggravating the problem.

Both trains were bound for New Delhi. I was probably the first and the senior most officer of the Allahabad Division to reach the site of the accident from Kanpur. The Divisional Officers and the DRM were yet to arrive from Allahabad.

Firozabad is 400 km away from Allahabad and 200 km from Kanpur. I could therefore reach prior to the team that was to arrive from Allahabad. I departed from Kanpur at around 4 a.m. It took me about 3-4 hours to reach Firozabad.

By the time I reached, the 140-tonne crane had already arrived. The medical team from Tundla was at the site. There was chaos all around. All of Firozabad seemed to have gathered there. Police was not able to control the crowd.

New DRM had taken over charge only about three weeks prior to the incident.

I stayed at the site of the accident for three days, supervising the restoration work and arranging relief to the next-of-kin of the deceased.

General Manager, and senior officers of Northern Railway also arrived from Delhi. As this was one of the biggest rail tragedies, the GM had to be at the site to supervise relief and restoration. GM was quite well versed and an expert civil engineer too. He had a bright career ahead of him. He rose to become the Chairman Railway Board (CRB).

What I observed at the site was that no single person was the overall in-charge, despite the presence of the General Manager, Principal Heads of Departments and the Divisional Railway Manager.

I was able to witness mis-management in different aspects of the relief and restoration work such as the working of the 140-tonne crane to remove damaged coaches, crowd management, separate set of staff and supervisors who could be deployed every eight hours for round-the-clock work, food and water for the staff, payment of diet charges to staff, coordination within and outside the Division to get track, traction and signalling material required to replace the damaged parts, shelter for the staff to take rest, medical team, and temporary toilets at site.

In my opinion, a lot could have been done better even in shifting the dead bodies to a civil hospital, providing ex-gratia to the injured and families of deceased passengers, arranging food for the affected passengers, arranging transport for the stranded passengers, dissemination of information to the people and regular update to the print and electronic media.

This might have been due to the DRM being new to the Division. Out of the officers present, it is assumed that the senior-most officer is the site in-charge as per standard Railways protocol. From what I saw, unfortunately this did not happen or was not visible.

The DRM has to be in full command of the site under such tragic circumstances. He is the only person who will be heard by the Branch Officers of the Division. They ultimately report to the DRM and deliver on the ground. The presence of GM and senior officers is only for the limited purpose of appreciation of the extent of the problem and providing necessary support for declaration of ex-gratia payment and handling the higher ups in the Government and, of-course, assessing the realistic target for the relief and restoration of traffic.

This was a huge learning for me. I was able to introspect – what if I were the DRM, how differently would I have handled the situation? The GM and DRM appeared completely helpless, probably seeing the sheer extent of the loss of lives and the colossal damage that had been caused by the accident.

This experience helped me to handle the fire tragedy of Doon Express in November 2011 very confidently and efficiently while I was DRM Dhanbad. Efficient handling of the situation brought a lot of appreciation not only from the media but also from the Australian High Commission and the Commissioner Railway Safety (CRS).

In the case of the Doon Express fire tragedy, the ex-gratia payment of ₹5 lakh was disbursed to the next-of-kin of the deceased passengers by the same evening. The affected passengers who decided to continue their journey were paid the ex-gratia of ₹25,000 each in the train itself between Gaya and Mughalsarai. Such a thing happened for the first time. Ajay Shukla, my Additional General Manager, deserves this credit. He helped in organising all this. All the affected passengers were provided food, tea and toilet kits. The CRS was extended full support to undertake his investigations. I was present myself all the time with the CRS.

This accident happened due to gross human error on the part of Cabin Man of West Cabin, Station Master of Firozabad, the Guard and Driver of Kalindi Express, and the Driver of Purushottam Express.

Kalindi Express had stopped between the Starter and the Advance Starter signals of the station due to 'cattle (nilgai) run over'.

The staff in-charge of the West Cabin, Firozabad, was supposed to give clearance for the despatch of the next train to the Station Master, Firozabad. For this he had to physically verify that Kalindi Express had passed Advance Starter. He made an error of judgement in giving clearance that Kalindi Express had passed the Advance Starter while it was stuck between the Starter and Advance Starter signals.

The train was stuck due to disconnection of vacuum pipes of the train, leading to brake application. It was monsoon season and raining that night. It is possible that the West Cabin in-charge was not able to see outside his Cabin due to poor visibility and did not make any conscious effort to listen to the buzzer that was supposed to sound when the train had crossed the Advance Starter. He made a gross error of judgement by giving clearance and lowering the Starter and Advance Starter for the next train by seeking permission from Station Master, Firozabad. It was possible to commit such an error as there had been no track circuiting between Starter and Advance Starter at that time.

This clearance from West Cabin meant that rail track was clear up to the Advance Starter signal for dispatch of the next train.

The Station Master gave amber light at Home signal for the Driver of Purushottam Express to enter the station. However, giving green lights at Starter and Advance Starter signal meant that the Driver could go to the next station – Hirangaon.

On seeing the amber lights of Home, and green lights of Starter and Advance Starter signal, the Driver of Purushottam Express understood that he was not supposed to stop at Firozabad, although amber lights at Home signal should have made him reduce the speed and be ready to stop at the Firozabad station. Instead, he ran at full speed and rammed into Kalindi Express at 100 kmph.

For dispatch of Purushottam Express, Kalindi Express should have reached Hirangaon, the next station. The assurance regarding the complete arrival of Kalindi Express had to come from the Station Master of Hirangaon, the station ahead of Firozabad, towards Delhi. This had not happened.

It was a mistake on the part of the Station Master Firozabad, who, although he gave amber lights at Home, gave green lights at Starter and Advance Starter signals at Firozabad station, without ascertaining from the next station Hirangaon whether Kalindi Express had arrived there or not.

Fatal but Not Fatalistic: Small Things Make a Big Difference

This error could have been averted if the track between Starter and Advance Starter had been track circuited. Had this technical solution been provided, the technology would not have allowed grant of clearance by the in-charge of the West Cabin at Firozabad to the Station Master Firozabad, and the accident could had been averted.

Also, if the Driver of Purushottam Express had been alert, he would have slowed down the speed of his train by seeing amber light of Home signal. In that eventuality, it is possible that he would have been able to see the red light of the tail lamp of Kalindi Express and stopped the train short of obstruction.

As per the rules, the Driver of Kalindi Express was also supposed to have conveyed to West Cabin or the Station Master Firozabad within 15 minutes of the detention of their train that the train had been disabled due to cattle run over. This would have alerted the Station Master about the incident and a major tragedy could have been averted.

After this tragedy, Railways decided to provide track circuit right from Advance Starter to Advance Starter on both sides of the station for movement of trains in both the directions. To the best of my knowledge, there has been no such incident since. That is what technology does – provides backup protection for foolproof working.

On a section fit for 130 kmph train operation, every station has a signalling arrangement wherein the Driver approaching the station first sees a Distant Signal followed by an Inner Distant Signal and then the Home Signal. All these signals have approximately one km distance between them. Distant and Inner Distant signals are permission signals and therefore a Driver is not supposed to stop at these signals; these signals have three aspects – Yellow, Double Yellow and Green.

Home signal is a stop signal and has three aspects – Red (stop), Green (go) and Yellow (go with caution). This signal is provided to permit entry of a train into a station.

There are two other signals for the departure of a train called Starter and Advance Starter. Unless both the Starter and Advance Starter are green, a train cannot proceed to the next station. Home, Starter and Advance Signals are called 'stop signals'. These signals are green, yellow or red depending on the conditions specified for safe train movement.

Track circuit arrangement confirms occupation of a track in the station area by showing red light on the panel provided in front of the Station Master. Once a train stands on the track, the circuit gets shorted through the wheels of the locomotives and coaches. After the train leaves the station, the light turns green, indicating that the track is not occupied. The logic for safe train movement is in-built in the working rules of the station to avert any accident and the staff is trained accordingly.

CRS is a statutory authority under Ministry of Civil Aviation and is supposed to conduct an independent enquiry into passenger train accidents where loss of human life is involved. This was done in this case.

The following directions were given from the Railway Ministry in 1995 to improve safety after this accident:

- Complete track circuiting from Fouling Mark to Fouling Mark on all trunk routes and main line by March 1996, and between Starter to Advance Starter on all trunk routes by June 1996.
- Provide track circuit ahead of Starter to make Starter signal red after the passage of train at roadside station.
- Distance between Starter and Advance Starter reduced to 180 m at roadside station so that the train can be seen by Cabinman if train had not crossed Advance Starter.
- Modify signal circuits to prevent lowering of signal for the next train till the level of Starter lowered for the earlier train, has not been put back to 'On'.

It is my opinion, irrespective of the seniority of the superior authority that might visit the site of an accident, the DRM should be the site in-charge and take all actions for relief and restoration work. The rule of 'senior-most officer to be the site in-charge' must go. This will provide unambiguous command-and-control under such circumstances. Superior authorities may give directions to DRM to act.

Resourcefulness: The Uses of Adversity – Tap Changer, the Heart of the Locomotive

Tap Changer is a vital equipment and considered the heart of a conventional electric locomotive. Its function is to increase or decrease voltage levels across traction motors to control the speed of a locomotive. There was only one source – Asea Brown Boveri or ABB (later AD Tranz, Bombardier and now River Engineering) – for the manufacture of this equipment and supply of components for its upkeep. The life of this equipment is 18 years, but it serves even beyond if repaired or reconditioned in accordance with guidelines of the OEM. Even experts take a lifetime to understand this equipment. It's an expensive part of the locomotive. It requires the highest level of attention, as any malfunction could result in a fire in the locomotive. It is filled with around 100 litres of mineral oil to ensure quenching of any electric spark inside during its operation.

All the spare parts of this equipment used to be procured from a single source, i.e., ABB, that too on payment of full advance. It was really a challenge to ensure upkeep of this equipment for a high order of reliability of the locomotive.

There was a perennial shortage of spare parts required for its repair during a major overhaul. Whenever a locomotive failed on this account, the responsibility was fixed. Off and on, there were cases of fire wherein the locomotive was badly damaged.

The staff used to agitate because complete overhauling kits were never available when required in one go. It was quite intriguing that despite the Railways willing to pay in advance, the OEM was not able to supply the material. Yet, there was no option. We used to have regular coordination meetings with the top management of ABB. The situation improved only incrementally. It was a crisis item for all the Sheds of Indian Railways due to shortage and high cost.

The problem was a lot more serious for locomotives more than 20 years old. These locomotives required major inputs to repair Tap Changers. Large sums of advance money were always outstanding with ABB for supply of spare parts. I thought of getting the complete Tap Changer repaired through OEM rather than buying spare parts in piecemeal. All the components used to be procured from ABB only.

RDSO had brought out a clear policy that all kits had to be procured from ABB. As the situation was simply out of control, sometime in 1998 I made a proposal to ABB to explore the possibility of repairing the whole Tap Changer as a unit and giving a warranty, like the purchase of a new Tap Changer. There was no response from ABB. Since I was continuously following up with their works at Vadodara, one Senior Executive from ABB visited the Kanpur Shed after 3–4 months. This executive of ABB belonged to Kanpur.

He wanted to ascertain the seriousness of the proposal and the commitment of the Shed's management in moving ahead with this idea. He had brought a questionnaire. The moot point in the questionnaire was: 'What will be the response of the labour unions?' At first, this annoyed me, but I seriously thought about it. The question did allow me to introspect.

The whole equipment was to be transported to Baroda Works for repair and the staff who were engaged in its repair and maintenance might feel redundant. This could also lead to progressive dilution in their skills. They would no more be doing this major activity. This is how people would portray the whole initiative. Although, such repairs would be carried out on some of the Tap Changers, the major work would remain with the Shed's workers.

I therefore consulted the Headquarters and my technical supervisors. Their response was overwhelming since there was no other source for its purchase and ABB was supplying these components with a lot of delays, despite getting advance payments. The matter was also discussed with RDSO and after protracted discussions, it was decided to lay down norms as to what could be repaired and beyond what level, the Tap Changer will have to be declared 'beyond economic repair' and condemned.

RDSO identified the 'must change' items and items which would get repaired or re-conditioned based on their conditions. It was legislated that if the repairs go beyond 60 per cent of the cost of a new Tap Changer, it would not be a good idea to have it rehabilitated or re-conditioned. In that eventuality the Tap Changer would be simply condemned. This exercise took two years. In the meantime, I got transferred as Director (Rolling Stock), Railway Board.

The Mission Rehabilitation of Tap Changer continued, as I was now looking after the Operation & Maintenance of around 2,500 locomotives from Railway Board, pan India. After persuasion of Members of the Railway Board and the Financial Commissioner Indian Railways, as a special case, a repair and rehabilitation work tender was issued from the Railway Board in the year 2000, for reconditioning of around 200 Tap Changers for the whole of Indian Railways – an unprecedented initiative by any standard. A.K. Jain was the Additional Member Electrical. I.C. Sharma was the Executive Director. Both were convinced. A.K. Jain had been my DRM at Allahabad and was a man with a lot of clarity and decisiveness. I.C. Sharma was a stalwart in rolling stock maintenance. He had worked as in-charge of Loco Shed, Mughalsarai.

This initiative was primarily aimed at improving the reliability of Tap Changers, eliminating the incidence of fire in the locomotives and optimising cost of maintenance. Alongside, another major decision was taken that Indian Railways would no longer procure new Tap Changers as Unit Exchange Spares (UES) for Railways. The rehabilitated Tap Changers were supposed to be as good as new, and ABB would provide similar warranty for the rehabilitated Tap Changer as for the new ones. A new era evolved for the Operation & Maintenance (O&M) of major high-end equipment.

UES was a concept wherein CLW would buy extra equipment (over and above their loco manufacturing need) in the range of 2.5 per cent to 5 per cent of the population of the major sub-assemblies in use, for supply to Sheds to ensure high level availability of locomotives manufactured by them. These spares were supposed to be a part of the supply of new locomotives from CLW to Loco Sheds.

Once the contract for complete rehabilitation was finalised by the Railway Board for repair of 200 Tap Changers, the Tap Changers were to be picked up by ABB from sheds of Zonal Railways. It so happened that ABB decided to lift the first Tap Changer from the Kanpur shed, where this idea had germinated. There was a big dispute between the administration and the Unions. This came to my knowledge in the Railway Board. I was reminded of the questionnaire prepared by the ABB management.

I decided to speak to Kishan Lal, the concerned officer in-charge who was fully associated with the project during my period of stay at Kanpur. He briefed me about the issues raised by the Unions. It took me no time to talk to Ram Bharosey, the secretary of the Union, who happened to be working in the Tap Changer section. When I spoke to him and reminded him of the difficulties that used to be faced when material was in short supply, and how some failures used to cause fire in the locomotive, he replied, 'Sir, we have no problem, but we should be sent for regular inspection of the repaired Tap Changers to ABB factory at Vadodara.'

Immediately, an agreement was reached that a roster would be made for doing such inspections. This would educate the staff and give them confidence that the job was being done well. Kishan Lal took all the necessary actions thereafter. A success was in the making. A very critical problem got resolved.

Maintenance philosophy with hand holding by the OEMs got settled and aligned amongst all stakeholders. From then onwards, it has become the stated policy of the Ministry of Railways that the Tap Changers will only get reconditioned or rehabilitated with OEMs. No new Tap Changers were sanctioned thereafter for maintenance. It was a major policy shift. It is being practised for the last two decades.

6

Hardiness and Grit: When You Stand Alone – Unprecedented Rains in 40 Years

Underfloor Wheel Lathe (UWL) is one of the most important plant & machinery of any loco maintenance depot, and is very vital for the safe running of a locomotive. This machine is installed in a separate covered shed, a little away from the main shed, for ease of working and to ensure that the steel scrap, generated because of removal of steel from the wheels of the locomotive, is kept away from the main working area. This ensured cleanliness and safety of the workers. Small, sharp steel chips come out of this process of metal cutting. This steel scrap is disposed at regular intervals along with other ferrous scrap of the shed. It is generally kept near the scrapyard in the depot.

The covered shed which houses the UWL is about 60 m long, 50 m wide and 8 m high. Within the covered shed there is a big rectangular pit which is about 33 m long, 13 m wide and 2.5 m deep. The machine is installed inside this pit. The locomotive stands on a rail track over the machine for the removal of unwanted steel using special tools. Locomotive wheels rotate on the rollers of the machine.

The wheels of the locomotive are re-profiled at regular intervals. Wear and tear of the wheels is a regular phenomenon. Wheels are checked during every maintenance schedule and action taken if the wheel profile is not as per the standard. If the wheel profile is not right, the locomotive may derail online and even cause an accident. This lathe machine is therefore always kept in the best of health all the time to ensure the safety of locomotives.

On July 6, 1998, while I was in-charge of the Shed, there were unprecedented rains. It was the highest rainfall in the past 40 years in Kanpur. The Kanpur Shed was flooded. This led to the flooding of the pit in which the machine was placed. Due to back flow of water from the main drain, the machine was completely submerged in water.

This happened on a Sunday night but came to our notice in the afternoon of the next working day. This covered shed is generally at one end of the main shed. We did not know what to do, as even draining of water, while the whole land mass was submerged in water, was a big task. Moreover, there was no electricity because of heavy flooding and continuous rains. A locomotive has two compressors of 1,500 litre per minute capacity to build pressure of 6 kg per square centimetre in the brake pipe of the train. The locomotive also has four air reservoirs of 1,000 litre capacity each. There was no 230-volt electricity but 25 KV traction supply was available. We therefore decided to use locomotive air supply to operate the pneumatic pumps that work on compressed air. This could avoid any chance of an electric shock to workers. A locomotive was placed near the Underfloor Wheel Lathe shed and it was energised to run compressors to generate air pressure and fill the air reservoirs of the locomotive. The water could be drained in about eight to ten hours.

This was a Heigensheigh machine made in Germany. Repair work for this machine was a serious question. This company made best quality machines. Till the development of the Indian model by HYT Pune, this used to be imported from Germany.

The proprietor of HYT was contacted to render assistance. They demanded airfare for their technicians, hotel for the stay and money for the repair and maintenance. Repair charges needed to be ascertained based on the extent of damage. I tried my best to persuade HYT and offered that we would provide the railway guest house in place of a hotel, and our own railway transport for their internal travel in Kanpur. There was no way we would be able to provide air fare for their travel. I also tried to persuade them to ascertain a fixed amount for the whole repair. HYT did not agree.

We lost two crucial days in this process. The Division did not have any powers to engage a private firm and pay for the air travel and hotel expenses without following a tender process. The Head office was quite angry and not providing any help as I was not willing to hold anyone accountable for the problem. It was an act of God, I felt.

I therefore decided that the best course of action would be to try and repair with the resources in the Shed. In the best-case scenario, we would have been able to re-commission the machine; in the worst case, it would remain as is.

The damage was only due to ingress of water in all the electrical parts, circuitry and control system. Many imported contactors were provided in the machine. The hydraulic oil had mixed with water and gone inside these sophisticated contactors. All these contactors were of German make and equivalent Indian models were not known to us. The concern was that if any of these hundreds of contactors went defective, it would not be possible to re-commission the machine.

Around 40 staff members and supervisors were identified and deployed to work in three shifts of 8 hours each, round the clock. Puran Chandra, Assistant Electrical Engineer, was made the overall in-charge of this operation. I decided to remain at site for at least 10–12 hours every day. After the water had been drained, we decided to dismantle all the motors and use petrol to clean the electrical windings and dry them using electrical heaters. This was done three times to ensure that the insulation resistance of the electrical circuits reach a high level. A similar job was done simultaneously on the contactors. After 10 days of strenuous work, all the machines and contactors were cleaned up and dried. We were extra cautious to eliminate any chance of a short circuit due to poor insulation, once the electrical supply was be switched on.

The energisation of the machine was done after 10 days, in a progressive manner and on the 11th day we were able to restore the machine to its full functionality. What an achievement!

The matter was reported to the Headquarters. The GM was also apprised. It was a commendable job done by the technicians and supervisors under the leadership of Puran Chandra. All the 40 staff members and Puran Chandra were awarded by the General Manager. It was an award of ₹21,000. It was unthinkable at that time as the GM's highest award used to be ₹500 per awardee, and a maximum of 2-3 staff members of a unit under the Division got such an award at the annual function. In this case the award was for 40 staff members and one officer. It was a big day for the shed.

Puran Chandra was a hardworking and self-motivated officer. I used to depend on him heavily for his technical opinion. If I had to remember any future event, I requested Puran to remember it rather than remembering it myself. He used to feed it into his electronic diary and remind me on that date. Such was my relationship with him.

He had excellent knowledge about mechanical systems. Even if he had to work for 24 hours in the Shed, he did it without blinking an eye. He was an old stalwart of the Shed. He had worked there in supervisory capacity as well. On his promotion to a gazetted cadre as Assistant Electrical Engineer, I made sure that he was posted at Kanpur Shed. He was quite thankful to me. We had an excellent personal chemistry. The staff always respected him for his competence and sheer hard work.

One afternoon, I was sitting in PPIO. Suddenly a staff member came from the HQ with a confidential letter. My initial thoughts were that the HQ was not happy about flooding of Underfloor Wheel Lathe, and maybe they had decided to convey the same. Confidential letters are generally about such matters. To my surprise, the letter was from the GM, and it had been signed on August 3, 1998. It was a letter of appreciation from S.P. Mehta who was the GM. It was quite a detailed letter. It was very motivating to read the feelings expressed therein: 'I am happy to record my appreciation of the successful management of the disaster by you. I am sure you must have derived personal satisfaction as an engineer in successfully meeting a challenge of this nature. Keep it up.'

This was the same Headquarter that was quite unhappy with my line of action regarding not holding anyone responsible for the disaster of flooding of Underfloor Wheel Lathe.

This letter was also placed in my service record.

Sheer perseverance can give you any result that you expect.

During this breakdown, a large number of officers had pointed out that this tragedy could have been avoided if the medical department had ensured proper cleaning of the main drain which ran by the side of the Shed. This drain had not been cleaned for a long time and a lot of silt had accumulated. I however decided not to blame any individual as this situation had arisen because of unprecedented rain. I decided to rather seek cooperation than apportion blame.

Health and hygiene had been the responsibility of the Medical Department in the Railways, and therefore cleaning of drains was squarely the job of the doctors through Sanitary Health Inspectors and sanitary workers. Needless to say, this job was not done well.

Not allocating any blame to the Medical Department also emanated from my inner feelings that the doctors are really those people I fall back upon any time for any assistance for the Shed's staff. They were always very helpful. If I didn't look at their yeoman service to my 1,100 strong staff and their families, it would be most ungrateful.

With 1,100 people working round the clock, there will always be some medical emergency. Unprecedented rain was certainly the prime reason for flooding. By coping with this adversity, I was sure to fetch all the cooperation at that time and ensure even stronger support in the future. The doctors also realised that for the present problem, the Medical Department was responsible. Withstanding the present pressure was therefore a better trade-off, I decided. This improved the goodwill at the Shed.

A tragedy of sorts became a virtue by sheer perseverance, collaboration and going above the call of duty. Without personal sacrifices, major changes are unthinkable. Personal sacrifice in the instant case was to work for 10–12 hours every day without a break, remain unruffled by the pressure of fixing responsibility, and remain at the site and have lunch and snacks with staff and supervisors.

7

Enabling Learning Agility: Chicago for Simulator

I had joined the working post after completing my probation in May 1985 in Delhi. After about six months, I was posted as Assistant Electrical Engineer (Operations) Tundla. My charge was operation and maintenance of electric locomotives between Ghaziabad and Kanpur section of Railways.

There were more than 500 drivers working under my control, mostly headquartered at Tundla. With progressive electrification of railway tracks, the diesel engine drivers were being trained for driving electric locomotives. They used to be given classroom training. On-the-job training for driving a locomotive used to be done either on locomotives under maintenance at the outstation pits or on locomotives working a train. This was always under the guidance of loco inspectors. They were however not allowed to drive a locomotive working a train. For driving a train, a driver had to be certified for the particular type of locomotive.

Even after passing the examination, the newly trained drivers initially drove a few trains under the supervision of a nominated loco inspector. It might appear quite scary as the driver who was yet to attain proficiency in driving trains, drove the first train under the supervision of an inspector. There was no other way to train a driver in Railways. This system had been going on for ages.

In the airline industry, pilots are trained on a simulator replicating real-life situations and only after they attain proficiency, are they granted license to fly as a trainee pilot. Finally, they are given the licence of a commercial pilot. Such a system did not exist in Indian Railways.

In 1990 an attempt was made to procure a simulator for loco drivers in Indian Railways. An order for the first electric and diesel loco simulator was placed on Tata Electronic Development Services, Bengaluru, who were to develop a simulator in collaboration with Illinois Institute of Technology Research Institute (IITRI), Chicago, USA.

My first experience with operations was at Tundla while N. Venkatesan was my DRM at Allahabad. He happened to be a Member, Railway Board when the simulators were to be commissioned.

In 1992, I was posted as in-charge of Traction Machine Shed, Kanpur. I had nothing to do with train operations. Yet, I was nominated along with a few drivers and other officers to undergo training on electric loco simulator at IITRI, Chicago. The mission was to fully understand the operational aspects of simulator technology. It was equally important to understand how to make the best use of new technology for training drivers, bring proficiency in train handling, optimising electrical energy consumption and ultimately improve safety. This was a two-month assignment in the USA. I was very fortunate as I was nominated by a Member, Railway Board to go to the USA.

Venkatesan had known me as Assistant Electrical Engineer (Operations) Tundla in 1986, almost six years earlier. He was my DRM. As DRM Allahabad, he used to talk to me every day about train operations. He would also talk to me whenever there was an accident or derailment or any unusual occurrence on the line. I used to attend all such events without fail and without anybody's directions. My intention was always to meet the driver and listen to his version. This helped me to identify the root cause. It also gave me confidence in my analysis. It was a great learning for me in my formative years.

I might have been considered for this assignment in the USA due to my straightforwardness, sincerity and professional honesty. It was a big motivator for me. I had put in just nine years of service at that time. We were a group of six railwaymen – three officers and three supervisors.

All formalities for the issue of official passport and visa were completed in July-August 1992. Our air tickets were issued just a week before our departure on September 5, 1992. I got foreign exchange released from State Bank of India, Kanpur. We got more than US$4,500 for this visit, at the rate of US$75 per day. It was an awesome feeling. I was to travel in an aeroplane for the first time in my life.

I had a huge fascination for aeroplanes. In fact, I had done my two months Industrial Training in Indian Airlines in Delhi in May–June 1980. This was a part of my BTech degree course. One of my uncles who worked in Indian Airlines in New Delhi had organised this training for me. I used to love going inside the aircraft and understand its working. I had made a project report on 'Aircrafts' which was very much appreciated by the General Manager (Personnel) in Indian Airlines.

Enabling Learning Agility: Chicago for Simulator

I remember the day I was at the Safdarjung Airport, when Sanjay Gandhi, son of Indira Gandhi, the then Prime Minister of India, had died in a plane crash, on June 23, 1980. He was flying a new aircraft of the Delhi Flying Club and had lost control while performing an aerobatic manoeuvre. I was a witness to this unfortunate accident.

On September 5, 1992, we boarded the flight to New York, from where we were to finally fly to Chicago. At Chicago, the Indian Embassy had arranged our stay at Hotel Residence Inn, very close to the Chicago Lake and a very beautiful hotel. The hotel had all the facilities with an equipped kitchenette attached. The lake used to freeze in winters, and people used to drive cars over it. It was a very windy city.

The Institute was on 35th Street in Chicago. On the first day itself we were told not to go beyond 35th Street due to security reasons. The classroom training started. There was a diesel locomotive simulator already there. This was regularly used to train drivers. Drivers used to be issued a licence like a car driving licence by IITRI, Chicago. It was simply fascinating.

During the training at IITRI, a World Railway Meet, which was held every four years at Chicago, was going on. We tried to get an opportunity to visit this Railway Meet and were fortunate enough to get the chance. We saw many simulators. These were on display by different manufacturers from across the world.

We discovered that a scorecard was generated by the simulator system. This was, in fact, a numerical score of the performance of the driver regarding energy consumption, train handling and response time to react to any unforeseen circumstances.

This feature was not a part of the purchase order placed by Indian Railways. We requested our professor in-charge at IITRI to include this aspect in the software design. There was some resistance. However, we insisted and got this feature included in the design of the simulator for the Indian Railways. The training was over in two months time. During this period in Chicago, we also saw how Presidential elections are held in the US. Bill Clinton was elected the US President in 1992.

After this training, an electric loco simulator was commissioned at Kanpur along with the new features. Simulator training became mandatory for drivers of high-speed trains and for drivers undergoing a diesel to electric conversion course.

I always cherish this training as I was a part of the new technology that was inducted by Railways. We were able to have unique features included in the system software that had not been thought about initially.

Thereafter, I had the chance to upscale the provision of simulators through the Corporate Safety Plan, evolved in 2002. I was working as Director (Rolling Stock), Railway Board at the time. I was able to get the sanction for about 15–16 simulators.

Recently, as Head of Transformation in the Railway Board, I got simulators worth ₹350 crore (US$50 million) sanctioned for Lobbies and Zonal Training Schools. Simulator training has helped tremendously in improving train handling skills and optimising energy consumption. Jeetendra Singh worked with me on this project while he was Executive Director in the Transformation Cell.

Desire to do well and lifelong learning are the most important aspects of one's behaviour to transform not only one's own self but also the organisation. Formative years are very important in life to establish one's reputation and top management's trust. Never breach that to your detriment.

8

Quiet Leadership: The Relentless Way – A Policy Revamp

I had worked in Kanpur for close to ten years since 1989. I had become well-adjusted there. One day, Yash Pal Gupta, the Chief Workshop Manager (CWM), Charbagh Workshop, Lucknow, visited my place and had breakfast with me. During discussion, he asked me why I was there for so long. He almost reprimanded me. He told me that life would be far better outside the Shed. This haunted me for quite a few days and then started making sense to me. I was in my comfort zone and therefore found it a safe haven. Undoubtedly, there were great challenges of working in a place having labour concentration. In fact, challenges increase as one goes on staying at the same place.

Yash Pal Gupta was a tall, handsome, energetic and a dynamic mechanical engineer and a great leader. He had worked as DRM Sambhalpur. Quite often he narrated to me the success stories of his stay at Sambhalpur, and those were quite inspiring. Sambhalpur is a division of East Coast Railway (ECR) and was formed on November 5, 1951. It is a district in the Indian state of Orissa It is the headquarter of Mahanadi Coalfield Limited. It is 300 km from the state capital, Bhubaneshwar, and 550 km from Kolkata. Yash Pal often told me about the pride people used to feel once a logo for the Division was created. That was 'Coal as Black Diamond' with a beautiful picture of a diamond. That was a unique way to enthuse and motivate people. They would have a personal connection with the place. A substantial portion of the business of Sambhalpur Division was coal loading.

Locomotives of my Shed used to be repaired at the Charbagh Workshop. Yash Pal Gupta's interaction with me was therefore quite frequent. Charbagh workshop was established in 1867-68 by Oudh and Rohilkhand Railway during British rule. It was established primarily to maintain steam locomotives. Maintenance of diesel locomotives started in 1975. Electric locos maintenance started in

1987. During Yash Pal Gupta's tenure at the workshop, centenary celebrations were held in the workshop. A lot of renovation activities were undertaken during this period. Electric loco maintenance also started.

One day in December 1998, A.K. Jain, the Additional Member, Railway Board, called me and asked me if I would like to work in the Railway Board as Director (Rolling Stock). I gave my assent in the blink of an eye. Orders were issued in December 1998.

But I was not relieved by Northern Railway as the CEE wanted me to be posted at HQ which I had not agreed to, prior to the issue of orders for posting in Railway Board. His anger was therefore genuine, as I was willing to work in Railway Board and not in Northern Railway. Both these places were in Delhi. With the intervention of the Railway Board, I was relieved in April 1999 and joined as Director (Rolling Stock).

I had worked in the field for around 14 years and during this period I was in-charge of two Depots – Electric Loco Maintenance and Traction Machine. Keeping this background in view, my field experience led me to be posted as Director (Rolling Stock), Railway Board.

The job required looking after manufacture, maintenance and operation of electric locos of entire Indian Railways. With progressive electrification of railway tracks, the requirement of electric loco was increasing and, hence there was a focus on maintaining a high level of reliability and availability of electric locos. We had a mix of old and new technology locomotives in the system: four axle locos of 1960s vintage, the majority of these being imported ones, and the newer 3-phase locos of the latest 1990s vintage with the Gate Turn Off Thyristor (GTO) technology. The GTO technology enabled regeneration of electrical energy when brakes are applied. Four axle locomotives were imported from the 50 Cycle Group of companies (Kraus-Maffei, Krupp, SFAC, La Bourgeoise & Nivelle) in Europe. Some of the four axle locomotives were from Hitachi, Mitsubishi and Toshiba, Japan. The four-axle technology had become outdated by the early 1980s.

Old Technology Out

Four axle locomotives were literally a drag on the rail operations, as these were frequently failing on the one hand and required extra maintenance effort and money for their upkeep on the other. Some of these locomotives had been in use for more than 30 or even 36 years. The codal life (life of an asset defined in railway code) of electric locos is 35 years. While working as in-charge of Electric Loco Shed, Kanpur, I had already phased out 40 locos of this variety after taking a lot of personal initiative by convincing Finance and the Headquarters.

A methodology to phase out old locos had been put in place by me in the Kanpur Shed after a lot of research, and that had become the norm now. The main component of this methodology was the measurement of Camber of the locomotive. Camber is the convex or arched shape of the underframe of the locomotive body. This is supposed to be positive all the time during the lifetime of the locomotive. This Camber had become negative to the extent of 20 to 30 mm in a majority of four axle locomotives. A Camber of less than zero was considered unsafe for a locomotive. When a new locomotive is manufactured, Camber is kept as 15 to 20 mm on the positive side. In some of the locomotives one could see negative camber even without any measurements.

In the new assignment, I had an opportunity to replicate the same concept on pan India basis and, so a conscious decision was taken with the approval of the Board to phase out 7 classes of four axle locomotives: WAG 1, 2, 3, 4 and WAM 1, 2, 3.

Here 'W' stands for broad gauge, 'A' stands for alternating current, 'G' stands for goods, 'M' stands for mixed and 1, 2, 3, 4 represent the series of manufacture with '1' being the oldest and '4' being the latest.

Over a period of three years, from 1999 to 2002, all the 392 locos (WAG 1, 2, 3, 4 and WAM 1, 2, 3) were phased out. These locomotives were 2,800 to 3,800 HP. It gave a big respite to operations. Ultimately, this initiative was applauded across Indian Railways. A new era of condemnation of locomotives was institutionalised.

New WAG 7 locos from CLW were getting inducted in the Railways system as a replacement of these old ones. WAG 7 locos proved to be the workhorse for Indian Railways. These were 5,000 HP locomotives and indigenously designed and manufactured.

End-to-End Running

There was an age-old practice of running Mail Express trains wherein the train engine used to be detached at the Zonal boundaries. This used to be done to ensure higher reliability. For a long time, there was a concept of ownership of a locomotive by a particular Zonal Railway. A locomotive belonging to Northern Railway running on Central Railway was referred to as 'foreign railway locomotive' by Central Railway. It was quite intriguing to me.

Detachment of locomotives from a running mail express train at the boundary of two adjoining Zones was leading to significant failures in the proximity of such change over. It was also causing loss of time required in the swapping of locos of either Zone. A mail express train had to be run by locomotives belonging to its own Zonal Railway within its own Zonal boundaries. It was like a colonial footprint.

Similar was the practice in freight operations, although a shade better. Freight locos used to be extended to adjoining Zonal Railway, but these locos also could not transcend beyond the adjoining railway. A freight locomotive extending beyond the adjoining railway, due to exigency of operation, used to be declared as 'non-permitted territory'. Ownership of locomotives for undertaking major schedules in the Home Sheds and trip schedules at outstation pit was a primary reason for such operating protocols. This was a serious constraint in operations but was business-as-usual.

Over a period of time, the quality of batteries and reliability of vacuum exhausters and air compressors had improved, which made us think that the topping up of distilled water in the battery and topping up of oil in the exhausters and compressors could be deferred as it would last longer than seven days between successive maintenance interventions. Moreover, end-to-end running of freight trains was making it difficult to detach locomotives for trips or weekly schedules, in order to avoid excessive detention to trains.

It was therefore thought that locomotives must run end-to-end in coaching operation, without detachment at the Zonal boundaries and there should be no embargo on movement of freight locomotives beyond the adjoining railways to make train operation seamless in the overall interest of industrial relations. This was a massive shift in operating strategy.

This, however, meant that the Coaching Links for Mail Express trains for locomotives had to be revised and the attention to freight locomotives needed to be organised far beyond the Home Sheds. Coaching Link is the programme of attachment and detachment of a locomotive from a train, and allocation of locomotive time for servicing or maintenance of the same at an out pit or in a regular Shed in between commercial operations.

Home Shed means the mother shed of the locomotive to which a locomotive is allotted for the purpose of maintenance and upkeep of all the records of its equipment including the day-to-day monitoring of its performance. Locomotive number and the name of the Loco Shed is written on the front face of the locomotive.

In fact, the concept of ownership of a locomotive by a particular Loco Shed of a Zonal Railway had to be translated into ownership of all the locomotives by all the Sheds and Railway Zones. For some reasons this could not be implemented.

Running of locomotives without detachment at interchange points was a major change in the pattern of operation of locomotives, which the officers of the Electrical discipline were not very happy with. The Traffic Officers in the Board were also sceptical, thinking that it might lead to surge in failure of locomotives and their associated dead movement.

One day, all the Executive Directors of the Traffic Department called me to understand this concept. It was more with apprehension than with a sense of purpose. However, after the meeting, everybody got convinced that this was the best way forward for the overall operation of Railways.

A suggestion of this nature coming from me was really welcomed. Slowly, quite a few outstation pits were closed and the staff redeployed in the Sheds. The Coaching Links were reworked on end-to-end basis, and accordingly Mail Express locos were transferred from one Shed to another Shed to meet the new operational requirement of running trains. What a major change it was! It took almost 6–8 months to stabilise the new normal. The officers of the Electrical discipline however remained very critical of this decision.

Alongside, it was also decided that the locos needing repairs would not 'haul dead'. We identified components and sub-systems that would be replaced in the Shed nearest to the place of failure of a locomotive.

This also enabled us to respond to the objections of the Audit Department (the objection was excessive dead movement without attention, nearest the place where failure had occurred), as it was in the overall interest of the Railways.

Both passenger and freight operations improved substantially as the detachment of locomotives at Zonal boundaries completely stopped. However, running of overdue schedule locos substantially increased, as locos in the Southern Region to which attention was overdue were not able to reach the northern part of the country within a week's time. Therefore, there was huge criticism of end-to-end running.

Periodicity of Maintenance

The maintenance schedules which were being followed for minor and major inspections had been laid down in the 1980s. These needed a hard look because of changing technology besides keeping in view the capacity to home locomotives in a particular Shed.

I had worked for ten years in the maintenance Shed and had a fairly clear idea that a locomotive which was due for maintenance after 30 days could as well wait for 45 days for the same maintenance, if the topping up of oil and water had been done in time.

Similarly, a major annual overhaul that was due could as well be done after one-and-a-half years without much loss of reliability, if the four-monthly schedules had been undertaken with perfection.

I was also pretty sure that the periodic overhaul, presently planned at the end of six years, could be deferred by another three years and undertaken after nine years. Drawing upon the same logic, intermediate overhaul could be undertaken after four-and-a-half years instead of three years. I followed this practice to some extent while working as in-charge of Kanpur Shed.

Sudesh Kumar was the Chief Electrical Loco Engineer at the Headquarters then. He was an extremely competent rolling stock engineer, and like a teacher to all of us working in the Sheds. He was convinced that this was the way forward to enhance availability of locos and homing capacity of Loco Sheds in order to maintain extra locomotives, utilising the same infrastructure.

These were the major issues we tried to resolve from the Railway Board in consultation with the field units. We were not able to reach any consensus, as everyone was happy with the status quo.

One day, we had a long discussion with N.K. Chidambaram, Member, Railway Board, along with I.C. Sharma, Executive Director, who was my boss (a very competent rolling stock engineer). A decision was taken that all minor and major schedules would henceforth be undertaken with revised timelines as brought out above.

Instructions were issued to all concerned in Indian Railways. It was a major shift in our maintenance philosophy. As a result, the capacity increased since the number of schedules to be undertaken in a Shed reduced substantially.

The flip side was that the feed of locomotives to workshops suddenly dropped, which led to a lot of hue-and-cry in the workshops. Major infrastructure works that had been sanctioned in the past were proposed to be dropped by the Mechanical Department as we had generated 50 per cent additional capacity in the existing depots and workshops.

Even the Electrical Department was unhappy during the turmoil. The 6–8 months that followed after the change of periodicity of the schedules were bad as there were no supporters except N.K. Chidambaram and the Traffic Department. Eventually, this got stabilised. It became a part of the culture in the railway system.

Instead of homing 100 locos in a Shed as in earlier times, today the same Sheds, with a little modification, home 250 locomotives. What a sense of satisfaction I have!

In order to provide constructive and proactive support to the shed to handle a large number of locos with the same set of manpower, we legislated a policy that high-end systems and sub-systems and major assemblies of locomotives could be off loaded for their repair and rehabilitation, preferably to the OEMs.

These major shifts in the pattern of operation of locomotives – running on end-to-end basis and change in periodicity of maintenance schedule – led to a substantial increase in productivity of electric locos in the Indian Railways. It was a hugely satisfying experience as Director (Rolling Stock) Railway Board.

The bottom line is: Question the status quo, be professionally honest and understand the domain well. As soon as you a get a chance to work in the area, market your ideas in a collaborative and persuasive manner for a wider impact, and you could transform the organisation in a major way.

Decisiveness Matters: ARNO Convertor for 50 Years

In conventional electric locomotives, an induction motor, which is a rotating machine, is used to convert single-phase alternating current (AC) to 3-phase alternating current (AC). This machine is called ARNO converter. This has a rating of 120–150 Kilo Volt Ampere (KVA). The 3-phase supply from ARNO is used to run 3-phase induction motors employed to operate blowers, exhausters, compressors and oil pumps in an electric locomotive. This electric supply was however quite unbalanced and caused frequent failure of 3-phase induction machines. The voltage unbalance could go up to as high as 22.5 per cent. Due to high incidence of failure of the 3-phase induction machines, we were looking for a good technology solution that could reduce these failures.

ARNO is a very old concept in locomotives for converting single-phase to 3-phase. All the initial imported locomotives of the 1950s also had an ARNO converter. This is one machine which would generally fail after the locomotive passed a Neutral Section on the electrified rail network due to malfunction of some of the associated circuitry and control mechanism.

A Neutral Section in 25 KV power supply system is that section on the railway track where two different phases of AC supply are separated by a portion of overhead wire which does not carry any current or voltage, and therefore the locomotive gets switched off on its own or is switched off by the driver before approaching this location. There are big sign boards at 500 and 250 m before the location of the Neutral Section to draw the attention of the driver. The driver is supposed to switch off the locomotive before entering the Neutral Section.

This portion of Overhead Equipment (OHE) which does not carry 25 KV voltage is called the Neutral Section. The length of this wire could be either 5.5 or 40 m depending on the type of technology. The short 5.5 m sections are called Short Neutral Section and made of Teflon material, and the long 40 m ones are called Conventional Neutral Section. Railways decided to have Short Neutral Section for better operational efficiency.

Once the ARNO failed there was nothing that a driver could do to haul the train. If ARNO failed, the loco would fail. Trains would lose time on run and reach late, affecting a large number of passengers. Sometimes even prestigious trains like Rajdhani and Shatabdi were affected. During Parliament sessions it used to cause a lot of embarrassment. The rate of failure of the ARNO itself was about 8–10 per cent. For a very long time there was only one manufacturer of this equipment – Jyoti Limited at Vadodara. The repair of ARNO was also difficult as it was a heavy-duty machine of 120 to 150 KVA rating. The problem was serious, but the alternative solution was based on Power Electronics. Moreover, a new product had to be developed for the needs of the Railways. Any new development takes its own time. The alternative arrangement was not being tried due to the complicated design based on electronics. ARNO was a simple device. Moreover, the ARNO was a cheaper product compared to what Power Electronics based solution might cost. A debate regarding this was going on for quite some time.

The invention of Power Electronics led to the development of Static Inverter for conversion of single-phase supply to 3-phase supply with balanced voltages and higher level of energy efficiency. This was expected to reduce the failure of 3-phase induction machines, used to run blowers, compressors, oil pumps etc. It took almost 50 years to have new technology replace ARNO with a Power Electronics based Static Inverter. Chidambaram took the decision to change the status quo.

I was the Director, Rolling Stock in Railway Board, and I.C. Sharma, my boss, was the Executive Director. We discussed the matter with N.K. Chidambaram who was Member, Railway Board and was always willing to try out new solutions. Chidambaram had worked as General Manager CLW, and therefore had a good understanding of locomotive design. He got convinced, as the trade-off was in favour of improved reliability of locos, even if it were to cost more vis-à-vis ARNO.

We prepared a policy to replace all the ARNO converters of the locomotives with Static Inverter (SI) units, in a programmed manner in order to improve the performance of locomotives. This was done in 2002. It became a standard product for provision in conventional electric locomotives, produced at CLW. RDSO Lucknow framed the specifications and took keen interest in developing the new SI unit. It took a year or so to have the product ready for trials.

The efficiency of ARNO was around 85 per cent while the SI unit had an efficiency of about 92–95 per cent. The unbalance of voltage with SI unit reduced to about 7–8 per cent from a level of 22.5 per cent. Failure of machines therefore reduced from about 11–14 per cent to about 4–5 per cent.

It was seen as a major innovation. But the initial design of Static Inverter (SI) was not without teething problems. It took time to improve and stabilise. Yet, some old design locos are running with ARNO converter due to cost considerations. Indian Railways discontinued manufacturing conventional locomotives in 2015 and switched over completely to manufacturing 3-phase electric locomotives. Requirement of ARNO or Static Inverters therefore reduced drastically.

Silo-Bridging: The Heart of Collaboration – Cadre Restructuring Forgotten

I belonged to the 1981 examination batch of Indian Railway Service of Electrical Engineers. There are eight Group A services in Railways recruited through Union Public Service Commission (UPSC). Five of these services – Electrical, Mechanical, Civil, Signal and Telecommunication, and Store – are recruited through Combined Engineering Services Examination. Three services – Traffic, Personnel and Accounts – are recruited through Civil Services Examination. A majority of the officers of different services of the 1981 examination batch had been promoted to Senior Administrative Grade (SAG) by 2001-02.

Some of the services such as Electrical and Mechanical were lagging behind other services of the same batch by more than two years for SAG promotion. Promotion to SAG is considered very important in one's career as it opens avenues for postings in various central government organisations at the level of Joint Secretary. Once you are empanelled in SAG, the Department of Personnel and Training (DOPT) considers you for empanelment as Joint Secretary, and then you may get an opportunity to work in any of the Ministries of the Central Government. The opportunities multiply. Disparity in promotional avenues was quite demotivating and frustrating.

I was the senior most Director in Railway Board in 2002, with 19 years of service, awaiting promotion to a SAG. In most other services, even junior batch officers had been promoted and posted in Railway Board. The impact on the morale of the officers was obvious. High-ranking officials were concerned about it

S.C. Gupta belonged to the Indian Railway Service of Signal Engineers and had taken over as Member, Railway Board. He was heading the Electrical discipline. No officer of electrical discipline qualified, as none of the General Managers of Electrical discipline had more than one year of residual service at that time.

There was serious stagnation in promotion in the Electrical and Mechanical disciplines.

In order to ensure career progression, similar to other Services in Government of India, the cadre restructuring is undertaken every five years. The purpose of cadre restructuring is to bring parity within different services in Railways, and parity with similar services outside of Railways, and create additional posts for senior level promotions to ensure career progression.

In Railways, the cadre restructuring was pending for more than ten years. Out of all the eight organised Group 'A' Services, the most affected Services were Electrical (IRSEE) and Mechanical (IRSME) services.

DOPT decided that the cadre restructuring of these two Services be undertaken on a fast-track basis. It was therefore decided in the Ministry of Railways that one Director from each of these two Services would undertake an exercise in consultation with Cadre Review Division of DOPT and the Ministry of Railways. These Directors were supposed to prepare a self-contained proposal for submission to DOPT, Ministry of Finance and thereafter to the Cadre Review Committee (CRC). CRC is headed by the Cabinet Secretary.

Since I was the most affected of the 1981 batch, I volunteered to prepare the proposal and submit it to the Railway Board. It was to be processed for the consideration of CRC and subsequently the Union Cabinet.

Arun Arora, Director Mechanical Engineering (Freight) was nominated from Mechanical Directorate. After a few rounds of meetings with Karan Singh, Director (Cadre Review), DOPT, self-contained proposals for IRSEE and IRSME were prepared and submitted to DOPT. These were processed by DOPT for approval by the Ministry of Finance. Karan Singh was a very competent officer of the Personnel Service of Railways, working in DOPT on deputation. He helped a lot at all stages of the exercise.

Usha Mathur was the Joint Secretary (Personnel), Ministry of Finance (MOF). She belonged to the Indian Railways Accounts Service. I used to frequently visit DOPT and MOF for discussion on behalf of Ministry of Railways. After protracted interactions, MOF agreed with the proposal and issued a memorandum indicating their concurrence for creation of additional posts for IRSEE cadre which included 11 additional posts of Higher Administrative Grade, 31 for Senior Administrative Grade and 91 for Junior Administrative Grade, while retaining one post each of Additional Member and Member Electrical Railway Board.

Silo-Bridging: The Heart of Collaboration

It was therefore time to submit these proposals to the CRC. The Office Memorandum was similarly issued for IRSME cadre as well a few days later. A meeting was fixed by the Cabinet Secretariat to consider the proposals.

A day before the meeting that was to be chaired by the Cabinet Secretary, I briefed S.C. Gupta, Member Electrical, Railway Board, about the proposal. As soon as he came to know that the proposal had reached the stage of penultimate approval, before consideration by the Cabinet, he became a little hesitant and, in fact, a little irritated. He was not able to see its value. The proposal contained only two Services, instead of all the eight Services that were there in the organisation. I was however not deterred by his response. I remained polite and persuasive.

I further briefed him about the Frequently Asked Questions (FAQs). These were well researched 25–30 questions along with their responses. He then got quite interested in the proposal. He considered that some of these questions could be a clincher at the meeting. He prepared well for the meeting. My job was done.

The two Additional Members – M.Z. Ansari, Additional Member Mechanical, and B.M. Lal, Additional Member Electrical – were also briefed and FAQs handed over. They were supposed to attend the meeting as they were the senior most officers of the two cadres, Electrical and Mechanical. Member Mechanical had submitted his resignation for personal reasons. B.M. Lal was known to take bold decisions and cared about the well-being of the junior officers. He was a tall, handsome human being.

M.Z. Ansari was a sober and soft-spoken person. He once told me that he had been the topper of Joint Entrance Examination (JEE) of IIT but preferred to join Special Class Railway Apprentice (SCRA) at Jamalpur as SCRA was considered superior to IIT at that time. In the FAQs, I had therefore indicated that Railway Services were at one time considered so superior that candidates used join this service to pursue a fulfilling professional career.

The CRC meeting was held the next day, and the two proposals were approved by the CRC. While the meeting was going on inside the Cabinet Secretary's office, Arun Arora and I were quietly waiting in the visitors room. The moment the meeting was over, we all left the Cabinet Secretariat. The first thing S.C. Gupta did after getting into the car was to congratulate me. He appreciated my efforts as the FAQs prepared came in very handy during the discussions in CRC and in fact decided the fate of the proposal.

After the receipt of the minutes of the meeting, the Cabinet Note was prepared by Pillai, of Establishment (Gazette Cadre) branch in

Railway Board in consultation with me. Pillai had a positive attitude and was like a pivot at the Cadre Review Division in Railway Board.

There was a lot of resistance in granting approval for processing the Cabinet Note as the proposals were processed only for two Services, Electrical and Mechanical. Normally, the Cadre Review proposals are processed for all the Services together. It was, however, the decision of DOPT to process these proposals in the first phase.

Somehow, the Cabinet Note was approved by the Minister of Railways (MR) in the third week of August 2003. B.S. Sudhir Chandra, the Member Staff of the Railway Board was superannuating in August 2003. I persuaded B.M. Lal to have the Cabinet Note signed by B.S. Sudhir Chandra before his superannuation. On Friday, August 29, 2003, the Cabinet Note was signed by B.S. Sudhir Chandra. This happened to be his last working day in Railway Board as August 30 and 31 were Saturday and Sunday. So, the Cabinet Note could be sent on August 29, 2003, for final approval. We were very happy as major hurdles were over. B.M. Lal and B.S. Sudhir Chandra were good friends and batchmates. Both of them had a soft corner for the proposal as it was going to give some relief to Electrical and Mechanical officers and motivate them.

Despite repeated attempts with Cabinet Secretariat, the proposal could not be listed on any day in September and October 2003. Along with Arun Arora, I decided to meet the MR, Shri Nitish Kumar, for consideration of the proposal by the Union Cabinet, as the officers of these two Services were feeling quite dejected due to serious stagnation. To the best of my memory, on October 27, 2003, we met the MR, who immediately spoke to Kamal Pandey, Cabinet Secretary. It was decided to list this proposal for consideration of the Union Cabinet on October 31, 2003. The proposal was approved on October 31 and brought a much-needed relief to these two Services. Some of the officers, who were completing their tenure as DRM, were expected to get promoted to Higher Administrative Grade (HAG) immediately. There was a sense of huge accomplishment.

But the story doesn't end here.

After the receipt of the approval of the Cabinet, the Railway Board was not willing to allow its implementation. R.R. Bhandari was the Secretary, Railway Board at that time. Both, Arun and I met the Secretary and briefed him about the stagnation of these two Services and pleaded for implementation of the Cabinet's decision. R.R. Bhandari was also very supportive of the initiative. He therefore pushed for its implementation.

Ultimately, in December 2003 it was decided that the decision of the Cabinet would be implemented. Accordingly, promotion orders were issued in bulk for HAG and SAG, for both IRSEE and IRSME cadres in December 2003. The officers of two batches (1981, 1982) got promoted to SAG, and 11 officers got promoted to HAG.

IRSEE had only ten posts of HAG prior to this Cadre Review and got more than 100 per cent additional posts of HAG (11 posts) pursuant to the approval of the Cabinet. This was something unexpected and it was a big day for the two cadres.

I felt quite satisfied as I was able to contribute to the overall good of the cadre. Post of Members – for Electrical and Mechanical – were also en-cadred for IRSEE and IRSME in accordance with the approval of the Union Cabinet.

I got my much-awaited promotion to SAG and was posted as Chief Locomotive Engineer in Northern Railway. A very satisfying contribution for the overall good of Electrical cadre had been accomplished. It created a lot of positive vibes in the department, which further encouraged me to think of out-of-the-box solutions.

After this, we had to wait for 17 long years for the next Cadre Review that materialised in 2020. It speaks volumes for the apathy of the organisation towards career progression. Without a motivated team of individuals, no transformative agenda can be driven in an organisation. For this to happen, career growth and selection of individuals is vital, which the Railways will need to look into.

With the full support of the Minister of Railways, Shri Piyush Goyal, the cadre review proposal was approved by the Cabinet in February 2019, but the implementation was delayed by more than a year. The career progression and putting the right person for the right job is very important for a high growth trajectory of the organisation.

V.K. Yadav, CRB, brought the leadership pipeline issue to the centre stage and pushed hard to make Cadre Review his top priority. But ultimately, the much-needed change – the positive act of selection for key positions – has not materialised. Most of the officers had high expectations from him. Even now, the date of birth and the date of joining the service are the key criteria for selection. How can we expect any major change? There is a need to introspect; possibly 'first who then what' could be a guiding mantra. As our Prime Minister, Shri Narendra Modi, says: 'We cannot achieve 21st century results with a 20th century mindset.'

11

Last Man Standing: Who Really Matters? Baroda House

It was a hard-earned promotion. I had worked for the cadre review for more than one year to create alignment within and outside the Ministry of Railways and had to go to the highest level of decision making – the Union Cabinet – for the much-needed cadre restructuring. This benefited those officers the most who were completing their tenure as DRM as they got promoted to HAG in the shortest possible service length. The sense of satisfaction that I felt was amazing. Someone else was getting promoted, and I was feeling elated! I had made an unimaginable change in their career.

For two months after my promotion, I was not relieved of my charge in the Railway Board. Even my batchmates and those junior to me got the working SAG assignment, but I was still waiting. The promotion orders were issued in December 2003, but I was relieved on February 26, 2004. I was posted as Chief Electrical Loco Engineer (CELE) in Delhi.

At CELE the biggest challenge that I faced in Northern Railway was the utilisation of a newly electrified track by taking mail express trains from diesel traction over to electric traction. The intention was to fully harness the benefits of electrification and lower the unit cost of transport. It meant running these trains with electric locomotive on the newly electrified tracks. This was difficult to do as there was a serious shortage of Assistant Loco Pilots (ALPs) and Loco Pilots (LPs) who could drive electric locomotives.

Around 1,100 ALPs had been recruited by the Railway Recruitment Board (RRB). They were to report for training in 2004. Every new trainee had to undergo 39 weeks of initial induction training in one mode of traction – electric or diesel. This training was approved by the Railway Board. Every Zonal Railway had to follow it uniformly.

A key decision was to be taken as to whether the initial training could be organised for both modes of traction together to ensure flexibility in their posting, either in electric or diesel traction, on any of the Divisions after the completion of the training.

Since the period of training and its modules were mandated by the Railway Board, I discussed the matter with Mathew John, the Chief Operating Manager. I gave him a way out to tide over the problem if all Principal Heads of Department cooperated.

In consultation with the Chief Operating Manager, Chief Safety Officer, Chief Personnel Officer, Chief Mechanical Engineer and Chief Electrical Engineer, I proposed that the initial induction training could be organised for both the modes of traction 13 weeks for diesel traction, 13 weeks for electric traction and 13 weeks for Safety and Traffic Transportation disciplines.

While Electrical, Traffic and Safety wings were happy with the progressive proposal, Mechanical officers were not aligned. The first reason was that some of the newly recruited Assistant Loco Pilots would have been allocated to work in electric traction, and the second reason was that the proposal was against the Railway Board orders for conducting such dual traction trainings. I persuaded them and mentioned that it would serve the interest of the Railways best, as trains were getting detained, and this initiative would help us tide over the crisis of shortage of drivers.

The proposal had to be approved by the General Manager. It was a fact that Zonal Railway had no power to change the training modules. So I thought of informing the Railway Board. The change that we were resorting to was under special circumstances, to mitigate the immediate crisis. The Railway Board was informed accordingly.

After continuous persuasion and humble submissions, everyone, right up to the GM, approved the proposal and a serious shortage of Assistant Loco Pilots was thus circumvented. Other Railways also followed suit. This helped Northern Railway substantially by ensuring free movement of trains on electrified routes. The assets created by electrification could be used efficiently.

The solution that we evolved was out-of-the-box, and we could implement it by bringing alignment amongst the stakeholders, and with the collaboration of all concerned.

12

Where There Is a Will, There Is a Highway: 25 KV Overhead Wires at 7.2 m

In April 2005, India and Japan announced their collaboration for undertaking a feasibility study and possible funding of dedicated rail freight corridors. This was followed by the formation of Planning Commission's task force to prepare a concept paper on Delhi–Mumbai and Delhi–Howrah Dedicated Freight Corridor (DFC) projects, and to suggest a new organisation structure, financing strategy and construction as well as operation of the same. Rail India Technical and Economic Service (RITES) was entrusted to undertake a feasibility study. RITES is a PSU of the Ministry of Railways that undertakes consultancy projects in India and globally besides other work like O&M of rolling stock and export of rolling stock from Railways Production Units etc.

Nasik is an ancient city in the northern region of the Indian state of Maharashtra, situated on the banks of the river Godavari. It is a well-known Hindu pilgrimage site. A Kumbh Mela is held here every 12 years. The city is 190 km north of the state capital Mumbai. It is also known as the wine capital of India as half of India's vineyards and wineries are in Nasik.

It was in the hot summer month of June 2005 that I was nominated for a two months training programme at the Indian Railway Institute of Electrical Engineers (IREEN) in Nasik. This institute had been established in 1988. I was supposed to undergo training specially designed for SAG officers of Indian Railway Service of Electrical Engineers (IRSEE). I was then working as CELE in Northern Railway, New Delhi. I had just a week's notice to join.

I was very happy to get a break after a very long time. I really wanted to read and explore areas that I had not been able to in my career so far. I wanted to pursue LLB while I was Director (Rolling Stock) in the Railway Board. I had even taken admission in Delhi

University in 2003, but the pressure of work did not allow me to pursue it beyond 3-4 months. I had to quit. The training therefore appeared to be quite exciting.

Since the training was to start from Monday, June 6, 2005, I decided to travel on Sunday by Nizamuddin-Ernakulam Express which takes about 21 hours to cover 1,360 km from Nizamuddin to Nasik, and goes via Agra, Gwalior, Jhansi, Bhopal, Bhusaval and Manmad.

I boarded the train at Nizamuddin on Sunday, June 5 at 9 a.m. and reached Nasik at 6 a.m. on the following day. A car sent by IREEN was awaiting my arrival at the Nasik railway station to ferry me to the IREEN hostel. There were 12 officers of my Service from Railways who had reported for this training at Nasik. We were supposed to stay initially for one week at Nasik, followed by six weeks in the Zonal Railway where we were posted to do project work, and thereafter come back to Nasik for one week and submit the project report. Lectures were generally taken by guest faculty on reliability, asset management and leadership.

During the first week of stay at Nasik, each one of us was to identify a project related to either improvement in the operational efficiency of the Railways or search for a future technology for improved train operation. However, I decided to undertake a project that did not fit with the scheme of the things being followed as a matter of convention.

As the Japanese team had started visiting our offices to obtain our views on the choice of traction for the Western corridor, I thought of doing a project which might give insights into the making of 25 KV system fit for double stack container operation.

I therefore chose a project to demonstrate a Proof of Concept (POC) for running a Double Stacked Container Train (one container over the other) under 25 KV traction wires (OHE). The standard design of traction wires in the Indian Railways system did not allow trains loaded with double stacked containers (DSC) since the height of traction wires was limited to 5.5 m while the height of DSC (with High Cube) itself was around 5.8 m.

A new design of OHE was required for DSC operation. We searched the internet but did not see such an operation except for one picture in the United States with a very high pantograph. US railroads predominantly work on diesel traction due to abundance of diesel oil there. So, even this picture did not offer a credible alternative.

These containers were called High Cube International Standard Organisation (ISO) Shipping Containers. They were 20 or 40 feet long and 8, 8.5 or 9.5 feet high. They were carried on the top of flat wagons, having a platform height of 1,000 mm and worked on diesel traction where there was no wire on top of the train. This worked well because height was not an issue.

A group of 45 BLCA/BLCB flat wagons are combined to form a Container Train. These 45 wagons comprise 9 units of 5 BLCA/BLCB wagons each; 9 units of 5 wagons each means 9 x 5 = 45 wagons. One unit of flat wagons consists of 1 BLCA flat wagons at each end and 3 BLCB flat wagons in the middle of the unit as shown below:

BLCA 1st wagon – BLCB 2nd wagon – BLCB 3rd wagon – BLCB 4th wagon – BLCA 5th wagon

All this, coupled together, makes one unit.

BLCA stands for Bogie Low Wagon for Containers (air brakes). These are flat bed wagons. 'A' wagon is the end wagon and 'B' wagon is the middle wagon. The height of the platform of the flat bed wagons is 1,000 mm on which the containers rest.

The project proposal was debated at IREEN and in the Railway Board, to evaluate its desirability and utility. Each project was supposed to bring out some tangible outcomes for the organisation. The Director of IREEN was to approve the project.

A.K. Dutta, the Executive Director (Development), Railway Board, was quite excited about this idea as he was looking for somebody to undertake a POC that would help him have conceptual clarity in the design of Western DFC.

Dutta was in fact a member of the committee working on the choice of traction for DFCs. He became the driver of this project.

Two separate DFCs were being planned for running freight traffic on the Indian Railways in order to boost the freight revenues and tide over the congestion on existing route between Delhi–Mumbai and Delhi–Howrah routes. The corridor connecting Delhi to Mumbai, in the western part of the country, was to carry primarily domestic and international containers. It was referred as Western DFC. The corridor connecting Delhi to Howrah, situated in the eastern part of the country, was to predominantly carry coal, and was referred as Eastern DFC.

Showcasing a POC was no doubt a difficult task. It was to be completed within a short time of six weeks as otherwise I would not be able to complete my training. With full support from the Railway Board, it was decided that this POC would be developed. This required all-party collaboration. The model had to work and demonstrate the real-life situation. The DSCs were to run under high-rise OHE and the locomotive had to come out under normal OHE with smooth transition from high-rise to normal OHE. I had to fully excite and energise the team.

DSC operation of High Cube (9.5 feet high) under electrification required shifting of OHE upwards to 7.2 m height. Existing maximum height of OHE was 5.5 m.

The Ministry of Railways had to choose between diesel and electric traction for the Western DFC. This corridor was to run from Rewari, a city in the state of Haryana, 80 km from Delhi to Jawaharlal Nehru Port Trust (JNPT) near Mumbai in the state of Maharashtra. The total distance between Rewari and JNPT is 1,337 km via Ajmer and Vadodara.

The mode of traction for Eastern DFC was not under debate, as height was not an issue. Container operation was not the focus in the Eastern route. The Eastern route was to cater to coal traffic. The hush-hush thinking in the corridors of the Railway Board was to have one DFC on electric and the other DFC on diesel traction.

Nowhere in the world such a high-rise OHE existed to run freight trains in DSC configuration.

Diesel traction provided better flexibility and could carry containers of any height since diesel traction operation was not constrained by any wire over the train; it was rather constrained only by the height of road over the bridges crossing the railway line.

This project generated adequate enthusiasm amongst Traffic, Mechanical and Electrical officers. Mechanical officers wanted Western DFC on diesel traction while Electrical officers wanted it to be on electric traction. Traffic officers wanted to understand the feasibility of running DSC operations with electric traction and were therefore neutral.

This was basically a fight to look for better technologies that would provide more opportunities and professional satisfaction to both the disciplines in rail operations.

I was, however, dispassionately looking at the technology and the economics of train operations. Electric traction had better economics and was more environment friendly.

When we sat down at the drawing board along with the concerned Directorates of RDSO, we were able to finalise the design of High Reach Pantograph, modifications required in the overhead wires to accommodate two High Cube containers (total height 2 x 9.5 feet = 19 feet or 5.8 m) and a dummy container. A Test Train was to be formed with BLC A/B flatbed containers.

In a way, all the three modifications were to be carried out in-house within two weeks. This required identification of a railway line with electric traction where the overhead wires could be modified without disruption to traffic. An electric locomotive had to be identified where the pantograph could be raised such that it was able to contact high-rise overhead wires to draw electric supply to run the electric locomotive. Equally challenging was to identify at least one unit of BLCA/BLCB wagons and a High Cube (9.5 feet high container) mounted on one of the flat wagons.

A team was constituted to identify a patch of railway track about 300 m long which had 25,000 volt electric traction. Super masts, 2.5 m high, were provided over the existing masts to raise the height of contact and catenary wires such that the contact wire was raised from a height of 5.5 m to 7.2 m. This was done by R.K. Rajput, the officer in-charge of the maintenance of OHE on Delhi Division. He was very hard working and was quite passionate about doing this work. He got this work done within a week.

The pantograph of one of the electric locomotives was also raised by 400 mm at Electric Loco Shed, Ghaziabad under the supervision of Vivek Agarwal, the in-charge of the Loco Shed. This work was done in tandem with the modification of overhead wires. Vivek had a high regard for me. He came from the same university as I did. This also had an impact.

The biggest challenge, however, was to identify one unit of five flat wagons and one High Cube of nine-and-a-half feet. It was to be placed in Electric Loco Shed, Ghaziabad. Madhusudan Rao, the Chief Freight Traffic Manager of Northern Railway, was a good friend of mine. He was keen to see whether a traction system with high-rise overhead wires was possible. He was the key person who made this project successful and I was able to project this POC and the possibility of running trains with DSCs on Western DFC.

Madhusudan Rao arranged five flat wagons along with a nine-and-a-half feet container and got them placed in the Electric Loco Shed, Ghaziabad while the work of modification was in progress. This was very crucial for the POC as it was just touch-and-go.

The dummy container was fabricated using iron sheets and channels after climbing on top of the existing container, resting on the flat wagon. This was done by the Shed's technicians. This was one of the most difficult jobs but was done with the cooperation of every single member of staff and supervisors of Electric Loco Shed, Ghaziabad. Thanks to Vivek.

I saw a high degree of enthusiasm amongst all the railwaymen associated with the project. Everyone was aspiring to see a new system of railways working in an electrified section with high-rise OHE and high-rise pantograph.

The team was fully aware of the fact that this POC would have an impact on the decision on the type of traction (diesel or electric) to be adopted for Western DFC. The enthusiasm was therefore palpable, and the work was being executed at jet speed.

I used to reach the Electric Loco Shed, Ghaziabad sharp at 10 a.m. every day, and spend the whole day up to 4 p.m. there. This continued for almost four weeks. Finally, the modified OHE, the modified pantograph of a locomotive and a dummy fabricated container were all ready for trial a week before my return to Nasik.

Madhusudan Rao, the Chief Freight Traffic Manager, and V.K. Dutt, the Chief Electrical Engineer (my boss) were invited to witness the trial of the Test Train in the second week of July 2015.

On the day of the trial, we all assembled at 10 a.m. in the Loco Shed, Ghaziabad. The Loco Driver came a bit late from the lobby. The moment the pantograph was raised to energise the locomotive, it was a great feeling amongst all those present as the OHE and the pantograph had been modified locally and it was working well. This was the first ever trial of such a Test Train on Indian Railways network. The container fabricated on the top of the High Cube looked very imposing. Everyone held their breath. What if something went wrong!

The moment the first notch was taken by the driver and the train started moving, it was a great moment for Rajput, Vivek, Rao and of course for me. Dutt was also very happy. Our POC was getting executed in a real-life situation. The Test Train ran very smoothly for about 300 m, and then the locomotive was detached and taken from 7.2 m OHE to normal OHE of 5.5 m height. This was to demonstrate that transition from high-rise OHE to normal OHE would work well. It turned out to be a picture-perfect trial. I thanked everyone who had contributed to the success of this POC.

The run of the Test Train was filmed. The report was written. It was time for me to go back to Nasik. The video and the Power Point Presentation were seen by all the trainee officers and the Director IREEN quite enthusiastically, and the initiative was well received. The project was highly appreciated across the departments in the Railway Board and RDSO.

This video film and the project report were seen by Sudhir Kumar, Officer on Special Duty (OSD) to Minister of Railways and also the Planning Commission. Later, RDSO and various committees referred to this project report. It really helped them in firming up the decision with respect to the type of traction to be used on Western DFC that was to run DSC trains. A full-length trial was subsequently also done in East Coast Railway with high-rise OHE over 8–10 km.

The debate over the type of traction continued for almost a year, and finally in 2006 it was decided that the DSC would be run on electric traction with high-rise OHE at 7.2 m height.

It was an extremely satisfying experience. I felt elated to see a new design of pantograph of the locomotive and high-rise OHE in operation in the Western DFC. The mission was well-accomplished.

The infrastructure created in Western DFC continues to remind me of my simple initiative of June 2005 that led to a full-fledged network for DSC operations at 2 x 25 KV electric traction. The POC turned into a reality.

North Star: The Best Is Often Elsewhere Too – Leadership Development at HEC Business School Paris

It was March 2006. I was in an operating meeting with Mathew John, Chief Operating Manager (COM), Northern Railway, Delhi. This meeting was conducted by COM every day at 11 a.m. to take stock of the operations of the previous day and plan for the current day. It was also to take any corrective action, if needed, for the smooth functioning of the railway system.

Mathew John was a nice human being and used to love meeting officers and resolve their issues then and there. If I did not attend this meeting, he reprimanded me, but only out of his affection and love for me. He always respected my professional advice.

I was the Chief Electrical Loco Engineer of Northern Railway, based at Delhi. One day, while I was attending the daily meeting, I got a call from the Director (Training & Manpower Planning) Railway Board to submit an application for selection by HEC Business School, Paris, for a course – World Railway Manager's Programme – organised by International Union of Railways (UIC) based in Paris, France. This was a joint effort of HEC Business School and UIC. It was a leadership development programme.

The railways of Europe originated separately, and each country had its responsibility towards its own railway. There were issues related to interoperability between adjoining countries. UIC, an international rail transport industry body, was created in such an environment, on October 17, 1922, after World War I. UIC's mission is to provide rail transport at world level and meet the challenges of mobility and sustainable development. UIC facilitates sharing of best practices, promotes interoperability, creates new standards and develops a centre of competence for its member countries. It has

194 members across five continents, including Japan and China, at present. India is also a member of UIC.

The application was to be submitted like one for any other business school – write two essays stating personal contributions made in the organisation and a statement of purpose (SOP). Based on these, the selection was to be made by HEC Business School. I wrote essays on 'End-to-End Running of Locomotives' and 'Change in Maintenance Philosophy of Rolling Stock'. These were the issues I had personally handled and therefore both the essays on these subjects were well articulated. I had the passion to do these things.

The formalities were completed well in time. I was selected from Indian Railways along with five other officers. Six of us went to Paris to attend this six-week programme. There were two components of three weeks each – one in Paris and the other in India. In all, we were 18 officers from railways all over the world – UK, South Africa, India, Italy, Denmark and Saudi Arabia. A comparison of the size of the network of these countries is mentioned here:

Comparative Rail Network

Country	rkm	Gauge (mm)	RErkm	Year Opened	Locos	Coaches	Wagons	Million GTKM	Million PKM	+250 km/hrkm
India	67,868	1,676	25,403	1853	11,453	69,321	2,77,987	6,20,175	11,49,835	0
UK	16,294	1,435	2,134	1825	856	15,985	22,000	19,342	66,594	113
South Africa	21,268	1,067	9,467	1860	2,368	5,902	71,173	1,13,342	13,865	0
Italy	21,529	1,435	13,332	1839	1,563	19,993	26,305	20,781	52,207	1,350
Denmark	3,058	1,435	626	1847	86	2,351	N/A	2,603	6,507	0
Saudi Arabia	4,577	1,435	902	1908	132	696	5,406	1,852	135	449

Note: Data derived from past UNIFE World Rail Market Studies
(Unit quantities for rolling stock are total procurements since 1950)

The faculty comprised professors from Harvard, London Business School, University of Oxford and HEC Paris. It was one of the most inspiring programmes I ever attended.

I remember having worked on a project 'Empowering DRMs in Sustaining Growth of Indian Railways' for the turnaround of Railways. The other officers who worked on this project were Purushottam Guha, Arvind Kumar and N. Malhan. Arvind belonged to the Personnel Department and the other two were Traffic Officers.

In 2007, the turnaround story of Railways was making rounds in various Business Schools globally as Railways was on the upswing. The policy of loading wagons at Carrying Capacity (CC) + 8 + 2 had been introduced. This meant that every wagon could legitimately carry 8 tonnes more than the normal load of 58.8 tonnes of payload (the commodity) and on top of it, 2 tonne of extra allowance was permitted. It paid rich dividends.

Railways charged tariff based on the CC of the wagons (which was 58.8 tonnes). Now, Railways started charging tariff at rate of CC + 10 tonnes. Thus the revenue increased by 10 tonne per wagon. For one freight train carrying coal, the freight was now charged at the rate of 68.8 tonnes per wagon. Every rake started earning revenue worth around 600 tonnes extra (17 per cent extra revenue per train) without doing any extra marketing efforts. This brought a massive increase in Railways revenue. It also circumvented the rules of overloading of wagons. Wagons had the capacity of carrying 10 extra tonnes of coal and overloading was taking place in the wagons for known or unknown reasons. For legitimising it and issuing it as a policy, the Civil Engineers had to be convinced. Commissioner of Railway Safety had also to give his assent. All this was done.

It was something like a low-hanging fruit for the organisation. The surplus generated by the Railways was available for undertaking a large number of infrastructure projects.

The two DFCs were in the process of being sanctioned since the Japan International Cooperation Agency (JICA) study was over. I remember an article brought out by *India Today* in 2006 about the turnaround of Railways. In fact, I had carried a copy of that article to HEC, and this was one of the cases discussed in the group at HEC, Paris.

The second half of this course was conducted in India, with Railway Managers from all over the world assembling at Staff College, Vadodara. Many subjects were covered in the course, right from strategy to marketing, finance, and leadership. This was one of the most invigorating courses I had done in my career till then. A three-day programme was conducted by Professor Roger Hallowell from Harvard on Change Management. He is presently a Professor at HEC, Paris

I vividly remember his class where he distributed a book *Leading Change* by John Kotter. He discussed all the eight steps of the framework on Change Management. The eight steps of this framework are – establishing a sense of urgency, creating and guiding a coalition, developing a vision and strategy, communicating the change vision, empowering the broad-based action, generating short term wins, consolidating gains and producing more change, and anchoring new approaches in the culture.

The class had a tea break of 15 minutes. During the break Hallowell changed the seating plan of each one of us randomly. When we came back to the lecture theatre, we were all searching for our notes and our badges. For a few minutes there was chaos. This was the way he introduced Change Management.

I experienced every step of this framework while leading the transformation journey of Indian Railway. Actually, Indian Railways needed something even beyond this framework.

Who knew I would not only be heading the Transformation Cell of the Ministry of Railway in India a decade later but also be engaged in empowerment and delegation of powers to DRMs and GMs? Most of the ideas I had presented in the project report at HEC Business School turned into reality.

These were the most satisfying six weeks with Railway Managers coming from different countries. One of the most interesting things to learn from the participants was the simplified method of recruitment of drivers by South African Railways. They were able to recruit drivers in about 3–5 months whereas we took not less than 18–24 months. Similarly, UK's Safety Board was much more independent and professional in conducting accident enquiries as they had simulation tools.

I was nominated by Ramesh Chandra, Member Electrical in the Railway Board, and selected by HEC Business School Paris based on the strength of my application and past contributions that I had made to my organisation. Hard work always pays. It was an excellent global exposure which gave me an opportunity to understand how other railway systems in the world worked and compare them with Indian Railway. It enabled me to prepare myself to set a vision and strategy for better service operation, culminating in better service delivery. I got an opportunity to bring a change in the organisation at different positions. Most of it took place when I was working as Divisional Railway Manager and as Head of Transformation in the Ministry of Railways.

14

Mining Insights from the Gemba: The Astonishing Kalka Hills – 1:40 Grade

After completing my tenure as Director (Rolling Stock) in Ministry of Indian Railway, I was posted as Chief Electrical Locomotive Engineer (CELE) in Northern Railway. I got this promotion after the Cadre Review of the Electrical and Mechanical disciplines of the Railways – something I was fully instrumental in pursuing from start to finish in October 2003. I commenced serving in this position on February 26, 2004.

Immediately after taking over as CELE, I visited Ambala Division and met Keshav Chandra, the DRM. He mentioned about a serious operational constraint of providing a locomotive in the rear of a mail express train at Chandigarh in order to push the train from behind while the front locomotive continued to work the train. This operation is known as banking operation.

This was a regular practice between Chandigarh and Kalka. This section had the steepest gradient of 1 in 40 (this means that if you travel 40 km horizontally, you climb 1 km vertically).

Kalka railway station is located at a mean sea level of 658 m. The Ambala–Kalka section was opened in 1891. The section beyond Kalka, up to Shimla, a narrow gauge, was first opened to traffic by Viceroy Lord Curzon with 2-feet-wide narrow gauge on November 9, 1903. It was later re-gauged to 2½-feet-wide narrow gauge in 1905 at the request of the Indian Army, for strategic reasons. Kalka to Shimla is 96 km by rail. Shimla was the summer capital during British Raj. On July 8, 2008, UNESCO added the Shimla–Kalka Railway, as Mountain Railway of India, to the World Heritage Site list.

All the trains going to Kalka had to be worked with a locomotive at the rear of the train (called as Banker Locomotive). The attachment of a Banker Locomotive to a train requires 30 minutes. This was mandated to ensure safety and prevent the train from rolling back. This was an age-old practice.

The distance between Chandigarh and Kalka is around 38 km. There is a continuous rising grade from Chandigarh to Kalka. Normally, the Kalka Shatabdi Express used to take 25–30 minutes more at Chandigarh for the attachment of a Banker before proceeding to Kalka.

The drivers running room at Chandigarh – the place where drivers used to stay after completing their duty – was not well equipped. This running room was meant only for the drivers engaged in Banking duty. Each eight-hour shift required a driver and an assistant driver. Three pairs of drivers were therefore engaged daily. Drivers used to agitate a lot due to the poor upkeep of this running room.

The DRM wanted deployment of more powerful locomotives like the latest WAP 7 class, having 6,000 HP, which would obviate the need for the Banker Locomotive. This would smoothen train operation in Ambala Division.

Normally, WAP 5 locomotive of 5,400 HP used to be employed for running Kalka Shatabdi, which had 12 coaches without any Banking Locomotive. But provision of any extra coach would require a Banking Locomotive.

This became a project of very high importance. We had not only to ensure safety but also to redeploy more powerful locomotives used elsewhere. These WAP 7 locomotives were being used on more demanding duty. There was a shortage of these locomotives.

We decided to scientifically ascertain the duty cycle of the locomotive and the electrical stresses to which the traction motors would be subjected in the event Bankers were withdrawn on this route.

The measurement of current drawn by the traction motors was done and was matched with theoretical calculations. It emerged that a single WAP 7 locomotive could run the train up to 16 coaches without the need of a Banker provided the RDSO agreed to the operation of this locomotive under the currently prescribed limits of one-hour duty cycle of the traction motor. It essentially meant running the locomotive under overload conditions. The duration of the journey between Chandigarh and Kalka was 40 minutes. This was within the one-hour duty cycle. Overloading was permitted in the design but this permission was not used regularly.

I personally visited RDSO and met I.C. Sharma, Senior Executive Director (RDSO), who was my boss when I was Director (RS), Railway Board. He got the issue examined and gave a clearance in writing on April 15, 2004, subject to physical verification based on a monitored trial in association with RDSO. Thereafter we conducted a trial of a

16 car Shatabdi Express hauled by WAP 7 locomotive with one dead WAP 7 locomotive attached in the rear. The dead loco had a weight of 123 tonnes (2.5 times the weight of a coach). This essentially meant we were running an 18.5 coach train during trial.

The trial was witnessed by N.K. Sinha, the Director from RDSO; Vivek Agrawal, the in-charge of Ghaziabad Shed; Pankaj Singh, in-charge of Operations in Delhi; and one officer from the Ambala Division. The train was stopped at the foot of the Home Signal at Kalka Station because that is the place the train normally stops before a platform is available at Kalka station and is the most difficult location on this section. I remember Vivek Agrawal and Pankaj Singh walking on the track alongside the train from the location of the Home Signal (where the train was stopped) right up to the platform where the train was to be received and relaying a running commentary to me on a mobile phone (I was in Delhi). The details of the real-life operation of the first such trial were known to me as both the dedicated officers kept me apprised of every aspect of the trial. We were trying to ensure that there was no wheel slip, excessive rise in the temperature of locomotive wheels or any unusual occurrence. RDSO officials were on the front locomotive and recording various parameters like tractive effort, current drawn by traction motors, energy consumed and speed.

The trial turned out to be successful. It was a moment of great satisfaction and relief as well, as nothing went wrong. The WAP 7 locomotive was able to successfully stop and start the train on the 1 in 40 gradient without any rollback. After the said exercise was done, trials were conducted on four or five trips. Loco Inspectors were made to footplate and run the Kalka Shatabdi Express between Chandigarh and Kalka without Bankers. This was done not only to instil confidence amongst drivers but also to make sure that it could be successfully repeated with stop and start of the train at the Home Signal of Kalka station.

A few days later, I went to see this operation on the section while reports were being finalised. It was for my personal assurance, and I was convinced that we were on the right track.

After the reports of trial runs on April 24 and 28, 2004 were prepared, it was legislated through an approval process, associating the concerned Principal Heads of Departments (Chief Electrical Engineer, Chief Mechanical Engineer and Chief Operating Manager), Chief Safety Officer and the General Manager, that Banker Locomotives were no more required if the Shatabdi Express was hauled by WAP 7 class of locomotives, up to 16 coaches. A notification was issued accordingly.

A joint procedure order was issued by the Ambala Division on April 27, 2004, withdrawing Bankers for the operation from trains running up to 16 coaches under fair weather conditions. Fair weather condition meant no rains and clear visibility. One special condition, in consultation with RDSO, was however imposed – that the signals in the section from Surajpur to Chandimandir to Kalka (a total distance of 9 km) would be kept Green. This was well within the competence of the Zonal Railway to implement. RDSO further ratified the same through their communication on June 3, 2004, based on the trials on April 24 and 28, 2004. Now the Banker drivers were also withdrawn from Chandigarh. It was a big relief to the drivers and the Ambala Division.

However, 2–3 weeks later, a complaint was made by the running staff to the Chief Commissioner Railway Safety that the Banker-less operation introduced with WAP 7 loco on the Chandigarh–Kalka section was unsafe. The complaint was examined by Chief Safety Officer and sent to me as I had been the person behind this initiative. The whole background including the approval of RDSO and the physical trial conducted was brought to the notice of all the concerned Principal Head of Departments, CSO and the GM. Chief Commissioner Railway Safety was accordingly advised, and the matter was put to rest.

Prior to the Banker-less operation, drivers rightly had a higher level of confidence while driving as they were not worried about the train rolling back, even if they did not have good driving skills. Also, in the event of something suddenly going out of their control, an additional locomotive and additional crew was available at the rear of the train to avert an accident. However, under the changed pattern of operation, the drivers needed to hone their skills and be more alert while driving. This was a psychological shock to them. Moreover, they did not have a clear understanding that a more powerful WAP 7 loco would provide adequate strength to hold a train on the gradient, something which the rear loco was doing earlier. A confidence building exercise was therefore required to be conducted over a long period of time with each and every driver. This was done for a few months.

The Banker-less operation continues even today under the conditions laid down. It has become a part of the standard operating protocol. It was an accomplishment, fully backed by engineering knowledge and detailed proof of concept, that got executed efficiently in the interest of safety.

Use of a Banker was an old practice when we did not have powerful locomotives. What comes out clearly is that it benefited the people travelling to Kalka. The journey time was reduced by about 20–25 minutes, as the time to attach a Banker Loco was not needed. This story used to be cited quite often by the DRM and GM as a success story of a new technology.

One must question the status quo if something transformative is to be achieved in life. But without solid professional domain expertise, safety could be compromised.

15

Collaboration Tales: Future Focused Solution Oriented – Nabinagar Power Plant

I had been working as Chief Electrical Loco Engineer (CELE) in Northern Railway for more than two years. I had expressed my desire to be posted back to the Railway Board. There was however no vacant post where I could have been accommodated.

In the meantime, a new post of Executive Director (Energy Management) was sanctioned for the Railway Board. I was appointed at this position in September 2006. I joined the Railway Board on October 6, 2006.

As this was a new post, work distribution had to be done between two Executive Directors – Executive Director (General) and Executive Director (Energy Management). All the matters which were not progressing were allocated to Executive Director (Energy Management) in order to give them a push.

Incidentally, setting up of a 1,000 MW Power Plant (four units of 250 MW each) at Nabinagar Bihar was allocated to Executive Director (Energy Management). This project had been languishing for more than five years, ever since a Memorandum of Understanding (MOU) was signed between Railways and National Thermal Power Corporation (NTPC) in February 2002.

Nabinagar is a city and a notified area in Aurangabad district in the Indian state of Bihar. It has a population of around 25,000. It is 9 km from Nabinagar Road railway station and is under Mughalsarai Division of East Central Railway. It is 100 km from Gaya airport. It has become the power hub in Bihar since a Super Thermal Plant of 1980 MW (three units of 660 MW) is being set up by NTPC; one unit was commissioned in 2019 and the second in 2021.

Shri Nitish Kumar was the railway minister at the time of signing of MOU in February 2002. Railways and NTPC were supposed to set up a power plant in Joint Venture (JV) to supply power to Indian Railways for its traction needs. The electricity that Zonal Railways was buying at that time from State utilities was quite costly. The tariff varied between ₹4 and ₹5 per unit (Kilo Watt Hour). Railways, as a bulk consumer, was charged the cross-subsidy charge of about ₹1.5 per unit of electricity which was a part of the ₹4–5 per unit tariff. The cross subsidy is charged to subsidise the electricity meant for agriculture. This was detrimental to Railways operations as its finances were being stressed to the tune of ₹2,500–3,000 crores per annum for energy consumption levels of 16 billion units for traction purpose, simply on account of cross-subsidy.

In the meantime, the new Electricity Act of 2003 came into force. A lot of unbundling of electricity operations was in the offing. The intent of the new Electricity Act was to give a choice to the consumer to buy electricity from any service provider, to provide a level playing field to government owned Electric Supply Companies and the privately owned power plants, to encourage private captive power plants with incentives in the tariff that could be passed on to the consumers and to provide open access for wheeling of power from power plants to the end consumers using the States transmission network.

The reason why the Nabinagar project was not progressing was the shareholding between NTPC and Railways in the JV company. Shareholding would provide control of the JV company to the party having majority equity share. Naturally, it would then be incumbent upon the party with higher share in the equity to own the responsibility to professionally run the power plant. Railways wanted a majority share of more than 50 per cent in the equity, but without having any responsibility of running the power plant. Railways did not have any domain knowledge to run a power plant.

On the other hand, NTPC was rightfully insisting on a majority stake in the JV company, because then only could the company and the power plant be run by NTPC professionally. This crucial decision was pending for five years. J.P. Batra was the CRB. R. Sivadasan was the Financial Commissioner of Railways. Sivadasan had also worked as Chairman, Kerala Electricity Authority. R.V. Shahi was the Secretary, Power, who was appointed Secretary as a domain expert. He had worked in the power sector and was not from the government. It was the first time such an appointment had been made by the Government of India.

A meeting was held at the level of Principal Secretary to the Prime Minister (PM), in January 2007 to resolve the issue. Ramesh Chandra, Member Electrical, attended this meeting. It was mentioned during the meeting that the new Electricity Act of 2003 provided for a power plant to be considered as captive power plant, even if the user of electricity had only 26 per cent equity in the project. It essentially meant that the power plant would be classified as a captive power plant of Railways and Railways would be eligible for non-payment of cross subsidy charge even with 26 per cent equity if Railways were to consume 90 per cent of the electricity generated by the power plant. It therefore became clear that no useful purpose would be served if Railways were to hold 74 per cent equity in the project.

The Railways equity with 74 per cent share was amounting to about ₹1178 crore. This would reduce to about ₹418 crore if Railways were to agree to an equity contribution of 26 per cent.

This was simple economics but had not been understood for so long by the Railways. I convinced J.P. Batra, CRB, to reduce the Railways equity from 74 per cent to 26 per cent. It meant lesser investment by Railways while having the same benefits in payment of electricity tariff for the energy to be consumed by the Railways. Ever since I had taken over as Executive Director (EM), J.P. Batra had nominated me to attend a number of conferences on power sector reforms, organised at the level of Ministry of Power, where Chief Ministers, Power Ministers, Power Secretaries, etc. of States were invited. I used to attend these conferences and submit brief notes on the takeaways. This was liked by Ramesh Chandra and J.P. Batra. This built a good trust and understanding. Once Ramesh Chandra and Financial Commissioner agreed with the idea of 26 per cent equity, J.P. Batra also agreed.

The question now was whether to do it with the approval of the Board or wait for the approval of the Minister. The Minister's approval would have taken time. I persuaded the CRB. The decision was therefore taken only with the approval of Member Electrical, Financial Commissioner and the Chairman. It was conveyed to the Prime Minister's Office (PMO) and the Ministry of Power. This was however not brought to the notice of the Minister of Railways. We should have done that.

It was also fully understood that reduction of cross subsidy surcharge would result in recurring savings of ₹400 crore annually. Payment of equity of ₹418 crore was a one-time payment, but savings were on a recurring basis. In any case, Nabinagar Power Plant was to be accorded Mega status and a Captive Power Plant of Railways due to the 26 per cent equity of Railways. It was supposed to directly feed power to 176 Traction Sub-Stations of Railways (of the total 400 traction sub-stations on Railways) in the eastern and western regions of the Railways for running trains in the states of Bihar, Jharkhand, West Bengal, Chhattisgarh, Maharashtra, Gujarat and Madhya Pradesh. Coal linkages were planned from the Central Industrial Chord (CIC) section of Dhanbad Division and water was to be sourced from the river Sone.

As a result of this above decision, the Cabinet Note which was being prepared by the Ministry of Railways was transferred to the Ministry of Power.

On January 31, 2007, the Cabinet Note was circulated by the Cabinet Secretariat, as it was listed for consideration of the Cabinet on February 1, 2007.

Around 3 p.m. on January 31, 2007, Sudhir Kumar, the OSD to the MR, called me and questioned me as to why Railways equity had been diluted. He was supposed to brief the MR for the Cabinet meeting the following day. The matter became very serious as the MR had not been briefed beforehand about the decision to dilute the equity from 74 per cent to 26 per cent.

Member Electrical was visibly upset that a grave mistake had been committed by not informing the MR. Along with Member Electrical, I went to J.P. Batra and briefed him about the matter, and about the reaction of the OSD to the MR.

Since the MR was in Mumbai that day, we were asked to meet him the next day at 8 a.m. at his residence. We all – Member Electrical, Financial Commissioner, CRB and I – went to the MR's residence the next day. It was ultimately decided that the MR would support the proposal in the Cabinet meeting. I was asked to go back to the Railway Board.

By 12.30 p.m. on February 1, 2007, the Board Members came back and informed me that the proposal had been approved by the Cabinet for 26 per cent equity of Railways. I breathed a sigh of relief as I had been at the verge of losing my job the previous day and Member Electrical had naturally been upset about the issue, as it had been done without informing the MR. But it was in the overall interest of Railways.

Almost seven months elapsed but the JV agreement between NTPC and Railways could not be signed because of objections raised by Finance. One day the Minister of Power talked to the MR and briefed him about the slow pace of progress of signing the JV agreement.

The file was called by OSD to the MR and the matter was discussed with Harsh Kumar who was the Executive Director, Finance Expenditure. It was decided that the Articles of Association (AOA) and Memorandum of Articles (MOA) would be cleared with the approval of the Board and sent back to NTPC.

I had done my homework and understood the Company Law. I had consulted Company Secretary, RailTel Corporation, while drafting AOA and MOA. This came in handy while finalising it in the chamber of Sudhir Kumar.

The JV agreement was signed finally on November 6, 2007, at a function jointly organised by the Ministry of Railways and the Ministry of Power. I happened to be one of the signatories and one of the founding Directors on the Board of the JV company. The company was incorporated as Bhartiya Rail Bijlee Company Ltd (BRBCL).

After a month, I was transferred out as Executive Director (Development). I was then asked to work on the Madhepura project. The Nabinagar Power Plant has become a reality now. The first unit was commissioned in 2016 and the second in 2021. The third unit is expected to be commissioned in 2022-23. While 90 per cent of the electricity generated from this plant is to be utilised by Railways, the rest is to be used by the state of Bihar.

Decisions must be taken at the most critical junctures, going far beyond the routine; otherwise, projects may not fructify.

A World Record, Quietly: Carbon Credits

I was the first officer posted as Executive Director (Energy Management) when the post was created in 2006 in the Indian Ministry of Railways. Prior to this assignment, I had only worked in Operation and Maintenance of Rolling stock. This was my first encounter with electrical general services.

Global warming was a topical subject of the time due to the high priority assigned by United Nations Framework Convention on Climate Change (UNFCCC). Developed countries had been assigned targets to reduce energy consumption or else adopt technologies that would improve energy efficiency. They could also buy Carbon Credits from nations successfully completing Clean Development Mechanism (CDM) projects and meet their targets of carbon footprint reduction.

The Kyoto Protocol mandated that industrialised nations cut their greenhouse gas emissions at a time when the threat of global warming was growing rapidly. This was adopted in Kyoto, Japan on December 11, 1997, and became an international law on February 16, 2005. The Protocol was linked to the United Nations Framework Convention on Climate Change (UNFCCC).

Industrialised nations made a promise under the Kyoto Protocol to reduce their annual hydrocarbon emission by an average of 5 per cent against the 1990 levels, over a period of four years from 2008 to 2012. The Kyoto Protocol also mandated that 37 industrialised nations and countries in the European Union cut their Greenhouse Gas (GHG) emissions.

Developing countries were asked to comply voluntarily, and more than 100 countries including China and India were exempted from the Kyoto Protocol. The Protocol separated countries into two groups – Annexure I contained developed countries, and Non-Annexure I nations contained developing countries.

Non-Annexure countries participated by investing in projects designed to lower emissions in their countries and earn Carbon Credits which they could sell to developed countries, allowing the developed nations a higher level of carbon emission than mandated for them.

The projects that developing nations were undertaking to reduce GHG emission were called as CDM projects. The CDM projects were incentivised by way of issuing Carbon Credits by UNFCCC, based on an approved methodology. If you reduced one tonne of CO_2 (carbon di-oxide) emission by reduced dependence on fossil fuels or adapt energy efficient technologies that required lesser consumption of grid energy (mostly sourced from coal-based plants), you earn one Carbon Credit.

CDM was the mechanism available with different countries to conceive projects that would improve the energy efficiency of their system. Often such improvement measures were not financially viable but support through Carbon Credits was available to fund them as an incentive for energy efficiency. This required approval from UNFCCC based on an approved methodology. These projects were to be monitored by an agency accredited by UNFCCC, before release of Carbon Credits. Carbon Credits were like a viability gap funding.

Replacement of incandescent lamps with Compact Fluorescent Lamp (CFL) was being talked about globally as one of the major initiatives to reduce GHG in the field of general lighting. While incandescent lamps used to cost ₹15–20 for a 60-watt bulb, a 12- or 15-watt CFL that produced equivalent light cost no less than ₹125. CFLs had a life of 10,000 burning hours as against the life of 1,000 burning hours for incandescent lamps. But households were not willing to buy the CFLs due to their high initial cost, and therefore this was incentivised by UNFCCC for effecting reduction in GHG emissions.

Quite a few CFL manufacturers were approaching Railways at different levels for procurement as Railways had a huge network in India and was consuming about 2.5 billion units of non-traction energy.

Ram Babu, a carbon specialist, wanted to meet me, but instead went to meet Sudhir Kumar, the OSD to the MR. This person had been working on energy efficiency technologies and had a deep understanding of Carbon Credits. OSD to the MR called me for a discussion in his chamber. The journey of Carbon Credit started.

Ram Babu presented the exciting idea that he could supply free CFLs if the project was structured in a manner that there was no theft and adequate monitoring mechanism was put in place.

A World Record, Quietly: Carbon Credits

In the first instance, it appeared unbelievable. In about a week's time I came to know that South Africa had completed an energy efficiency project for household lighting under CDM for their whole country. A methodology (AMS II J Ver 3) duly approved by UNFCCC already existed for this. In accordance with this methodology, one household could be given a maximum of four CFLs in lieu of four incandescent lamps at a substantially reduced cost.

I engaged with Ram Babu again on the condition that the project would have to be done through competitive bidding and the bidding parameters could be the amount of Carbon Credits the developer would pass on to Railways in addition to free CFLs. Railways would stand guarantee to the CFLs supplied free-of-cost by the developer. Even if it was a project for acquisition of free CFLs, it could not be done on a negotiated or nomination basis as we were to follow the Government of India guidelines of providing equal opportunity to everyone. We therefore brought out an advertised tender for this initiative. Ram Babu did not participate.

We assured the suppliers that Railways would ensure safe custody of CFLs from the moment the CFLs were received. Further, these would be taken on the Railways books and would become Railways property. This would be a sort of guarantee and a comfort to the suppliers to provide free CFLs. This clinched the deal.

All the necessary documentation for approval of the project through UNFCCC and transfer of Carbon Credits would however be the sole responsibility of the suppliers.

The Bureau of Energy Efficiency (BEE) in India had launched a scheme in India called Bachat Lamp Yojana (BLY) in which the CFLs were made available at ₹15 per unit on replacement and return of one incandescent bulb, for household use. This essentially meant handing over one working incandescent bulb and getting a CFL in return on a payment of ₹15.

We arranged to ensure safe custody of CFLs and their distribution through the Railways own depot. Return of an incandescent bulb and the guarantee that CFLs would be distributed internally by the Railways was another condition we wished to ensure. Railways was anyway to keep proper records.

Once these conditions were in place, tender documents were accordingly framed, and bids were invited in 2007. Only one bid, which offered around 2 per cent of Carbon Credits, was received. It was a big setback as a lot of work had been done on this project. We had even consulted the Planning Commission.

The tender was discharged with the expectation that more Carbon Credits than what had been offered by the single bidder could be received in addition to free CFLs.

Railways had six lakh households. Provision of four CFLs per household was envisaged. This was the maximum number permitted in the UNFCCC scheme.

The tender was re-invited for free supply of 2.4 million CFLs. The bid parameter was share of Carbon Credits. Yet again, only one bid was received from a company based in the USA which had an office in Malaysia.

This time the Carbon Credits offered were 3 per cent. There was a three-member Tender Committee. The Executive and the Finance agreed to award the tender on these terms. However, the third member gave his dissent and insisted that bids be invited afresh in the hope that someone would offer higher Carbon Credits. I was the executive member of the tender committee.

The tender was finally accepted by Member Electrical and the project was launched. Finally, C-Quest Capital Malaysia implemented this unique project successfully. It was completed with the distribution of about 1.8 million CFLs, as quite a few households did not participate in this voluntary scheme. Since this was a voluntary programme, some 600,000 CFLs could not be distributed. We decided to return these to the supplier, to be fair.

These CFLs were manufactured by Phillips India at their plant at Mohali with each CFL marked as Railway CDM Project to ensure that they were not stolen.

The project was planned for a seven-year cycle. It was envisaged that CFLs would have a life of seven years with about 5 per cent failures. The validation of the project was to be done by UNFCCC accredited agencies for issuance of Carbon Credits on an annual basis for all the seven years. The project was started in 2010 and came to an end in 2017. The Carbon Credits earned were deposited in Railways account at UNFCCC. Each year, all the four projects (Northern, Eastern, Western and Southern Region) earned Carbon Credits of approximately 100,000 in all. For seven years, Railways earned 3 per cent of these credits.

While the Carbon Credits were to be directly credited to the Indian Railways account, we found there was no mechanism to receive these credits in any department or offices of the Government of India. We therefore got our account opened with UNFCCC in Germany. This was the first project of this dimension, and the biggest in the world.

This project was given a Special Jury Award by the International Union of Railways (UIC), Paris, France, in 2012. This remains the biggest ever project of Railways, funded through Carbon Credits. The Carbon Credits business is presently at an ebb.

This was a contribution towards social, economic and environmental well-being of Railways employees, and sustainable development of the country. With the implementation of this project each employee who voluntarily opted for four CFLs, saved around 245 units (KWH) of electricity each year, saving approximately ₹1,000 per employee per year. With an emission factor of 0.8 kg of CO_2 emission per unit of electricity consumption in India, the reduction in CO_2 emission for the nation was about 0.3 million tonnes annually. It turned out to be a big game changer for improving the environment.

I, along with three colleagues of my team, were recommended by the Ministry of Railways for consideration of Prime Minister's award for Excellence in Public Administration in the year 2010. It did not materialise. There was no one to follow it up. However, a cash award of about one lakh rupees was sanctioned by the Minister of Railways, which was distributed amongst all those who had worked on this project – some of them had even been transferred from the Ministry of Railways by that time. When this prize money was handed over to those colleagues who had been transferred out, they were pleasantly surprised and had a huge sense of accomplishment. It was one of those initiatives where everything was uncertain from the very beginning, and everyone was sceptical about the project success. Yet it had materialised. The project details are available on UNFCCC website as 'CDM: Improving Energy Efficiency in Railways Residential Quarters for Northern, Eastern, Western and Southern Regions – UNFCCC'.

This was an out-of-the-box thinking as no parallel of this scheme existed in India. We could have lost this opportunity if we had got stuck in consensus building at the tender acceptance stage.

Opportunity knocks at the door, but once. Be honest in your approach and conduct to innovate in the organisation.

17

First Mover Disadvantage: Not Really – Escalators and Windmills

I was Executive Director (Energy Management) in the Ministry of Railways in 2007. J.P. Batra was the CRB. He was a very decisive and forward-looking person. Whenever he got an invitation to attend any of the major conferences on power sector reforms, he asked me to attend them on his behalf. I thus got many opportunities to meet the State Power Secretaries, Power Ministers and attend the Chief Ministers Conference on Power Sector Reforms between October 2006 and 2007. The power sector was under severe stress due to the poor state of its financial health. The Electricity Act of 2003 was already in place to reform this sector.

One such conference of Chief Ministers in 2007 was addressed by Prime Minister Shri Manmohan Singh, and Finance Minister Shri P. Chidambaram. It was during this conference in Vigyan Bhavan in New Delhi that I heard Shri Narendra Modi, the then Chief Minister of Gujarat. He talked about setting up solar cities in the State and about massive solarisation to reduce greenhouse gas effects. It was an inspiring address from the Chief Minister of Gujarat.

As the founding Executive Director (Energy Management) in Railway Board, it was my responsibility to give a new direction to the Energy Management Wing of the Railways and therefore it was decided to:

- Set up windmills for non-traction purpose as a renewable source of energy;
- Introduce CFL in a big way to reduce energy consumption;
- Set up 1,000 MW Nabinagar Power Plant in JV with NTPC;
- Ban the use of incandescent lamps except for decoration purpose;
- Introduce at least three-star rated products to reduce energy consumption; and

- Introduce the concept of Carbon Credits to carry forward CDM initiatives.

It was equally important to bring in escalators and lifts at railway stations to facilitate passengers and be in sync with the developments taking place in major cities. By then, Delhi Metro had adopted escalators in a big way at all of their stations. Indian Railways was viewed as a laggard. Some of my colleagues also talked about a major shift in thinking in the Electrical Department.

There was no regular Member Electrical in Railway Board at that time. Even the Additional Member Electrical's post was vacant. K.C. Jena had taken over as the CRB on August 1, 2007. He was a graduate of IIT Kanpur and had joined IRTS in 1971. As General Manager of East Central Railway, he was responsible for introduction of *litti chokha*, a popular Bihari delicacy, at Patna railway station.

Harsh Kumar was the Executive Director (Finance) who was in sync with my ideas – to use technology to reduce energy consumption and provide better facilities to passengers and at the same time, reduce the carbon footprint of the Railways. Earlier, we would resort to switching off lights and fans to conserve energy. This thinking had to be replaced by use of energy efficient appliances to reduce energy consumption. Harsh was a forward-looking finance officer.

Jena agreed with the proposal to provide escalators at major railway stations, similar to those in major shopping complexes and the Delhi Metro Rail Corporation (DMRC). This would convey our intent to modernise stations. Some 200 escalators were initially planned in the supplementary budget of 2007-08. However, the Chairman agreed to approve 100 escalators first and to have another 100 approved the next year.

Thus, for the first time in the Railways, escalators were sanctioned in bulk in the supplementary budget of 2007-08. This was a major decision taken to provide better passenger amenities at railway stations. Jena understood the need and the current trend.

We also decided to have an Energy Policy. The policy was – for 10 years, source 1 per cent of electrical energy from renewable sources every year to reduce carbon footprint. To achieve that end, it was also decided to set up a 10 MW wind farm for Integral Coach Factory (ICF), Chennai, in Tirunelveli district. The tariff for electricity at Chennai was quite high – of the order of ₹7-8 per unit. For wind energy there was an incentive and the tariff for wind energy was about ₹3-4 per unit. It made sense to use wind energy. This project was sanctioned on an out-of-turn basis at an estimated cost of ₹60 crore in 2007-08 budget. The work was done at a fast pace as we gave full freedom to ICF to go ahead and set up the farm. The Wind Farm was commissioned by ICF in July 2008. ICF's electricity bill reduced substantially.

We also decided to procure only three-star rated products, especially those electrical appliances where Bureau of Energy Efficiency (BEE) had provided a star rating. This policy was issued jointly by Executive Director (Energy Management), Executive Director (Store) and Executive Director (Finance), Railway Board. It was rare for all the three departments to collaborate and come to a common understanding to issue such a policy. No such policy existed in the Government of India at that time. I had pursued the proposal with both the Executive Directors. They found it creditable and therefore agreed with me. We also banned the use of incandescent bulbs in the Railways. These were major energy efficiency reforms implemented in the Railways.

In fact, I had discussed this subject with Ajay Mathur, the Director General of the Bureau of Energy Efficiency. But he had expressed his inability to issue such directives from BEE. He told me to do it directly as it was within the domain of the Ministries to decide on such issues. We therefore went ahead and took the decisions. It gave a new direction to the entire efforts. He was also happy.

When I look back, I find that Railways have so far provided 745 escalators at 260 major stations at the rate of ₹65–70 lakh per unit, and there is a provision for about 1,000 escalators in the pipeline. The policy in place considers its provision at stations where passenger footfall is more than 25,000 per day. Stations of tourist importance and stations at state capitals are exempted from these limits in this policy.

Similarly, windmills of 103 MW have been installed by June 2020. Windmills of 200 MW capacity are at various stages of installation. Windmills have been provided mostly in the states of Tamil Nadu (21 MW), Rajasthan (26 MW) and Maharashtra (56 MW). Wind energy is now used for traction purpose too.

Efforts have also been made by Railways to provide solar based power. As of June 2020, 105 MW solar power plants have been provided. The Capacity Factor (ratio of energy generated to installed capacity over a period) for wind and solar plants varies between 15 and 25 per cent and therefore only about 30–50 MW of solar and wind energy is consumed for Railway applications. Overall, out of 2,800–3,000 MW power requirement for the Railways, only about 1–1.5 per cent of the energy is being sourced from renewable sources. Over a 10-year period, our desire was to have at least 10 per cent of our power requirements from renewable sources and to that end we have not made good progress. This situation is due to regimental decision-making process in the Railways.

Rajesh Jain was my director at that time. He was a very competent electrical engineer and had worked mostly in Operation and Maintenance of Rolling Stock. He had a passion to look for innovative solutions for our age-old problems. In him, I had a stalwart. He was actively working on finding new business models for energy security and therefore energy efficiency. A robust plan of action was drawn out. Implementation has however been slow. It is nevertheless moving in the right direction.

I spent just over about 16 months on this assignment, and I think a good foundation was laid for Energy Management in Railway Board.

Audacity, Courage and Hope: Madhepura Public – Private Partnership

Way back in 2001, while working as Director in the Ministry of Railways, I was handling Operation and Maintenance (O&M) of an entire fleet of electric locos of Indian Railways. There were about 2,800 electric locomotives operating in the country at that time. We had 17 types of electric locomotives – old imported, indigenous conventional 25 KV, 1,500 volt DC, dual voltage AC–DC 25 KV / 1,500 volt DC, and the latest 3-phase AC.

New Era of 3-Phase Technology

The locomotives acquired from Asea Brown Boveri (ABB) Switzerland in 1996 with 3-phase propulsion technology was at the initial stage of its introduction. We were trying our best to assimilate the new technology in Indian Railways for manufacture, maintenance and operation.

The existing fleet of AC locomotives had direct current (DC) drive which meant that the traction motors used would run on DC voltage. The new 3-phase locomotives had 3-phase induction motor which would run on AC voltage. The unique feature of the new technology was feeding of electrical power back to the source whenever the locomotive would be braked to stop the train. This phenomenon is called regeneration of power. This improves the efficiency of the locomotive.

There was transfer of technology (TOT) from ABB to CLW to manufacture these locomotives in India. We had acquired only 33 locomotives of this technology. Technology was transferred to Railways to manufacture complete locomotives at CLW. Railways also had the flexibility to either manufacture in-house or outsource technology for the manufacture of the following major assemblies and sub-assemblies by the Indian industry:

- Loco car body (or, 'shell' as we call it);
- Bogie and transmission system;
- Traction motor;
- Transformer;
- Power and auxiliary converters; and
- Vehicle control unit (VCU) or vehicle electronics.

We were primarily manufacturing the car body, bogie and traction motors of the conventional locomotives at CLW. Some technical knowhow was available at CLW. It was therefore decided to continue manufacturing these parts of 3-phase locomotives also by upgrading the infrastructure at CLW and re-skilling the existing manpower to manufacture new locomotives. Whenever staff is trained in new areas, they feel empowered and motivated.

It was imperative to give licence to various Indian manufacturers to produce transformers, propulsion equipment and vehicle electronics. Traction motor was also included in the strategy to outsource in order to have an alternate source of supply. This was in accordance with the TOT agreement

Car body and bogie were retained for manufacture at CLW exclusively. CLW decided to undertake manufacture of traction motor since the existing manpower had some basic knowledge of its manufacture. A new traction motor manufacturing facility was established as it required different tools and equipment to manufacture AC motors. Indian Railways was undertaking to manufacture AC traction motors for the first time.

Warranty of ABB Locos

These locos were warranted for five years. They were homed at Ghaziabad Loco Shed of Northern Railway and Gomoh Loco Shed of Eastern Railway (now East Central) for maintenance and performance monitoring.

The five-year warranty was about to be over in 2001-02. I was Director, Rolling Stock. The problems persisted in the drive gear mechanism, bogies and the Gate Turn Off Thyristor (GTO). We were not able to resolve these problems even after five years. There were cracks in bogies. Hurth coupling membrane was failing. GTOs were burning.

Slowly, the hand-holding by ABB, which later became Bombardier Transportation (BT), reduced. Maintenance staff of the two sheds were still in the process of learning the new technology. We were finding it difficult to do justice to the maintenance of these locomotives.

The availability and reliability of the locos was not very good. Availability means how much time the loco remains in operation vis-à-vis total time available in the day, while reliability means the distance travelled by a locomotive between two successive failures. Lack of trained manpower was the prime reason.

About 50 supervisors and technicians were engaged by BT while discharging their warranty obligations. They were the best trained personnel as they had five years of on-the-job experience on this project. We ought to have recruited them but there was no rule which could permit Railways to employ them. We would have got a head start if we had those trained personnel absorbed by the Railways.

Some of the locomotives were getting stabled either for want of material or for want of failure investigation. Every day, the statistics relating to these 33 imported locomotives and a few indigenously manufactured locos used to be put up to Member Electrical, Railway Board. I used to get perplexed. I did not know how to improve the performance.

Outsourcing Taboo

The performance of these locomotives was inferior to the conventional locomotives. I had once even suggested to the then Member Electrical that we should give a ten-year comprehensive maintenance contract to BT. We would then have exactly understood the cost of maintenance per locomotive and its true reliability and availability index.

Outsourcing of maintenance of locomotive was considered a taboo at that time and the idea was struck down. With various ups and downs, the system continued in the business-as-usual mode and the production of these locos at CLW increased from 2–3 locomotives per year to 15–20 locomotives per year.

No one even agreed to outsource the maintenance of high-end technology products viz., propulsion system comprising power and auxiliary convertor and the vehicle electronics to the TOT partners. The underlying thought was – maintenance is our core competence. How could we outsource maintenance? We are electrical engineers, and therefore we should slowly learn and maintain. We were on a denial mode.

There was absolute dependence on RDSO to resolve the issues of frequent failure of GTOs, traction motors and the Hurth coupling. Support from OEMs was over.

It was decided to continue import of some of the critical items and live with suboptimal reliability and availability.

By now I firmly believed that if I ever got an opportunity, I would try my best to partner with the technology owner on a long-term basis for maintenance support. This would then provide possibility of continuous upgradation of technology. This is a global best practice – the one who designs is the one who maintains and upgrades.

By 2003-04, the Insulated Gate Bipolar Junction Transistor (IGBT) technology had been developed worldwide. This was an improvement over GTO. GTO had high incidence of failure compared to IGBT.

Indian Railways was however not thinking in this direction. Railways had hardly been able to assimilate GTO technology, so migrating to IGBT appeared arduous.

The thought of selecting a new technology partner and long-term hand-holding remained dormant in my mind even though there were no takers. These ideas were much ahead of the curve at that time.

Belief Turns into Faith

Belief is being convinced something to be true and it starts in your head. As it grows its roots, it settles in your heart. But faith is in your feet. Proceeding in faith moulds our belief and etches those truths in our hearts and matures into trust.

In December 2003, I was promoted to Chief Electrical Loco Engineer (CELE) in Northern Railway. It was then that I was able to closely monitor the performance of these ABB locomotives. I was certain that this was not a locomotive we could call a workhorse of the Indian Railways although it had many unique features like:

- The regenerative braking;
- Constant speed control that provided ease to drivers;
- Computer based fault diagnostics that was very easy for drivers;
- Driver's vigilance control every 60 seconds to ensure alertness of drivers;
- Speed control during shunting limited to 15 kmph to ensure safety;
- Energy consumed and regenerated could be seen real-time on board;
- Parking brakes.

These features did not exist in the conventional locomotives which used the technology of the 1960s.

In October 2006, I was posted in the Ministry of Railways as Executive Director (Energy Management). I was asked by Member

Electrical to work on setting up a new Electric Loco Factory. A new Diesel Loco Factory had already been sanctioned in September 2006 on a Public Private Partnership (PPP) basis. This was to be set up at Marhowra, Bihar.

I had no doubt in my mind that the new factory would usher a new culture of manufacture and maintenance. Although I was not associated with the locomotive portfolio, I was asked to pursue the same.

New Factory

For sanction of a new factory, consultations were to be held with the Planning Commission, Traffic Directorate, Finance Directorate and Rolling Stock Directorate in the Ministry of Railways.

After vigorous follow up with the Planning Commission, the Cabinet Committee on Economic Affairs finally approved a new Electric Loco Factory on February 1, 2007. This factory was to be set up at Madhepura, Bihar. Shri Lalu Prasad Yadav was the railway minister. He gave his OSD, Sudhir Kumar, full freedom to modernise Railways.

A 1,000 MW power plant at Nabinagar, Bihar, as a JV of Railways and NTPC, was also approved by the Cabinet on the same day. This project had been languishing for five years due to an unsettled issue of equity investment by Railways in the JV company. It was finally decided that Railways would invest an equity of only 26 per cent in the JV and NTPC would hold 74 per cent equity. The JV agreement between NTPC and Railways was signed on November 6, 2007.

After the signing of the JV agreement of Nabinagar, Sudhir Kumar asked me to work on the Madhepura project. It was very vital for the socio-economic development of this backward region in Bihar. The project was very close to the MR since this was his parliamentary constituency. Politically, it was therefore very sensitive. MR wanted to create a CLW-like establishment in Bihar to manufacture state-of-the-art electric locos to improve rail operations. CLW is spread over 1,300 acre of land and is a big township.

But this project was being handled by Shakeel Ahmad, the Executive Director, Railway Board. Shakeel Ahmad was senior to me and had the mandate to see all the new factories. I told Sudhir Kumar that I would not be able to handle the project unless the full Board unanimously took a decision and transferred the project to me. I was also to be posted as Executive Director in-charge of Development activities and shifted from the post of Executive Director (Energy Management).

Madhepura Journey

On January 14, 2008, I was posted as Executive Director (Development), Railway Board and the Madhepura project was duly transferred under me. My Energy Management portfolio was now to be looked after by another officer.

The real journey of the Madhepura project started. After many rounds of discussions between the Ministry of Railways and Planning Commission, it was decided to take the Madhepura project forward on a PPP model.

The estimated cost of this project was ₹1,300 crore. The locomotive for manufacture at this factory was identified as the 12,000 HP locomotives with latest IGBT technology. These locos were in operation in China. The 12,000 HP locomotive happened to be the most powerful locomotive in the world at that time. Viney Mittal and Kul Bhushan had gone to China and travelled on this locomotive some time ago. Viney Mittal became the CRB while Kul Bhushan became Member Electrical, Railway Board.

It was firmed up that the factory could be set up through private investment, only if an assured business for manufacture of a reasonable number of locomotives was committed to the successful bidder. Since an investment of ₹1,300 crore was to be committed by the private investor only for Railways rolling stock, Railways also had to make a firm commitment.

It was therefore considered essential to sanction the manufacture of 1,000 locomotives of 12,000 HP over 10 years at an estimated cost of ₹18,000 crore.

The same principle was considered for Diesel Loco Factory enabling a provision of ₹14,000 crore for 1,000 diesel locos of 4,500 and 6,000 HP.

More or less, it became certain that a committed offtake of 1,000 locomotives over 10 years will evince interest of the private sector, especially the foreign companies who were the primary source of locomotive technology. None of the Indian companies had the technology to manufacture electric locomotives.

Locomotives were manufactured in-house in our own Production Units at CLW and DLW with transfer of technology at different stages. The TOT for production of locomotives and its sub-assemblies at that time was considered as the only and best option since there was heavy dependence on in-house manufacture and maintenance. The transaction of around ₹20–25,000 crore had never been handled by this Ministry earlier. It was unthinkable to go to the private sector and commit this level of procurement to enable the world's leading companies to come to India and set up manufacturing facilities.

International Consultants

It was therefore considered essential to select an international consultant to prepare the procurement agreement, following global best practices. In August 2008, we selected Mott McDonald, UK, to prepare the technical and commercial transaction documents.

One of the key personnel was Bob Simpson. He was deputed by Mott McDonald UK for this assignment. Bob Simpson had worked on the English Channel Tunnel project for which more than £6 billion contracts had been issued.

Consequently, we thought that Simpson would provide good technical and commercial advisory for this mega project. This consultancy contract did give us confidence that such large procurement contracts had been undertaken globally. Such contracts were mostly pertaining to procurement with comprehensive maintenance, but not linked to setting up of a factory. We were able to understand global best practices relating to reliability and availability standards.

We figured out the contours of the project and clearly identified the responsibilities of the technology partner and Railways. Safety in train operations had to be the sole responsibility of Railways. In consultation with the Planning Commission, Ministry of Law and Justice, and Ministry of Finance, we drafted a Model Concession Agreement for the project with Railways equity being 26 per cent in the Special Purpose Vehicle (SPV). This was a new thinking.

The SPV was to be incorporated by the technology partner with commitment to set up the factory, maintenance depots and a training school. It was also clear that land would have to be provided on a long-term lease of 35 years to set up the factory. Any factory would have useful asset life of more than 25–30 years.

A token licence fee of ₹1 was fixed for the maintenance depots. I was certain that maintenance of these locomotives by the company would be done up to the major periodic overhaul and extended to three more years in order to assimilate the technology and ensure high reliability for a sustainable success.

We thought that the period for maintenance should be around 15 years, keeping in view the data we gathered from various sources and Mott McDonald UK.

The global norm was that OEMs provided maintenance support for the life of the rolling stock.

There was a lot of resentment within the Electrical Directorate as nobody was willing to part with the maintenance of the locos to the private sector due to the basic belief that 'maintenance is our core competence'. I had my personal experience of ABB locomotives. Railways did not have the capability and competence to assimilate the high-end technology even after five years. Our maintenance people did not have the basic technical knowledge by education or even by experience.

The Planning Commission was very supportive of the idea of long-term maintenance by the technology partner. It was the considered opinion of the Planning Commission that unless the risk of maintenance rested with the private sector company, government interest would not be adequately protected. Since this would be a major contract to a private sector company with complete autonomy, it was befitting to have the risk of manufacture and maintenance with the company. That was what was planned.

Finally, the bid documents were made ready for shortlisting of the bidders (Request for Qualification – RFQ) and for submission of financial bids (Request for Proposal – RFP). All the major companies in the world evinced interest in this project. Prospective bidders were somewhat scared looking at the size and duration of the project as this would be a 25-year contract – 10 years for supply of locomotives and 15 years for maintenance of all locomotives.

Three major global companies – Alstom France, Bombardier Germany and Siemens Germany – were shortlisted in May 2008. The financial bids were to be opened in October 2008.

The Planning Commission was fully on board despite several objections from Stores and Finance Departments within the Ministry of Railways.

Ten days before the opening of the financial bids in October 2008, Montek Singh Ahluwalia, Deputy Chairman, Planning Commission, met Minister of Railways Shri Lalu Prasad Yadav and suggested that in view of the size of the two contracts for setting up the two factories, it would be fitting to seek the approval of the Cabinet. These were going to be the biggest contracts ever in the history of the nation. Cabinet approval would require a high degree of due diligence amongst various Ministries and greatly enhance the credibility of the project – for the bidders and for Railways. Montek Singh Ahluwalia was an economist of repute and his word carried weight in the Government of India (GOI).

Immediately thereafter, the Financial Commissioner Railways convened a meeting with Member Electrical, Member Mechanical and all the officers looking after the two factories – Shakeel Ahmed, Sharad Mallik and me. A final decision was to be taken whether to go ahead with the opening of financial bids in October 2008 or to put the whole process on hold and approach the Cabinet for approval.

A majority of the officers were in favour of opening the financial bids as all preparations had been done and the date of opening was very close.

I was of a contrarian view. I suggested that obtaining the approval of the Cabinet would be in the best interest of Railways since the approval of the Cabinet would enhance the credibility of the project tremendously. This would entail more rigorous due diligence by all concerned in the Government of India.

Full Board, in consultation with the Minister, decided to put everything on hold and directed us to prepare a Cabinet Note in consultation with the Ministry of Finance, Ministry of Law and Justice and the Planning Commission.

Union Cabinet Approves: February 2009

I was made the nodal officer to prepare a common Cabinet Note for the two factories. In the whole process, there was lot of criticism. Rigorous work was to be done. We used to work from 9 a.m. to 11 p.m. Within two months we were able to prepare the Cabinet Note and place the bid documents before the Cabinet for approval. The Cabinet considered the proposal and accorded its approval on February 5, 2009.

The bids were thereafter invited quickly as the Model Code of Conduct was to come into effect due to the Lok Sabha term coming to an end.

Despite my repeated requests to postpone the opening of the financial bids, nobody paid any attention and finally the bids were opened on February 16, 2009.

No company participated in the Madhepura Project. One bid was however received for the Diesel factory. We were immediately asked to approach the Cabinet to convert this PPP project into a Production Unit (PU) like CLW. This was also approved by the Cabinet on February 18, 2009. Eventually the PPP initiative came to an end. It was a huge setback. I had thought of setting up a world-class infrastructure. This was no more possible.

Project Review by Dr Amit Mitra

After the Lok Sabha elections were over in May 2009, a new government was formed and Sushri Mamata Banerjee took over as the Minister of Railways. After the Railway Budget was presented in July 2009, all the major projects were reviewed. A committee headed by Dr Amit Mitra, Secretary General, Federation of Indian Chambers of Commerce and Industry (FICCI), with other expert members, was constituted to look into major infrastructure projects of Railways for their expeditious execution. Dr Amit Mitra was an economist and a very soft-spoken person. I used to go and meet him in FICCI house for discussions.

The Madhepura project was also reviewed by this committee. After protracted deliberations with the committee and the Members of the Railway Board, it was considered essential to approach the Cabinet again to obtain its approval for executing this project on PPP model rather than a PU model of Railways. The PPP model was the originally envisaged model approved by the Cabinet in February 2009.

The proposal for undertaking the project on PPP mode was approved by the Cabinet in February 2010. With this approval, we were excited that a world-class factory could be set up.

It took almost a year to undo the PU model and initiate the process again, keeping the same PPP framework. The RFQ process was initiated and shortlisting of bidders completed in May 2010.

Empowered Committee

A high-powered Empowered Committee (EC) comprising Chairman Railway Board, Secretary Department of Economic Affairs, Secretary Law, Member Secretary Planning Commission, Member Electrical, Member Mechanical and Financial Commissioner Railways was notified in accordance with the approval of the Cabinet accorded in February 2010 to consider and approve changes which had been requested by various bidders during the pre-bid conferences held prior to the opening of RFP in 2009.

After six rounds of meetings of the EC, the bid documents attained finality. It was almost certain that the process of holding pre-bid conferences for RFP would be completed and financial bids opened.

However, on the insistence of some of the members of EC, it was decided to approach the Cabinet for making a few changes that would make the bidding process yet more competitive. These changes were considered beyond the purview of the EC.

This essentially pertained to a reduction in the price of the locomotive from the fourth year onwards once the production of locomotives stabilised at Madhepura. The Cabinet had earlier approved a reduction in the base price by 3 per cent on a year-on-year basis, but the suggestion of some of the EC members was to reduce it to 1 per cent.

Executive Directors Review Union Cabinet Decisions

A Cabinet Note duly cleared by the full Board was put up to Minister of Railways Sushri Mamata Banerjee who did not approve it for six months. Instead, a Committee of Executive Directors of various Directorates in the Railway Board was constituted to review various terms and conditions originally approved by the Cabinet in 2009 and the changes approved by the Empowered Committee on six different occasions. I was not a member of this Committee. We were all aghast that the Railway Ministry could think of reviewing even the decisions of the highest decision-making body of the country. This Committee was at the level of the Joint Secretary.

The review of Cabinet approved documents and EC approved changes by a committee consisting of their juniors was unusual and it did demoralise everyone associated with the two factory projects. These were big-ticket projects.

The officers engaged in this Committee were not well versed with the project and the PPP framework. Again, the controversies relating to outsourcing of the maintenance and an assured offtake for 1,000 locos for 10 years each for diesel and electric locos started. We were back to where we were when the project was initiated in January 2008.

The committee was critical of these projects (Madhepura and Marhowra) and gave a negative report. Once the report was submitted by the Committee in September 2011, detailed comments were put up for the consideration of the full Board. I responded honestly and sincerely.

By the time a final view was taken by the Board, I was transferred on September 29, 2011 and posted as DRM Dhanbad. I left Railway Board on October 13, 2011, to take charge of the Dhanbad Division on October 14, 2011.

Cabinet Approves RFQ

N.R. Dash took over from me as Executive Director (Development). For the next two years, I worked as DRM Dhanbad and during this period, a Cabinet Note was put up to obtain the approval of the Cabinet for the Eligibility Criteria for setting up the projects.

For setting up the Madhepura factory, both electric and diesel loco manufacturers could participate in the RFQ. But for the Marhowra factory, only diesel loco manufacturers were allowed to participate in the RFQ.

This led to a serious controversy. To put an end to the controversy and adoption of different eligibility criteria for electric and diesel loco factories, even the RFQ had to be put up to the Cabinet for approval.

The electric loco factory project had an enabling arrangement, permitting both diesel and electric loco manufacturers if they had designed and manufactured diesel or electric locomotives of 4,000 HP and above with IGBT technology, and had produced locomotives equivalent to 1.8 million HP in the preceding five years.

For the diesel factory project only those manufacturers who had designed and manufactured diesel locomotives even with limited numbers of IGBT propulsion technology, were allowed to participate.

The Cabinet approved different eligibility criteria for the two projects on May 1, 2013. The controversy was put to rest.

Informal Group of Ministers

The changes approved by the EC and suggestions furnished by the Executive Directors Committee were again considered in totality by an Informal Group of Ministers (IGOM) headed by Finance Minister Shri P. Chidambaram, along with the Minister of Railways and the Deputy Chairman, Planning Commission. This IGOM was constituted by the Prime Minister's Office to review the provisions and give a final go-ahead to the Ministry of Railways. The recommendations were finalised and approved by IGOM early in 2013.

The RFQ process was initiated afresh as approved by the Cabinet. The RFQ was opened on September 2, 2013. But the process of evaluation could not be completed over the next four months.

In September 2013, I was posted back as Executive Director (Development), Railway Board, after completing my tenure as DRM Dhanbad.

I was hesitant to work again on the same project. No one paid heed to it. I took over as Executive Director (Development) on September 25, 2013. My immediate priority was to complete the process of RFQ which was pending and take the final bid documents for the approval of the Cabinet as early as possible, keeping in view the forthcoming Lok Sabha elections in May 2014.

As regards to the finalisation of the RFQ, I discovered that more than 40 Indian Embassies abroad had been requested to verify the credentials relating to the 'eligible projects' claimed by the bidders before the tender committee could even consider finalisation of its minutes.

Dissenting Tender Committee

The process of verification was not required in accordance with the intent of the RFQ wherein all the certifications were to be submitted by the bidders duly certified by their Statutory Auditors.

This happened due to a lack of understanding by the Finance, Stores and Electrical officers prior to my taking over as Executive Director in September 2013. With the best of my efforts, Indian Embassies abroad could verify only few projects, and therefore a decision was taken to short-close this process as it was serving no purpose except causing a delay.

The minutes of the tender committee for the RFQ were prepared to present all the logic with utmost due diligence. They were however dissented by the Finance and Stores officers, who were predisposed to stall the project on some count or the other.

Both officers, Executive Directors of Finance and Stores discipline, did not agree to commit to an offtake of 1,000 locomotives for 10 years. Some of the officers possibly perceived this project as taking away the work of year-on-year procurement of 10 years in one go. It was intriguing to note such views on a project which had been approved at the highest level of decision making in the Government – the Union Cabinet – after a very high level of due diligence across various ministries in the Government of India.

This was a split decision of the Tender Committee (2:1) wherein my recommendations were inconsequential. Finance and Store officers had decided to say what they wanted to say and completely disagree with my views.

I had the firm conviction that I was professionally right and therefore wrote a 43-page note justifying my stand and giving detailed and cogent reasons for not agreeing with the views of the majority. It needed courage and conviction, which I had. I knew what I was doing was in the best interest of the Railways. There was no bitterness about this on the part of any one of us, as all of us were professionally honest and doing what was our conviction at that time.

These tender committee minutes were forwarded to a higher-level Appreciation Committee comprising three Additional Members. There was a dissent again. Additional Members of Electrical and Stores discipline had their views 'for' and Additional Member Finance had views 'against'. This was again a split (2:1) Tender Committee recommendation. It was nevertheless accepted by the then Member Electrical on May 15, 2014. The Appreciation Committee agreed with my view, which was their majority view. This stage was, after all, only to decide which bidders to shortlist at the first stage, i.e., RFQ. At this stage no one even knew whether this project would move forward or not, and who could be the successful bidder after the receipt of financial bids.

The fate of the Diesel Loco Factory project was similar, wherein the Member Mechanical accepted the majority view (2:1). The following major international companies were shortlisted:
- Electric factory Madhepura: Alstom France, Bombardier Germany, Siemens Germany and GE USA.
- Diesel factory Marhowra: GE USA and EMD USA.

Cabinet Approves Agreement

Simultaneously, the Cabinet Note along with bid documents, was also finalised. After protracted deliberations, a Cabinet Note was put up for the approval of Minister of Railways, Shri Mallikarjun Kharge.

The Cabinet Note contained 1,170 pages, and 72 copies were to be made. Normally a Cabinet note contains 20–25 pages including annexures. It was unusually long as views of all the Ministries had to be represented and Railway Ministry's response on them recorded.

Moreover, the Cabinet Note had the complete agreement that was to be entered into with the successful bidder. Prior to this project, no such documents had ever been placed before the Union Cabinet, as the Director, Cabinet Secretariat, told me at that time.

The Cabinet Note was listed for consideration on January 20, 2014. Two days before the Cabinet meeting, Arunendra Kumar, CRB asked me to go to Bengaluru to brief the MR either at his residence in Bengaluru or during the flight from Bengaluru to Delhi on the day of the Cabinet meeting on January 20. I went to Bengaluru on January 19, 2014.

On January 20, 2014, I met the MR in Bengaluru in one of the election meetings. He asked me to brief him on board the flight from Bengaluru to Delhi.

In-flight with Railway Minister

While I was briefing the Minister during the flight, he made a very pertinent observation, 'We are in January 2014 and the Lok Sabha elections are due in May 2014. How will the process of bidding be completed during this period, as the Model Code of Conduct will come into force somewhere in February–March 2014?'

I very humbly submitted to the Minister that approving the bid documents for these extremely important Make-in-India and PPP would be in the best interest of Indian Railways. A lot of work had been done over the last six years with the best possible due diligence undertaken by various ministries. I also told him, 'We will make no attempt whatsoever to invite the financial bids during this period. It will not be possible to complete this exercise in a manner that would ensure success without the participation of international bidders. However, approval of Cabinet will vindicate our intent of making this project a success and our desire to bring private investment. There is no risk of any sort. In the event these documents are approved by the Cabinet today (January 20, 2014), the next Government may decide whether to take these projects forward or not in the interest of the country.

I also mentioned that these projects had created a lot of goodwill internationally. The Minister agreed. He was convinced that the approval of the bid documents by the Cabinet would not create anything negative for the outgoing Government. It could, in fact, create an enabling environment for the new Government. He assured me of his support for the project in the Cabinet meeting planned that day itself.

We landed at Indira Gandhi International Airport Delhi at 4 p.m. The Minister proceeded to attend the Cabinet meeting slated for 5.30 p.m. I headed directly to the Railway Board and briefed Arunendra Kumar, CRB, about my discussions with the Minister. That day there was a *gherao* of Parliament and Rail Bhawan by the Chief Minister of Delhi, Shri Arvind Kejriwal. I had to leave my car at Vayu Sena Bhawan and walk for around 3 km.

The Chairman also left for the meeting but told me to stay at Rail Bhawan till he returned. By 7 p.m., CRB came back and congratulated me that the project, as proposed, had been approved by the Union Cabinet.

Since the bidders had already been shortlisted, it was decided to issue RFP to the shortlisted bidders and follow a timeline which would give adequate comfort to all the parties for submitting an unconditional financial bid without deviating from the Cabinet-approved framework.

The process was to kickstart with proposed pre-bid conferences for the RFP and opening of the bids with a clear time frame of about 7–8 months from start to finish. There was some criticism that a far too relaxed timeline was being given, but I did not relent.

New Minister Briefed

After the elections, the new government was in place by the end of May 2014. We thought it prudent to brief the new Minister of Railways, Shri Sadananda Gowda, before releasing the RFP to the shortlisted bidders.

The project really got a fillip in the Modi government as it made all the sense to acquire the world's best technology for the movement of freight traffic at 100 kmph on Indian Railways.

This was a top-notch Make-in-India project and was reviewed by the MR before the receipt of financial bids on August 30, 2015.

In one of the Review Meetings with the Minister, I mentioned, 'If we want to run bullock carts, we do not require these projects. These projects will bring a paradigm shift in freight operations. Speeds of our freight trains today are around 22 kmph.' This was to stretch the arguments to their limit to drive home the importance of these projects. After all, I had been working on this project for about five years. The meeting was attended by full Board and both the Ministers. My statement was well-received.

It was decided in the meeting that if the Ministry required less locomotives in future, the requirement from Madhepura and Marhowra would not be curtailed. However, it would be adjusted against Railways own production programme for the manufacture of locomotives at CLW and DLW. All the issues were resolved and there was a total commitment at the highest level. I could see a positive change in the mindset of people in Railway Board.

The financial bids were finally opened on August 30, 2015 but were put on hold for communicating the decision after approval of the Tender Committee minutes on file because of the Model Code of Conduct in force due to Assembly elections in Bihar.

Agreement Signing

The result was announced on November 9, 2015, and the agreement was signed on November 30, 2015 in a function organised jointly by Minister of Finance Shri Arun Jaitley and the Minister of Railways Shri Suresh Prabhu. All the 50 Members of Parliament (MPs) from Bihar and all the Cabinet Ministers who hailed from Bihar participated in the function organised at Media Centre in Delhi. It was a big event. Even the Ambassador of France attended the function. The Ambassador of USA sent his representative to attend the function due to a last-minute engagement.

The highlight of the event was that the Minister of Railways Shri Suresh Prabhu mentioned in his speech that the projects had been awarded to the successful bidders Alstom, France–Madhepura project, and GE, USA–Marhowra project, *with a unique appreciation even from the unsuccessful bidders*. The unsuccessful bidders told the Prime Minister's Office and the Railway Ministry that though they had lost the projects, they had nothing against the bidding, as the bid process was conducted in a fair, transparent and competitive environment.

This was a big positive for me as the message was conveyed to everyone in an open forum by the MR. It gave me a great sense of accomplishment. I had conceived the project, and I was rewarded in such a grand manner.

Key Features

This was a ₹25,000 crore contract signed on November 30, 2015. I was the signatory from the Ministry of Railways. Some of the key features that defined the success of the project and international appreciation are mentioned here:

- **An assured offtake for 10 years and maintenance for 13 years:**

    Railways committed to buy 800 locos of 12,000 HP over 11 years with a provision to extend the contract by another 200 locos at 90 per cent of the price of the 800th locomotive. In the event Railways was not able to procure the loco quantities as agreed upon, a penalty was to be paid to the JV company. The Agreement also clearly defined the event of termination of the contract on account of either the JV company or Railways. The cap on this payment was fixed at ₹1,200 crore. The terms were such that either party would find it difficult to terminate the Agreement.

- **Setting up of factory, two depots and a training school:**

    The JV company was to set up a greenfield factory at Madhepura including a township for the staff and important facilities like shopping complex and a community centre. Railways was to ensure rail and road connectivity and the availability of 132 KV power supply within 500 m of the factory. This was done to ensure 'ease of doing business' as it would have been difficult for the JV company to get the permissions from the government. A full-fledged Training Institute with a Simulator and other training infrastructure was also to be set up. Two maintenance depots had to be set up – at Saharanpur and Nagpur.

- **Land on lease for 35 years for the factory, and on license fee of ₹1 for depot:**

  Since the factory would have a useful life of at least 30–35 years, the lease period of land was accordingly kept at 35 years for the comfort of the bidders, at a fixed charge for the 11-year supply period, and thereafter it had been linked to circle rates. The licence for depot land was fixed at ₹1 per acre per annum since these depots would return to Railways after the maintenance period was over.

- **Single bidding parameter:**

  This was a unique concept for such a mega project valued at about ₹25,000 crore (about US$3.75 billion). Maintenance fee was also linked to the bid price 'P'. This ensured simple bid evaluation and there was no need to do NPV calculations. This ensured elimination of any chance of gaming of the bidding.

- **Maintenance fee defined in the Agreement as a per cent of the loco price:**

  To ensure least total cost of ownership, the maintenance fees for each of the 13 years was specified upfront in the agreement, varying from 1.25 per cent of 'P' for the first year to 8.25 per cent of 'P' for the 12th year. Both 'P' and the maintenance fee were fully indexed to inflation to reduce any risk that bidders might consider and inflate the bid price.

- **KPIs: 95 per cent availability, 2,00,000 km per failure reliability:**

  These were the best global norms for performance of locomotives and were clearly defined. For underperformance, penalties were specified. The concept of epidemic defect liability for design failures were also specified.

- **Incentives for early payment by Railways @ 0.5 per cent of the price, and penalty for delay – interest at bank rate +3 per cent:**

  This was unheard of, that for any delay in payment of bills beyond 30 days, the Government would pay a penalty by way of interest at the bank rate + 3 per cent of the bill amount to be paid, and for payment within 15 days, the government would get a discount of 0.5 per cent of the bill amount. This was done with the approval of the Cabinet. This provided immense comfort to the JV company.

- **First time the Government invested equity of 26 per cent in private sector:**

    This was to ensure seriousness on the part of the Government. Unless you have skin in the game, seriousness will not be visible; and 26 per cent equity provided veto rights to Railways if the JV company wanted to change the business altogether.

- **Price of the spares linked to loco price:**

    This unique feature ensured that the spares were not priced exorbitantly. All spares put together would add up to the price 'P'. A markup of 30 per cent was kept to provide for cost of carrying the inventory and freight, if any. Normally spares cost 2–3 times the cost of the complete rolling stock.

- **Learning curve: Loco price reduction by 3 per cent from fourth year onwards:**

    From the fourth year onwards, the price of manufacture of locos at Madhepura would reduce by 3 per cent from the price of the preceding year. As the production increased, the productivity would improve, and it would reflect in reduced cost of production. This is what was captured in the learning curve. Due to successive reduction from the fourth year till the eleventh year, there would be an overall reduction of about 26 per cent in the price 'P'.

This was a defining project of my career and one of the biggest projects ever acquired by Alstom France in their history, globally. It taught me numerous intricacies related to Company Law and Finance.

Gajendra Haldea was an authority in PPP in India. He had written many concession agreements and books on a variety of subjects while he was in the Planning Commission. He guided us at each stage of the project. Ved Mani Tiwari was my Director between 2008 and 2011. Ved was a wizard who used to work late night almost all the days to do all the work related to the project. He had an amazing capacity for work and numerous capabilities.

S.K. Saha later handled this project with me. He knew this project inside out as he was Director Infrastructure in the Planning Commission during 2008–2010 when we had conceptualised this project. Saha is an amazingly competent officer who had absolute clarity on PPP. He became Executive Director (Development) and handled the project after I was appointed as Advisor (Rolling Stock).

We had a small team of two officers and 2-3 supervisors who worked on this project. We trusted one another immensely. The project predominantly succeeded due to the support of the Planning

Commission, not that other Ministries and other officers did not contribute in a substantial manner

It was the Modi government which made this project happen. The 12,000 HP loco has started working trains from May 2020. The PM inaugurated this project on April 10, 2018. This project also found mention in a book titled *Strategy for New India@75* released by Niti Aayog with a foreword by the Prime Minister. Extracts are reproduced here:

The Madhepura Electric Locomotive Project, a joint venture between the Indian Railways and the French multinational, Alstom, provides a good example of how mega projects can be leveraged to boost domestic production. The project enabled effective transfer of technology and the availability of state-of-the-art locomotives for the Railways. The Madhepura model is replicable in defence, aerospace, railways and shipping sectors.

Model Code of Conduct

It is a set of guidelines issued by the Election Commission of India for the conduct of political parties and candidates during elections, mainly with respect to speeches, polling day activities, polling booths management, election manifestos and promises, processions and personal conduct. These norms have been evolved with the consensus of political parties who have consented to follow them. It comes into effect immediately after the announcement of the election schedule by the Election Commission of India for ensuring free and fair elections. The main points included in the Code are:

- No new projects to be announced;
- No recruitment process to be initiated;
- No rallies to hinder road traffic;
- Refrain from distributing liquor;
- Public places like helipads, guest houses to be equally shared;
- Official machinery not to be used for campaigning;
- No announcements to be made by the ruling party that can influence voters;
- Seek permission from the local police for use of loudspeakers;
- No welfare programmes to be launched like – road construction, drinking water or ribbon-cutting ceremonies.

Complaints can be made to Election Officers of the State or Election Commission of India for necessary action.

Unintended Consequences: Benefits in Retrospect – Dankuni for Chittaranjan, West Bengal

Sushri Mamata Banerjee was the Minister of Railways in 2010. Sukhbir Singh was the Member Electrical, Railway Board. Sukhbir Singh had worked as the General Manager CLW. He was my DRM at Allahabad when I was in-charge of Kanpur Loco Shed in 1998-99. In fact, I moved to Railway Board in April 1999 during his tenure. He was not happy with my transfer to Railway Board as he had wanted me to be posted at Allahabad to look after Operations. He would always think big and wanted to create world class infrastructure. CLW had been given a massive facelift in terms of cleanliness, production of locomotives and staff welfare during his tenure as General Manager.

Sushri Mamata Banerjee is a very compassionate human being and was quite interested in creating infrastructure pan India, but the Indian state of West Bengal was very close to her heart as she came from there. There was a genuine need to enhance production of electric locomotives at CLW and upgrade its infrastructure.

CLW is a very old loco factory, set up in West Bengal in 1950. It had reached a capacity to manufacture 200 locomotives per annum. The capacity could have been further enhanced by outsourcing certain activities to private companies, but the unionised culture of the eastern region made it difficult to do so. It was better to maintain industrial peace and find alternate ways and means to ramp up production.

I was an Executive Director in the Railway Board, looking after various development projects. Augmenting the capacity of CLW had been discussed for quite some time. The thought of finding another location for the manufacture of locomotives was always a priority.

Sukhbir Singh called me to discuss the prospects of setting up a new factory at a distant place to augment the capacity of CLW. A new place with a new culture was being considered to start the new venture. After brainstorming, it was clear that the proposal would be approved and included in the forthcoming Rail Budget.

Railways land was available near Dankuni railway station. Eastern DFC was planned to terminate at Dankuni. Setting up the ancillary unit of CLW at Dankuni was therefore a natural choice. This was agreed upon by the Minister. This turned out to be a consensual choice.

Dankuni is about 200 km from Chittaranjan and it takes about 4 hours by road to reach CLW. It is 18 km from Howrah station. Dankuni was strategically very important due to DFC. It was therefore decided to set up a factory to manufacture 50 electric locomotives per year in the first phase at Dankuni. This could be enhanced to manufacture 100 locos annually in the second phase.

As soon as I was able to frame a project proposal, it was sanctioned at a cost of about ˋ350 crore and included in the Rail Budget of 2010. All this was done at a great pace as the Budget was to be presented to the Parliament in February 2010.

The Eastern and Western DFC projects had already been sanctioned in 2007. The High Horsepower 12,000 HP locomotive had been identified in 2008 itself for operation on Eastern DFC, which was also to be proliferated on a pan India basis to improve average speed of freight trains.

The Western DFC was planned for the movement of container traffic in double stack formation which necessitated a highrise OHE (7.2 m high) and a different locomotive. For ensuring right powering of trains to run at 100 kmph, it was necessary to provide 2 HP locomotive to haul one tonne of load. The laws of motion in Physics tell us that if a one tonne train is to be run at 100 kmph on a level gradient, we need 2 HP per tonne.

For a 4,500 tonne train with DSCs, we needed a locomotive of 9,000 HP. This was no rocket science. This had also been recommended by Japan Investment Cooperation Agency (JICA) in their report on DFC. JICA was also providing soft loan for the Western DFC project. We did not have the technology to manufacture 9,000 HP locomotives at CLW.

It was considered essential to set up a new factory at Dankuni, not only to augment the production of the existing ABB electric locos, but also to induct the new technology of 9,000 HP. Transfer of Technology (TOT) for manufacture of a new car body, bogie and traction motor at Dankuni was the need of the hour, if we were to think of 9,000 HP locomotives.

Here we did not want to follow the Madhepura model, although it was the best option, because we wanted to re-skill our own staff at CLW and migrate CLW to a completely new loco platform to modernise it. CLW was manufacturing locomotives with GTO technology of ABB, a design of the mid-1980s, that was 20 years old at that time.

It was considered important to set up a new factory with new culture at a new place which could imbibe new technology. This investment, directly and indirectly, was expected to lead to the development of that area as well.

All conceptual planning for this work was done under a high-level committee headed by Dr Amit Mitra, a noted economist, who was the Secretary General (1994–2011) of FICCI. FICCI is an association of business organisations in India, and established in 1927 on the advice of Mahatma Gandhi.

The beauty of this high-level group was that it had representatives of both the labour federations of Railways – the All-India Railwayman's Federation (AIRF) and the National Federation of Indian Railway (NFIR). This mechanism ensured that whatever decisions were taken, everyone was on board – from the management to labour federations.

In fact, I remember, a day before the foundation of the Dankuni factory was to be laid by Sushri Mamata Banerjee, the project was once again discussed threadbare with both the labour federations, and their opinions sought. They gave the go-ahead.

The critical part of this initiative was to relocate about 45 staff quarters from this land parcel to elsewhere till the new quarters were made ready. These staff members were to be brought back and housed in the new quarters constructed at this place. Relocating the staff was a big concern for everyone. Besides, there were a lot of unauthorised encroachments at this site. These were to be removed. We needed the support of both, the unions and the staff. A cooperative and congenial environment was the need of the hour.

The other critical issue that was to be resolved through the Amit Mitra committee was to get 40 acres of land close to the railway track so that the factory could be connected to the rail network to take out the locomotives manufactured there. This was a major issue as there were two competing parties claiming for this with equal force.

Another project that was simultaneously sanctioned at Dankuni in 2010 was an Ancillary Unit of DLW Varanasi for which 30 acres of land adjoining the land earmarked for the Ancillary Unit of CLW was allotted.

Varanasi is almost 650 km from Dankuni and it takes around 14 hours by road. The Dankuni facility for DLW was to manufacture the underframe for diesel locomotives. My argument was that the underframes could be transported by road and so they could be given a land parcel away from rail line.

However, the difficulty with the land close to the track was an encumbrance of 132 KV overhead transmission line crossing in the middle of the 40 acres land and a 25 KV Traction Sub-Station (TSS) of Eastern Railway.

I made several visits to resolve both the issues. It needed the support of the State Government. S.K. Saha, who was my Director, knew the Power Secretary of West Bengal. He mobilised all the support from the State Government. Once the 132 KV transmission towers were shifted, the job became easy. TSS also got relocated after a new TSS was made ready, opposite the railway tracks.

The land was allotted close to the Railway track for the CLW ancillary project, and the foundation laying ceremony was done with a lot of enthusiasm. Coordination and arguments worked well. Amit Mitra was quite happy with our professional approach.

For the 9,000 HP locomotive, Dankuni was also planned to be the Centre of Excellence for design and development.

The construction work of the factory was allotted to Rail Vikas Nigam Limited (RVNL), a PSU of the Railways, to fast-track the construction. RVNL had been doing the infrastructure work of Railways and executing projects faster than many other PSUs.

With continuous liaison, the factory construction got completed and the first freight locomotive was manufactured in 2015. This factory presently manufactures about 50 locos per annum.

A lot of work had to be done to post staff at Dankuni. All the Indian Railways Zones and Production Units were approached to identify staff interested in coming to Dankuni on transfer on request in accordance with the transfer policy. This exercise took almost a year. Some staff were also transferred on request from CLW. It was done on a voluntary basis. This was quite an onerous task as human beings were involved.

The contribution of S.K. Saha needs to be recognised in all earnestness as he was continuously tracking this work even during the period I was working as DRM Dhanbad. He provided the much-needed continuity for the completion of critical work in this major project. He belonged to Kolkata and naturally he had great affinity towards this project. Saha's perseverance and leadership were of high quality.

This mission was accomplished over a period of five years. Development of the 9,000 HP locomotive project, with Transfer of Technology from Japan under Special Terms of Economics Partnership component of JICA loan for Western DFC, has however not taken place. But the Dankuni factory is manufacturing WAG 9 freight locomotives. It gives me much satisfaction to see this initiative fructify.

Cutting the Nose, Spiting the Face: Kanchrapara, West Bengal

Indian Railways runs about (as of January 2020) 13,000 passenger trains daily, 6,000 of these are commuter trains which operate locally in Mumbai, Chennai, Kolkata and Hyderabad. The fast-moving, long distance and intercity mail express trains account for about 3,500. And about 3,500 trains are the slow-moving, short distance, passenger trains which substantially eat up the line capacity of Indian Railways network.

These slow-moving passenger trains are the top priority target of the Railways for conversion into self-propelled Electric Multiple Units (EMU) and Mainline EMUs (MEMU) as they have higher rates of acceleration and deceleration.

EMUs and MEMUs are globally employed for suburban and intercity operation. By design, the distributed power in the train provides better adhesion as the large numbers of axles in the train provide motive power for train movement, unlike the locomotive where the axle loads are high, and the number of axles is limited.

However, the production of EMUs and MEMUs has always been a problem with the Production Units (PUs). These PUs manufacture coaches of a different variety. Manufacture of a self-propelled coach takes longer. General Managers of these PUs were therefore not interested in manufacturing EMUs and MEMUs. Departmental biases also had their share of blame for such a situation. Coaches were maintained by Mechanical Engineers while EMUs and MEMUs were maintained by Electrical Engineers. This silo culture was a big reason for the slow development of Railways.

It was decided in 2010 to set up a separate PU to manufacture self-propelled coaches at Kanchrapara. This site is well connected by air. It is just 42 km from Netaji Subhash Chandra International Airport, Kolkata and is right on the Kalyani Expressway. A railway station is near the site. Sushri Mamata Banerjee was the railway minister. The project was sanctioned at an estimated cost of ₹900 crore.

Kanchrapara also had a railway workshop to repair locomotives, wagons and coaches. This workshop was established in 1863. It had overhauled and repaired aircrafts during World Wars and manufactured armoured cars and hand-grenade shells.

A big rail yard was available to set up this coach manufacturing facility but had about 360 big, grown-up trees and a few water bodies. Environment clearance was a major issue.

The project was to be undertaken along the lines of the Madhepura Factory and on the PPP. This was to be approved by the Cabinet Committee on Economic Affairs (CCEA) and the Expanded Board on Railways (EBR).

EBR is a mechanism to appraise and clear railway projects requiring investment in excess of (at that time) ₹500 crore (this limit has now been raised to ₹1,000 crore). All proposals costing more than ₹500 crore are to be approved by a select Cabinet Committee headed by the Prime Minister and is called CCEA. This committee comprises CRB and representatives of the Planning Commission, Ministry of Finance and Ministry of Programme Implementation.

It was decided that 5,000 coaches would be manufactured over 10 years and accordingly the project was sanctioned with the approval of the CCEA.

Despite many rounds of bidding (RFQ/RFP) and preparation of all the bid documents and the Agreement that was to be signed between Railways and the SPV, the project could not be taken to its logical end due to difference of opinion in the Ministry of Railways. One group of officers had been recommending manufacture of these EMU/MEMU coaches in the Railways existing PUs while others wanted a new factory, and to this end ten years had been lost.

The availability of EMUs and MEMUs would have greatly enhanced the passenger train operations on Indian Railways, as these would have replaced loco-hauled slow-moving passenger trains, thereby improving line capacity and terminal capacity. This would have brought a paradigm shift in train operations. It was a lost opportunity.

The unfortunate part of this initiative had been the difference of opinions between the various stakeholders. The quantum of work done on this project can be judged from the fact that 360 fully grown trees on 110 acres land were cut with the permission of the Forest Department and twice the number of trees planted at the boundary of the site. The 33 KV sub-station required to feed the factory was ready.

The rail and road connectivity were provided. The water bodies were filled with earth. The unauthorised shanties were relocated. A primary school nearby was provided separate road access. All this required massive effort on my part. I made several visits to the site. Dr Amit Mitra Committee was reviewing this project on a regular basis. This provided an impetus to fast-track the work. Allocation of land for setting up new depots and identifying space within the existing depots was done extremely quickly with the cooperation of Zonal Railways and the Traffic Department.

At one stage we thought that this project would be executed faster than the Madhepura project. Rightly so, as we had gained a lot of experience from the Madhepura project.

I remember that this project was being monitored by the PMO. I had made a presentation to the PMO in August 2015. I was asked why this project was moving slowly. I had replied that this would be taken up after completion of Madhepura project; the bids for Madhepura would be opened on August 30, 2015. This was not liked by the PMO. A letter followed from PMO, indicating that Railways should take serious action to complete this project without linking it with Madhepura. Railways did take action to issue fresh RFQ in October 2015. All the work related to preparation of agreement and processing of note for seeking approval of the Union Cabinet for investing into the equity of a private company had also been done. But the project did not move forward as inter-department differences derailed the bidding process again.

It would have been as beneficial to Railways as the Madhepura loco factory project was, wherein the country received Foreign Direct Investment (FDI). It also created wealth for the nation by way of socio-economic development of that backward region and generated direct and indirect employment. The Kanchrapara project would have provided avenues for induction of the latest technology for manufacture of new design of EMUs for faster train travel. Major hurdles relating to environment clearance, rail and road connectivity, and power supply had already been removed.

In my opinion, with the success of T-18 Train Set manufactured by ICF, the project has perhaps lost its relevance now unless Railways decide to chart a new strategy.

Inner Engineering and Leadership Programme, June 2017, at Isha Yoga Centre, Coimbatore with Sadhguru.

Front row from left: Tushar Pandey (4), Anurag Tripathi (5), Ved Prakash (6), Pradeep Sikdar (7), Jeetendra Singh (10), Sagarika Patnaik (11).

Second row from left: Niraj Sahay (2), Naveen Kumar (3), Sudheer Kumar (5), Dr Suchitra Kumar (6), R.K. Verma (12).

Third row from left: Manoj Pandey (2), Greesha Unnikumar (3), V. Arun Kumar (5), A.K. Chandra (7), S.K. Saha (8), Alok Gupta (9), Mamta Gupta (10).

Fourth row from left: R R. Prasad (4).

Addressing officers of South-Central Railway, October 2018.

From left: V.K. Yadav, GM SCR; Sudheer Kumar; A.K. Chandra, Executive Director Transformation Cell, Railway Board.

SCR became the laboratory for generation of transformation ideas.

Delegation of railway officers to France and Switzerland for tunnel ventilation and seeing Gotthard Base Tunnel (longest in the world: 57 km long with electric traction), June 2007.

From left: D.K. Sharma (2); S. Kubba (3), Sudheer Kumar (6), Dr Suchitra Kumar (7), P. Guha (8), B.P. Awasthi (10), Kalpana Awasthi (11), R.K. Chaudhary (13), P.V. Vadiyalingam (14).

Delegation to Japan to finalise STEP component for Western DFC, December 2010.

First row from left: Sudheer Kumar (3), Naveen Shukla (4), Jagmohan Gupta (5).

Others in the photograph are senior executives of Kawasaki Heavy Industry.

JV agreement for setting up a 1,000 MW thermal power plant Nabinagar signed in November 2007. R.S. Sharma Director Commercial NTPC (left) and Sudheer Kumar.

Power Minister and Railway Minister are seated on the dais.

JV agreement signed between Alstom and Railways, 30 November 2015.

Bharat Salhotra of Alstom (left) and Sudheer Kumar. Finance Minister Shri Arun Jaitley and Railway Minister Shri Suresh Prabhu along with other Cabinet Ministers are seated on the dais.

An MOU for writing case studies, signed between Indian School of Business Hyderabad and Ministry of Railways, October 2019.

Seated, from left: Prof. Chandan Chowdhary; Prof. Milind Sohoni; Prof. Rajendra Srivastava, Dean; Vinod Yadav, Chairman Railway Board; Vijay Kumar, Financial Commissioner.

Standing, from left: Mamtha Reddy, ISB (2); Sudheer Kumar (3); Alka Misra, Indian Railways (4).

Indian School of Business, Hyderabad, for writing the case study on Madhepura, December 2019.

From left: Dr Phil Zerrillo, Deputy Dean, ISB; P. Srinivas, DRM Vijayawada; Sudheer Kumar; Dr Rajendra Srivastava, Dean, ISB.

My wife and I at our residence in Dhanbad while I was DRM during 2011–2013.

Visit to Tulip Garden, Amsterdam, with my wife, 2008.

Meeting after formation of Transformation Cell, January 2017.

From left: S.K. Saha; Sudheer Kumar; G.S. Singh; Railway Minister Shri Suresh Prabhu, A.K. Mital, Chairman Railway Board.

Award of Change Agent to Mukul Mathur, DRM Waltair, at Bhopal, 2018.

From left: Tushar Pandey; Sudheer Kumar, Railway Minister Shri Piyush Goyal; Chief Minister of Madhya Pradesh Shri Shivraj Singh Chouhan; Minister of State for Railways Shri Manoj Sinha; Ashwini Lohani, Chairman Railway Board.

World Railway Managers Programme at HEC Business School, Paris, May 2006.

Officers from Indian Railways, South Africa, UK, Saudi Arabia, Denmark and Italy.

Second row from left: Arvind Kumar (1), Sudheer Kumar (2), P. Guha (3), Sanjive Roy (8), Lalit Trivedi (9).

World Railway Managers Programme at Staff College, Baroda, October 2006.

Officers from Indian Railways, South Africa, UK, Saudi Arabia, Denmark and Italy.

Second row from left: Arvind Kumar (3), Sudheer Kumar (10), Sanjive Roy (11), Lalit Trivedi (12), P. Guha (13).

National Award by Ministry of Railways, 1994.

From left: R.S. Grover (2), Sudheer Kumar (3), A.J. Gupta (4), my wife.

National Award presented by M.K. Rao, Chairman Railway Board, 1994.

World Trade Centre, New York, USA, October 1992.

From left: Sudheer Kumar and B.B. Singh.

This was a part of our visit to Illinois Institute of Technology Research Institute, Chicago, for ToT of Drivers' Simulator for Indian Railways.

General Manager's annual inspection of Dhanbad Division on 22 December 2011.

With Varun Bharthuar, GM, East Central Railway. The special train derailed while returning to Dhanbad.

No Deal Is Also a Deal: Tokyo, Japan

Western DFC was an important project under the monitor of Ministry of Finance as well as the Ministry of Railways. The company Dedicated Freight Corridor Corporation of India Limited (DFCCIL) was incorporated in October 2006. Two DFCs – Eastern DFC from Ludhiana in Punjab to Dankuni in West Bengal, and Western DFC from Dadri in Uttar Pradesh to Jawahar Lal Nehru Port Trust (JNPT) in Maharashtra – were sanctioned in February 2008.

The Dankuni factory had already been sanctioned keeping in view the enhanced loco production and future technology of the new 9,000 HP locomotive based on the latest technology of Insulated Gate Bipolar Transistor (IGBT).

IGBT operates at 3–4 times higher switching frequency than Gate Turn Off Thyristor (GTO) which reduces the heat generated in the device. The weight of an IGBT module is about 30 per cent lower than that of a GTO module. The noise produced by IGBT controlled AC motors is around 10 per cent lower than the GTO counterpart. The efficiency of IGBT is 5–6 per cent better than GTO. IGBT can handle higher currents. These are the advantages of IGBT technology.

I was dealing with the setting up of the new factory at Dankuni. In December 2010, Ministry of Railways decided to send a delegation comprising four officers to Tokyo, Japan, for finalising the contours of Special Terms of Economic Partnership (STEP) of the Japanese Overseas Development Assistance (ODA) loan. I was one of the members of this delegation. The Western DFC is substantially funded by JICA.

The terms and conditions of this loan included that 30 per cent of the goods and services for the project must be sourced either directly from Japan or from companies in India with more than 50 per cent of the equity of Japanese origin. The components of the Special Terms of Economic Partnership were:

- Locomotives of 9,000 HP for Container Train Operation – 200 locomotives;
- Head Hardened Rails for WDFC;
- Signalling System for WDFC; and
- Scott connected Transformers for 2 x 25 KV OHE for WDFC.

However, the major component of this 30 per cent was 200 locomotives of 9,000 HP for WDFC.

The purpose of this visit was to meet the Ministry of Economic Trade and Industry (METI), Ministry of Land Infrastructure and Tourism (MLIT) and other stakeholders to firm up the breakup of the transactions in respect of the STEP components.

The 200 locomotives that were to be procured had to be maintained by the successful bidder on a comprehensive basis by setting up a depot at Rewari in Haryana in accordance with the maintenance requirement of the technology for 9,000 HP locomotives. The industry in Japan was not ready to set up the depot and maintain these locomotives over a long period of time (12–15 years). They perceived setting up a depot and long-term maintenance as a major risk.

Their argument was that they were not in the business of setting up the depot. As regards the maintenance of the locomotives, even if the depot was to be set up by Railways, their intention was to maintain these locomotives initially for 3–4 years only. My experience with ABB technology was quite bitter. I was convinced that new technology locomotives had to be maintained by the designer for a longer period of 10–15 years to ensure development of full skill sets in our employees. All types of major maintenance schedules were also supposed to be undertaken on at least a few new locomotives by the OEM. This was the only way Railways interest could be protected properly.

Similarly, regarding the model of transfer of technology for manufacture of locomotives, our desire was to have only a few locomotives imported in fully assembled conditions and the rest of the locomotives were to be assembled in India from Completely Knocked Down (CKD) and Semi Knocked Down (SKD) kits. Thereafter, locomotives would be fully manufactured utilising the manpower available at CLW, under the supervision of the Japanese technology partner.

We also wanted a Centre of Excellence to be established at Dankuni to undertake changes in software to upgrade various systems and sub-systems. A long-term hand-holding by the OEM was essential. This was planned to ensure full understanding of the design aspects along with TOT for Loco Bogie, Loco Shell and Traction Motors by RDSO and CLW.

We also wanted development of at least two vendors in India for the manufacture of major equipments like Transformers, Traction and Auxiliary Converters and Vehicle Electronics.

For other major sub-systems wherein technology was being transferred to CLW, such as Bogie, Shell and Traction Motor, we desired to have at least one additional vendor developed in India, in addition to CLW itself.

The whole transaction was structured in a manner that would ensure upgrade of CLW to manufacture 9,000 HP locomotives with IGBT technology and have at least two vendors in India who could competitively supply major systems and sub-systems for smooth manufacture of these locomotives in future at an optimal cost. Thereafter, we were to progressively phase out the existing WAP 5 and WAP 9 class of locomotives. We wanted to fast track the ramp up of indigenous production of these locomotives. In case of ABB locos, we were not able to do that, and therefore our strategy was clear from the very beginning.

We also tried to get the human resource of Indian Railways well trained in maintenance, over a longer period. Our experience with 3-phase ABB technology for manufacture and maintenance of locomotives, even with a warranty for five years, was not good. As soon as the warranty period was over, there was a substantial dip in the performance of these ABB locomotives. We wanted to avoid that situation – and for the right reasons!

As can be seen, we wanted to fully secure ourselves, mitigating all the difficulties and, naturally, the Japanese vendors were not coming forward to agree with our proposition. Meetings continued for three continuous days in Tokyo and the negotiations almost failed. Finally, on the last day of this trip, the Japanese Government agreed to our demand for the manufacture of some of the locomotives at CLW/ Dankuni to ensure that the TOT was fully demonstrated. Along with that, a Maintenance Depot would be set up at Rewari undertaking maintenance for 12 years with major overhaul of 10–15 locomotives.

Rewari is a city in the Rewari district in the Indian state of Haryana. It is 82 km from Delhi. It has a population of about 1.5 lakh. It is famous for brass metalwork and ornamental shoes. The brass industry began here in 1535 with the help of the Portuguese. Rewari also homes a Heritage Steam Locomotive Museum and a surviving steam shed. The shed was built in 1893.

This was a breakthrough after a lot of brinkmanship by both parties. We returned to India, fully satisfied with the negotiations. In February 2011, an MOU was formally signed in Delhi between the Ministry of Railways and Government of Japan based on these negotiations.

My thought process for undertaking the Madhepura project was reflected in the framework that we prepared for acquisition of the 9,000 HP locomotives from Japan. The only difference between the two transactions was that Japanese locomotive technology was being inducted with limited competition for discovery of the price of the locomotive.

This locomotive deal has not succeeded so far due to various reasons including very high cost. We had signed a deal in case of the Madhepura loco project at a price of ₹24.88 crore per 12,000 HP loco as a weighted average price for 800 locos, which also included the capex for setting up a Factory, two Maintenance Depots and a full-fledged Training School.

The unit rate offered by the single Japanese bidder was ₹52 crore for a 9,000 HP locomotive. The cost of setting up the Rewari Depot, Centre of Excellence and TOT was to be paid additionally. The Japanese bidder was a consortium of Kawasaki Heavy Industry, Toshiba, Mitsubishi Electric and Mitsubishi Corporation. It is my understanding that a good alignment was missing amongst the parties forming the consortium to submit the financial bid. We had estimated that the whole contract would be worth ₹5,500 to 6,000 crore.

There was no way Indian Railways could have paid such an exorbitant price. We organised two rounds of negotiations with the sole bidder. The price was reduced by the Japanese consortium from ₹52 crore to ₹34 crore per unit. This could not have been considered as even this price was far beyond the market determined price for the Madhepura locomotive which, in fact, was the price for a higher HP locomotive.

The tender was therefore discharged. Keeping in view of the circumstances, it was agreed between JICA and the Indian Government that this procurement would be held through International Competitive Bidding (ICB). The process has not been initiated even now (June 2021).

I sincerely hope that this locomotive will be inducted in the Railways in future, as it is very much required to upgrade the CLW factory and to replace the existing 6,000 HP ABB locomotives. ABB technology is three decades old now.

Moreover, for Western DFC we need a locomotive that can provide 2 HP per tonne for running container trains at 100 kmph on level track. The container trains that will operate on Western DFC will have 4,500 tonnes of load in Double Stack Configuration and will therefore require a 9,000 HP locomotive. This will bring a paradigm shift in freight train operations of the Indian Railways.

Acres of Diamonds: Transforming Coal – Dhanbad, the Coal Capital of India

It was Thursday, September 29, 2011. I was Executive Director (Development) Railway Board. The Madhepura project was at a very crucial stage of decision making. This was the project I was handling. I would have completed my tenure of five years in the Ministry of Railways on October 5, 2011. This was the maximum period you could be posted in a Ministry. Beyond this you needed the approval of the Minister of Railways.

Orders for my posting as DRM were issued on this day. Although I had an inkling that I would be drafted for DRM, I didn't realise that it would happen so soon. I had a desire to work in the Baroda Division. I was therefore a little unhappy that I was posted in Dhanbad.

Normally, officers are given three choices before an important posting. This was an unspoken rule in vogue for a long time. No one ever gave me an option to choose from the list of the Divisions that were vacant.

The day the posting orders were issued, I came home very late as I had got stuck due to some issue pertaining to Madhepura. For some time, I did not even share the news of my posting with my wife and my son. I broke the news after we had our dinner. Obviously, it was not liked much, the moment it was conveyed. My argument was that someone had to go to Dhanbad, and therefore I had been asked to go.

I knew that Dhanbad was the second biggest freight loading Division in Indian Railways. I had never worked in the eastern sector of the country. It was therefore an opportunity to work in this part of the country for the first time in my career. I started looking at it as an opportunity in more ways than one.

Viney Mittal, CRB, told me that far too many accidents and breakdowns had been taking place in this Division, and the performance needed to be substantially improved. That was the reason I was picked up for this assignment. Viney Mittal knew me well. He was a hard taskmaster. He was a good friend of Kul Bhushan, who was the Member looking after the Electrical Department of Railways and was my super boss. Kul Bhushan complimented me for getting the second biggest Division of Indian Railways. Kul Bhushan had worked in the Katihar Division during his time.

Tryst with Dhanbad

I was the second non-traffic officer posted in Dhanbad Division, ever since it came into being in 1958. I belonged to Electrical discipline. The last time a non-traffic officer had been posted was ten years earlier when A.K. Vohra was appointed as DRM Dhanbad in the year 2001. He was also an officer of Electrical Engineering discipline. In 53 years, only two non-traffic officers were posted at Dhanbad as DRM.

I had visited Dhanbad in April 1979 during a study tour while pursuing my engineering degree. We were a group of around 50 students who had gone to the eastern part of India. We had a fully reserved rail coach, with one professor in-charge of the tour. We had visited the fertiliser plant at Sindri, near Dhanbad. We had seen the exciting Prilling Tower in the plant from where molten urea is dropped to convert into small urea balls. We had also gone to see the Heavy Engineering Corporation at Ranchi. I was reminded of my old memories.

Dhanbad is an important Division as it loads about 20 per cent of the coal produced in the country and is situated on the Grand Chord (GC) route connecting Delhi and Kolkata. It contributes to about 10 per cent of the total freight revenue of Railways. It is also known as the 'Coal Capital of India'.

In earlier times, in the 1970s, the top four Divisions used to be called ABCD Divisions of Indian Railways. ABCD stood for Asansol, Bilaspur, Chakradharpur and Dhanbad. Normally, officers used to be posted in these Divisions after they had done one posting as DRM elsewhere in a smaller Division. In those times, DRM used to be known as Divisional Superintendent (DS).

After ten days of the issuance of my orders, I was asked to leave Railway Board. I joined the Division on October 14, 2011. I reached there by Rajdhani Express. Quite a few officers had come to receive me at the station. After meeting the Branch Officers and some of the staff, I realised that there was a lot of scope for improving the infrastructure, asset reliability and operations, which would ultimately improve safety and freight loading.

Initial Diagnosis

The Division had quite a few operational problems. Some of these were:

- Low average speeds of freight train;
- High incidences of yard derailments, accidents;
- Poor speed of trains in coal sidings;
- Frequent failure of overhead traction distribution equipment;
- Frequent panto-entanglement;
- Frequent stalling of freight trains in the section;
- Higher number of signalling failures; and
- Stagnant freight loading for 4–5 years.

A.S. Upadhyay, the outgoing DRM, had not prepared any formal handing-over notes. He instead handed over the Morning Position papers, which used to be put up to him daily. These papers did not make much sense to me and did not give me any idea about freight loading in million tonnes, and the revenue earning, in crores of rupees. The information contained in the Morning Position did not clearly bring out the strengths and weaknesses of the Division.

Ved Prakash was the Senior Divisional Operating Manager and therefore head of operations of the Division. I told him that the Morning Position should clearly bring out the transport output in terms of freight loading and passengers booked, and revenue earning both for freight and passenger business. The factors that were our operational bottlenecks and potential safety risks should be brought out in the Morning Position.

Morning Position in Railways is quite a typical brief containing 15–20 pages that brings out the previous day's performance and the current day's plan. It is prepared between midnight and 6 a.m. Papers start getting compiled only after midnight, as a Railways day lasts for 24 hours – from midnight to midnight. Morning Position is delivered at the residence of DRM by 7 a.m., like a morning newspaper. It is a must. This is the first thing the DRM looks at in the morning.

It took a week before I could get the information in the desired format. Ved Prakash ensured it. He was a very dedicated officer. I was able to figure this out in my first meeting itself on October 14 when I arrived. He had a very good understanding of the operations. He had earlier worked as head of operations in the Mughalsarai Division, which is considered quite a challenging Division from the standpoint of operations.

Within 4–5 days, I conducted my first window trailing inspection from Dhanbad to Gaya station, which is about 200 km. I had a good touch and feel of the section. The Division needed massive inputs in track maintenance and in the upkeep of stations and the three tunnels that we had in the ghat section, from Gurpa to Gujhandi – 22 km long.

As against the permitted speed of operation of 60 kmph inside the tunnel, trains were working at 30 kmph due to poor upkeep of the track. Similarly, in the ghat section, trains were permitted to run at 65 kmph only, whereas the whole section was operating at 130 kmph. I asked my civil engineers to do the calculations and show me the results as to why this limit had been imposed. The speed of a section is decided by the design criteria for a particular type of track and the terrain, primarily based on physics.

The ghat section was very critical for the operation of the Division. It had a gradient of 1 in 80. A section is called ghat when it had a gradient steeper than 1 in 100. Gradient means rise or fall of track on a vertical plane. If you travel 100 m horizontally and, in the process, rise 1 m vertically, then the grade is defined as 1 in 100.

Window trailing inspection means travelling by an official inspection vehicle, called saloon, with Branch Officers sitting in a cabin together and observing the condition of the rail track, signals, overhead wires, stations and other infrastructure on the section. The saloon is attached to a train as the rear-most bogey. It provides complete visibility through a full-size glass window, equal to the width of the coach. It is fully equipped with a bedroom, drawing and dining room, inspection cabin, and can accommodate a private secretary to do official work and a cook to prepare meals while on inspection.

This is the biggest efficiency multiplier of a DRM. I fully used it to do inspections. It would have not been possible to discharge my duties as DRM without this facility, especially due to the vastness of the Division and the law-and-order problems prevailing at that time.

First Yard Derailment

Within a week, a locomotive derailed in the yard at Dhanbad, at about 11 a.m. This loco was supposed to work prestigious trains like the Rajdhani. It could have caused a major accident if it had derailed while working a train. The loco belonged to the Mughalsarai Division. This means that this loco was maintained by the Mughalsarai shed.

I went to the site and examined the derailed locomotive and the track where it had derailed. I directed the concerned officers to establish the root cause without any divided responsibility. What I meant was that the primary responsibility must be clearly identified. I had myself identified the reason but did not disclose it to anyone.

By 8 p.m., the two officers responsible for the operation and maintenance of locomotives came to my chamber and explained the cause of derailment. Excessive wear on one of the six wheels was established as the root cause. Five wheels were on track and one wheel had derailed. This was exactly in line with what I had observed. The cause of derailment was conveyed to K.K. Srivastava, the General Manager East Central Railway who had taken over as Member Traffic at Delhi.

I was clear that there could be no dilution of responsibility. The condition of the railway track in the Dhanbad yard was quite bad. The Route Relay Interlocking (RRI) work planned ten years ago had not been completed. This was the main reason for the poor track condition in the yard. In the instant case, the responsibility was clearly fixed on the Electric Loco Shed, Mughalsarai. This was also conveyed to Kul Bhushan, Member Electrical, as derailment of a locomotive used for Rajdhani Express was too serious a matter to be left without being highlighted.

RRI is a system of working of signals, points and crossings in the station area through remote control using relays, point machines and logic circuits. The logic circuits take care of any conflicting movements and therefore do not allow any manipulation by human beings. The whole yard is controlled from a single place in case of RRI. A special purpose building is constructed to house all the equipment of RRI. One can keep an eye on the yard, to a large extent, from this building.

Prior to the advent of RRI, the signals and points on the track used to be set manually for the arrival and departure of a train from small cabins made at different places. This used manual labour and would cause delays, human errors and higher failures, leading to derailments and accidents.

The Dhanbad station had the manual system of 1937 (75 years old, codal life 30 years) vintage and was a cause of frequent failures and derailments. The work of converting the station to RRI type system had been sanctioned in 2001. But the work could not be executed due to lack of collaboration between departments and lack of assigning highest priority for the work by the Division.

Five DRMs had completed their tenure prior to me, but this work had always been deferred for some reason or the other. We had reached a point where no more delay was possible. I realised this within a week of my taking charge of the Division.

Fixing responsibility for the cause of derailment of the locomotive in the very early days conveyed a clear message that irrespective of the department, the responsibility will be fixed without any hesitation.

Word spread that the DRM, who belonged to the Electrical discipline, had held the Electrical discipline itself responsible.

First Passenger Train Derails

Within 15 days of this incident, there were two derailments of passenger trains and in both these cases the cause of derailment was clearly identified as entanglement of buffers of the coaches. These coaches were maintained by the Dhanbad Division. I attended the site of accident in both these cases.

There was lot of resentment at the HQ because East Central Railway had been held responsible in all the three recent cases: Mughalsarai Shed for excessive wheel wear in locomotive, and Dhanbad Coaching Depot for buffer entanglement. Both maintenance centres belonged to East Central Railway. It was not the business-as-usual way of working. As the statistics of the Zone deteriorated, it led to resentment. All Zones look at their Key Performance Indicators (KPI) and strive for improvement. To my mind, finding the root cause and taking appropriate action was the only way forward to improve KPIs; hiding failures would not serve anyone.

The buffer entanglement was a result of poor maintenance of buffers and side bearers of the coaches. The concerned officers of the HQ visited the Division to investigate the root cause and to ascertain that there was no bias. The message was loud and clear – responsibilities shall be fixed without any regard to the department. An action plan to avoid the recurrence was also clearly identified.

There was a serious shortage of buffers and their repair kits. Action was taken to improve the availability of spares of buffers. The pit wheel lathe of Mughalsarai Shed had been non-functional for 7–8 months. The repair proposal was shuttling between Finance and the Executive. No one was bothered. As a result, locomotives were frequently sent to Kanpur Shed and Ludhiana Shed for re-profiling of wheel-sets. Re-profiling of the wheels is done on a regular basis to bring their shape to the original dimensions to avoid any risk of derailment at points and crossings.

During meetings with the Branch Officers, my message used to be clear – 'Do not be in denial, accept your problem if you want to find a solution.'

I also told my officers that if any Senior Supervisor gives a dissent note in a preliminary inquiry for an accident, all the signatories to the inquiry will be taken up under Discipline and Appeal Rules. The primary responsibility for any failure or accident had to be clearly fixed. This would help the Division plan an action to improve operational efficiency. There was no other way.

In between, there were a few cases of safety breaches during shunting operations. Coaches used to derail while shifting them from platform lines to the washing lines for cleaning, repair and maintenance. The main reason used to be the communication over walkie-talkie for this operation, which was against the standing operating procedure as it would compromise safety. As per the operating procedure, staff were supposed to give hand signal and work based on written communications from the Station Master. But this would have caused delay, and therefore the practice was to follow instructions on a walkie-talkie so that the job would get done faster.

Walkie-talkie communication used to confuse the staff as it was not a secure communication between one-to-one; rather, it used to be between one-to-all.

The concerned staff and supervisors were always getting called for my personal interview to clearly understand the cause. This became the new normal identify the root cause of an accident or derailment or any other unsafe practices on the same or the next day and take remedial measures. This used to give me an opportunity to understand the psyche of the staff involved in any unsafe operation. It also gave the staff confidence to follow rules and not be worried about delays if delays were due to procedures. Staff also used to tell me about other associated operational difficulties fearlessly, which would not have come to my notice, otherwise. In the process, inter-departmental disputes used to get resolved. I understood the root cause clearly. I was able to understand the safety culture and firm up my mind as to what needs to be done to bring a change.

Within 15 days of joining the Division, I was able to physically visit the entire Division and meet many staff members. The Division was spread over four states and 13 districts and was badly affected by Naxalite activities.

State Officials

On the second day of my joining the Division, I wrote a demi-official (DO) letter to all the Deputy Commissioners (DC) and the Superintendents of Police (SP), highlighting the importance of the Division and the cooperation I was seeking from all of them. The law-and-order situation was in disarray, and therefore the support of State Governments was very vital. I also reached out to the Chief Secretary and the Director General of Police (DGP) of the state of Jharkhand and met both of them in their offices within two months of taking charge of the Division. They appreciated this gesture.

Doon Express Tragedy

On November 22, 2011, around 3 a.m., I got a call from my Control Office that two air-conditioned coaches of Dehradun Express had caught fire between Parasnath and Nimiaghat stations. This train was going from Howrah to Dehradun.

I reached Control Office immediately. It was at a stone's throw from my residence. I left for the site with all the concerned Branch Officers after ascertaining the location of the incident and the extent of fire. By 4.15 a.m., I was at the site of the accident. I reached the site by road. Two coaches had been completely engulfed in fire. On the way, I had briefed the Chairman. I also informed the Deputy Commissioner, Dhanbad, and sought the assistance of fire brigade and police for handling fire and for ensuring law-and-order at the site.

The Deputy Commissioner is supposed to provide necessary assistance to maintain law-and-order, provide fire brigade, arrange medical assistance from the State Government, arrange police clearance to undertake restoration in case any medico-legal issues are involved and to look into any sabotage angle. Law-and-order is a State subject. In case of death, post-mortem is also done by the Civil Hospital. Therefore, the State Government's assistance is very vital under such circumstances. I had developed good relations with State Government officers.

There was chaos and confusion at the site, but I maintained my cool. By 5 a.m., two fire brigade parties had arrived. In the intervening period, we tried to rescue the passengers who had got off the affected coaches. They either wanted to continue their journey or go back to Howrah. It was difficult to ascertain the casualties as the coaches were still on fire. The overhead wires of traction power supply just above the place of fire had melted.

Incidentally, the Parliament session was to begin from November 22, 2011.

A few Australian ladies were also standing near the track. One of them was in a very critical condition due to carbon monoxide toxicity. All the vehicles available at the site including my staff car were utilised to transport the stranded passengers to Dhanbad. Some buses were also hired. By 6.30 a.m., I decided that the unaffected track should be made fit for the movement of traffic. This would ease out the pressure on the Division from the Railway Board and the Headquarters. We therefore decided to stop operation of fire brigades. Both the fire brigades were positioned on the opposite side of the unaffected railway track. By around 7.30 a.m., one track was declared fit for movement of traffic. The unaffected coaches were shifted to Parasnath where arrangement was made for drinking water, tea and biscuits for all the passengers.

Two passengers – one Australian lady and another person – were rushed to Bokaro Hospital with doctors for treatment. The concerned Police and Civil authorities also arrived by 7.30 a.m. As soon as the fire was put out, I made an attempt to enter the burnt coaches. However, due to toxic pungent gases, I was restrained by the Chief Medical Superintendent (CMS). Finally, at around 9 a.m., along with the CMS, I entered these coaches with body bags. Seven body bags were filled in our presence, with details of seat numbers marked for identification. It was a really sad and tragic incident.

Assessment of Casualties

It occurred to me that there might be some controversy about the number of fatalities, and therefore it would be fitting to have a joint note prepared between the State Government, Dhanbad Division and the Government Railway Police (GRP). This was a tragedy of a very large magnitude and people may not believe whatever number of casualties that were reported by Railways, despite the best efforts to be accurate.

I therefore talked to the Deputy Commissioner and the Superintendent of Police of the area who were at the site to help me undertake a joint verification of the casualties. Looking into the gravity of the situation, they all agreed. This is normally not done at site. The onus to furnish details rests with Railways. This agreement was quite important for me.

The joint note clearly brought out that seven lives had been lost. In the meanwhile, Bharadwaj Chaudhary, my Branch Officer, came running to me and requested me to meet one of the passengers who was travelling in the affected coach, and had seen the initiation of fire after boarding and starting of the train from Parasnath station. Chaudhary was a very sincere and competent electrical engineer. He was the one who had clearly identified the root cause of derailment of the locomotive which I have mentioned earlier. I trusted him a lot.

I accompanied Chaudhary and met this gentleman. He was extremely angry and abusing the railway administration. While I was trying to engage with him, I told Parag Goyal, my Senior Divisional Signal and Telecommunication Engineer, to record this conversation. Parag had a high-end Nokia E71 mobile phone.

The passenger narrated that he had seen a fellow passenger carrying a handbag which he had kept on the side upper berth of the affected cabin. As per his version, something had fallen from the bag which led to the fire. He was suggesting some chemical substance. The curtains of the side berths had started burning. This conversation was recorded by Parag. This was a very important piece of evidence that could give us some idea about the cause of fire. Everyone was suspecting electrical short circuit as the cause of fire. The staff had checked the condition of the battery and the fuse, which did not indicate any possibility of a short circuit. But, under such circumstances, no one would believe them.

The adjoining AC 3-tier coach had also got completely gutted, mainly due to strong wind blowing that day and the flames from the AC 2-tier had caused this fire.

This man was immediately taken away by the State police after my brief interaction. By now, I was a little less uncomfortable as I had some preliminary idea about the cause of fire and the number of casualties.

Ex-gratia

By 10 a.m. we decided to leave the site along with the Accident Relief Train (ART). This was necessary to allow restoration work on the affected line and shift the two burnt coaches for further investigation and examination by the CRS Eastern Circle, Kolkata.

Both facts available at that time – the number of casualties and the eyewitness account of the travelling passenger – were conveyed to the Railway Board. By 10.30 a.m., information was also conveyed by the officers of concerned department to Minister of Railways Shri Dinesh Trivedi and Viney Mittal, the Chairman Railway Board.

The moment the passenger's version was heard, the prima facie reason became known well before the start of the Parliament Session at 11 a.m. The Minister of Railways made a statement in the Parliament based on the available inputs from the Division. This was done with great precision. I knew the sensitivity of the accident, that too just before the Parliament came into session.

After handling the immediate crisis, I got in touch with Anup Kumar, DRM Mughalsarai, my adjoining Division, to take care of the passengers travelling to Delhi. Dehradun Express left Parasnath at around 10.30 a.m.

I requested Anup Kumar that ex-gratia of ₹25,000 per passenger may be paid to those passengers travelling to their destinations and were in the two ill-fated coaches. This was to be paid between Gaya and Mughalsarai. Anup had 2–3 hours notice to arrange cash at Gaya station. The affected train was to reach Gaya in 2–3 hours.

Acres of Diamonds: Transforming Coal

I also requested him to arrange toiletries and bathroom slippers, at least by the time the train reached Mughalsarai. This was well organised by the Mughalsarai Division and all passengers of affected coaches were paid ₹25,000 each and handed over a kit containing toiletries and bathroom slippers.

This was completely unusual. Ex-gratia is generally paid either at the destination or at accident site. In the instant case, it was done while passengers were travelling.

After completing all the formalities, we reached Dhanbad at around 5 p.m. Ex-gratia of ₹5 lakh was to be paid to the families who had lost their loved ones. By 7 p.m. the next-of-kin of five passengers were paid ₹5 lakh each. One Australian lady and one unidentified passenger could not be paid ₹5 lakh.

All the body bags were handed over to the Government Railway Police, Dhanbad, who in turn took them to the Civil Hospital for post-mortem. By 8 p.m., all the paper formalities were completed. Except for two body bags, all bodies were handed over to the next-of-kin of the passengers.

By 8 p.m., the representatives of the Australian High Commission had also reached Dhanbad. The parents of the deceased Australian lady passenger wanted her body to be flown to Australia. It was quite a difficult situation. After a lot of persuasion, they agreed for her cremation at Dhanbad itself.

It was practically impossible to clearly identify the charred bodies, except for their identification from the berth number mentioned on the reservation chart. And that was done with the berth number from where the remains were collected and kept inside the body bags.

The next morning, the relatives of one of the unidentified deceased passengers arrived and the body of the passenger was handed over. The ex-gratia of ₹5 lakh was also paid. The job of disbursing the ex-gratia to six deceased passengers and the affected passengers was over. We were yet to pay ex-gratia to the relatives of the deceased Australian lady through the Australian High Commission.

Three Australian ladies who were staying in the retiring rooms and were a part of the group, were fully taken care of for their medical needs and everything else including their outfits, food, telephone, etc. One of their colleagues was hospitalised in Bokaro Hospital. It took three days for her to be discharged. Gita Mohapatra, Divisional Commercial Manager, was fully empowered to take full care of these lady passengers.

New Claimants

However, two more claimants surfaced the next day. The relatives of two missing passengers made a written claim that they had also lost their loved ones in the fire incident. This created an embarrassment as only seven body bags had been filled, which was jointly witnessed by the officials of the State Government and the Railways. The joint note was a big strength for me.

Search for the Lost

As regards the claims made by the relatives of two missing passengers who could not be traced, it was decided to form two teams comprising Commercial, Personnel and RPF Inspectors to confidentially investigate the matter. Their mandate was to visit the hometowns of both the passengers and ascertain the facts in consultation with the local police, village Pradhan and the local people. These teams returned after 2–3 days and furnished their reports that the last rites of both these missing passengers had been performed in their respective villages.

There was no other way possible to handle such an unusual situation. If we had decided to stick to the joint report of seven deaths, the relatives of these two passengers would have gone to Railway Claims Tribunal or any other competent Court or Authority to seek justice and wait for a decision for years together. They would have suffered another tragedy (through the delay) and that would have been simply horrible. I wanted to figure out an easier and a humane solution and have faith in the Indian system to have confirmation about their death. Last rites can only be performed if the person is no more. That is what I firmly believed in, and therefore those teams had been formed.

Based on the reports of the special teams, it was inferred that these passengers had lost their lives and therefore ex-gratia of ₹5 lakh needed to be paid. It was simply a humanitarian approach to deal with the situation. Ex-gratia was paid, taking care of the bona fides. I had no one above me to approve or disapprove it. I was squarely responsible and accountable.

I had decided to go beyond the traditional protocols and be humane in my approach. It was a question of ethics in public service. After all, the tragedy happened on the railway system, and it was only incidental that we had a joint verification done. I had seen the burnt coach from inside when we were trying to fill the body bags with the remains of the bodies.

What haunted me was the doubt that maybe we were not able to fill all the remains of the passengers involved in the tragedy. The benefit of doubt must go in favour of the deceased. The teams in fact gave much more confirmatory evidence than what was available at the time of ex-gratia payment. In this case there was a positive act of ascertaining the facts. This was appreciated by one and all. The claims turned out to be genuine. It gave me immense relief and great satisfaction. We finally concluded that nine lives had been lost and the matter was closed.

Commissioner Railway Safety

From the second day onwards R.P. Yadav, Commissioner Railway Safety (CRS) Eastern Circle, started conducting its statutory inquiry at Gomoh. I decided to be present all through the inquiry and not delegate this part to anyone else. The affected coaches were first examined by the forensic team of the Government of Jharkhand from Ranchi and thereafter the coaches were lifted for a thorough examination by CRS.

The CRS was completely satisfied that nothing was left to chance. All possible help was rendered to R.P. Yadav to conduct the enquiry in a fair and transparent manner. There was no intent on the part of the Division to suppress any facts. Rather, we fully cooperated with the CRS. After two days of my stay and engagement with the CRS at Gomoh, the enquiry was completed. The CRS left the Division, and I came back to Dhanbad.

It was clear that there was no fault in the electrical system, including the coach battery. The forensic experts also gave their report. The extent of damage was huge and that led to an inference that something external must have been the cause and source of the fire.

Some bottle openers of wine bottles and a burnt mobile handset were recovered which were taken away by the CRS. It was being inferred that the wine bottles somehow got opened and the wine spread out on the floor of the coach. Maybe a spark from the mobile phone battery had fallen on the floor and triggered the fire. In those days cases of mobile phone battery explosion were being reported in the media. It is also possible that as per the eyewitness account of the passenger, some inflammable material had fallen on the floor and caught fire either due to a lit cigarette or some other thing. It was not possible to locate that passenger whose statement we had recorded on Parag's mobile.

A comprehensive report was prepared by the Division and sent to the Railway Board and HQ in accordance with the law.

After a lapse of a week, a letter of appreciation was received from the Australian High Commission thanking the Division for all the assistance rendered to the Australian ladies. A month later, another letter came from the Australian High Commission, addressed to the Chief Secretary of Jharkhand with a copy to the Chairman Railway Board, highlighting the good work done by the Division.

CRS submitted its report subsequently and appreciated the efforts of the Division. This was my satisfaction.

Normalcy Returns

The Division returned to normalcy after around ten days, overcoming the trauma of the fire accident.

This was the peak loading season of Dhanbad, and I had envisioned the Division crossing the magic figure of freight loading of 100 million tonnes and become the second 100 million tonnes Division after Bilaspur. Even in 2020, there were only two 100 million tonnes loading Divisions in Indian Railways – Bilaspur and Dhanbad. Dhanbad became the highest loading Division in 2019-20 with freight loading of 142 million tonnes.

By 2011, we had been loading around 82–84 million tonnes for the previous 5–6 years. In fact, the loading was almost stagnant due to several reasons – poor mobility in the Division due to frequent derailments, many speed restrictions, poor track maintenance, frequent stalling, poor condition of sidings, failure of TRD (Traction and Distribution), failure of signals, poor working conditions in Dhanbad Control Office, rail fractures and no addition of new sidings for additional loading points.

During the first week of December 2011, during the Monday meeting, I suggested that a system of on-the-spot reward be instituted that could encourage alertness of the train passing staff and in turn help the Division in improving safety. The train passing ought to be a sacred activity.

Every 4–5 km, there is a railway staff passing the train either at the level crossing gate or at the cabin or the station. I had a firm conviction that more the number of eyeballs looking for a defect in a running train, better would be the safety. The train passing staff ought to be alert and understand what they needed to look for.

Persistence of Vision

During every inspection, I used to silently stand a little away from the train passing staff and watch what they were doing while the train was running. I realised that the staff was not doing the work effectively as they did not understand the concept of persistence of vision. If an event is seen by the eyes for less than 1/30 seconds, it won't be understood by the brain. This is known as the persistence of vision. I used to guide them on how to watch a running train. I frequently taught them to watch a running train from an angle and tell them that following that practice they would be able to see the train for a longer duration without getting stressed.

Staff Empowered: Spot Award

Quite a few officers rejected the idea of the on-the-spot reward saying that this would severely impact the operation as trains would get frequently stopped. The majority believed that stoppage of trains merely based on the judgment of an unskilled person may not be in the best interest of the Division.

I was, however, firm and wanted a system of identifying a defect in the running train to run for at least three months to instil a feeling of responsibility and concern for safety.

I said that if it turned out to be detrimental to the operations, we would revert to the old system. I wanted to give authority to the train passing staff that if they detected something unsafe, they could stop the train and avert an accident. It would bring a sense of ownership for safety in everyone's mind. It was a big empowerment to enhance safety and change the culture of the organisation. Spot awards would serve as a skill as well as a will or motivation raiser. The flip side was some possible disruption in train movement.

Under the scheme, anybody on duty or off-duty noticing anything unusual in the train and communicating the same to the Control Office or to the station on real-time basis was to be rewarded ₹1,000. There were no restrictions as to the number of times this award could be given to the same individual.

All the apprehensions turned out to be unfounded. In a matter of 15–20 days, we realised that serious defects such as hot axle and part hanging had been detected by the train passing staff. In fact, a case of hot axle, if it had gone undetected, could have caused a major accident leading to serious damage to rail infrastructure.

This was quite encouraging. Staff members were being rewarded almost the same day or the next day. It gave us substantial respite as we were able to avert serious accidents and motivate many employees to become ambassadors of safety. Everyone became part of this safety drill. It turned into a mass movement. The spot awards, therefore, continued.

Some of the operating officers started objecting to this practice, but I did not relent. I remember the day when Deepak Nath, the head of operations at the HQ, telephoned me and spoke sarcastically, 'Division *bahut achha chal raha hai, traine ruk rahi hain*' (Division is doing very well, trains are stopping). I told Deepak, 'Safety is my responsibility and if you think something wrong is being done, please tell the General Manager and get the system reversed. From then on, you will be accountable for the safety.' My message was a little terse, but clear and upfront. He was a good friend of mine and we had worked together in the Railway Board. He did not call me again on this issue, ever.

After a short while, this system became the talk of the entire East Central Railway. Some of the train passing staff got the ₹1,000 award 10–15 times in two years. To the best of my knowledge, around 860 such awards were given to the staff over 23 months and nobody ever made a false claim.

We averted 15–20 major accidents over two years. The culture of the Division changed. Safety became the first priority, and getting an award was very enjoyable to the person who had correctly identified and stopped the train. He used to feel highly elated.

I had analysed that one derailment of a goods train in the Division used to cause a loss of loading of 3–4 rakes. Each rake used to fetch a revenue of ₹55–60 lakh. Accidents were that expensive.

Hundred Million Tonnes Slogan

The target of loading 100 million tonnes per annum became a t-shirt slogan. Even the families of the railwaymen started talking about it. One day one of my Chief Controllers told me that his mother was trying to understand 'What is 100 million tonnes which the DRM talks about every day?' I was quite happy that this was also becoming a mass movement like the spot award.

Another fact that got widely disseminated was – 'Loss of one minute due to any disruption to traffic leads to a loss of revenue of ₹1.5 lakh'. Value of one minute was calculated thus – we were earning ₹24 crore daily, and therefore the opportunity cost of one minute was ₹1.5 lakh.

At the beginning of December 2011, it was decided that the General Manager's annual inspection, a big event for the Division, would be organised. The section selected was Central Industrial Chord (CIC) section, which had not been inspected for 13 years because of Naxalite activities. Any section which is planned for annual inspection gets a lot of inputs in terms of attention to track, signals, Traction and Distribution (overhead wires) and other infrastructure. Such a section gets an overall facelift. I requested Varun Bharthuar, GM, that my Division may be inspected first. This was done to have a stress-free period during January–March 2012 and concentrate on loading.

There were genuine difficulties in completing various jobs in the CIC section as there were serious law-and-order problems. Sometimes, officers felt that we had ourselves invited trouble, firstly by identifying a difficult section, and secondly by organising it at a short notice of three weeks.

GM Special Derails

December 22, 2011, was the date scheduled for the annual inspection. A lot of good work was done even in the short duration. Inspection was done from Garwa Road station to Patratu station, a 224 km section. The section was fully barricaded with Central Reserve Police Force (CRPF) and Jharkhand Police to ensure safety and security. A lot of coordination was done by Shashi Kumar, my Senior Commandant RPF. He was very friendly with State officials. He was a professional cricket player. Everyone knew him well. He had the sportsman's spirit. I depended on him for going online for inspection.

The inspection was over by about 5 p.m. The run from Patratu to Dhanbad was a non-inspection track. All the officers had returned either to their own inspection carriages or had come to my inspection carriage, which was next to the train engine. While we were about to reach Dhanbad, at around 8 p.m., my carriage suddenly derailed, and our train stopped. Luckily, nobody suffered any injury.

Naturally, there was chaos, but I calmed everybody down and walked up to the last carriage in which Varun Bharthuwar was travelling. There was panic all around because the GM's Special is run with the highest level of care, safety and alertness. This train is just not supposed to derail. But it had.

My priority was to detach my carriage and reach Dhanbad with rest of the train. All senior officers and CRS were also travelling in the train. Dinner and a cultural function had already been planned in the Officers Club at Dhanbad. Officers and their families had been waiting anxiously. Despite the best efforts, we reached Dhanbad at around 11 p.m. These were unique and intriguing circumstances. Print and electronic media, and staff were waiting with apprehensions. In no time, it became global news because very soon I was able to listen to the GM's daughter speaking to him from the USA and talking about the incident.

I kept my cool and briefed the media at Dhanbad about the incident and also the sense of satisfaction with which the section had been inspected after 13 years. I told my officers not to engage with anybody and not to panic but find out the root cause after careful examination of the inspection carriage, the locomotive and the track, after the visit was over.

The moment I reached the Club with the GM and all other officers, the first job I did was to come to the podium and brief all the officers and their families about the inspection and the incident of derailment. I told the GM that whatever had happened, I held myself responsible as head of the Division. I also said that corrective measures would be taken as soon as possible and communicated to the HQ. Everyone got relaxed. There was nothing beyond after this.

The cultural evening was organised in a very cool and calm atmosphere. I did not allow anybody to feel any stress because of this incident.

The GM's Special left Dhanbad at 2 a.m. on December 23, 2011, after the dinner. The event was well organised. I thanked each person and came back home.

The next day, I met the Driver and the Inspector who were on the locomotive and inspected my inspection carriage in the maintenance depot. It became clear that the inspection carriage had not been maintained as per the laid down standards for a long time and the side bearers had worn out. Side bearer is a hemispherical shaped bronze component. One coach has four such pieces. It allows unrestricted movement of the coach over the curves. These had worn out and had not been replaced for a long time.

But the prime responsibility was that of the Driver who was running at more than 30 kmph on a curve. He suddenly applied regenerative brakes instead of pneumatic brakes when an Inspector escorting the train shouted in the loco cabin. This caused the locomotive to halt without train brakes and, as a result, the carriage jumped and derailed. All this happened out of panic.

The concerned staff and Driver were counselled, but nobody was taken to task because the Driver had performed well during the day while the inspection was in progress. Identifying the root cause was vital to eliminate such incidents, rather than reprimanding any staff member.

A few days later, one of the Senior Supervisors met me in my chamber and very humbly suggested me that I should organise some *hawan*. Ever since I had taken over the Division, something or the other had been going wrong. It was as if I had brought bad luck to the Division. I readily agreed and organised the hawan in December 2011 itself at my residence.

The next three months passed off peacefully and the Division was able to load 98.5 million tonnes, almost 14.5 million tonnes more than the previous year. It was a record for the Division. Soon everyone forgot about the tragedies and accidents.

During my inspections, I used to meet many officers and staff and most of them would either request for the payment of their arrears relating to travelling allowances or other allowances or would mention about the poor condition of their houses with leaking roofs. I could hardly respond to these as there was a serious shortage of funds for these activities. This was a serious constraint I had.

Flash Strike: Guards

One night, while I was on site attending to the derailment of a goods train, around 11 p.m., a message came that the guards had gone on a flash strike in the Gomoh Lobby. The reason was an altercation the Guards had on phone with one of my traffic officers.

The Guards were also demanding payment of their arrears which had been long overdue. After talking to D.K. Pandey, President of the Union, the matter was resolved. After two hours, the operation was restored to normal. The traffic officer involved in the altercation was asked to go to the Lobby and seek an apology from the Guards for their unacceptable conduct.

The next day happened to be a Saturday. The Guards wanted to meet me. I readily agreed. They were around 40 in number. I met them in my conference room. They were all highly agitated. I allowed everybody to speak while maintaining decency. Finally, I spoke and told them that they have to ensure and assure not to repeat their behaviour in future such as stopping trains as it would attract disciplinary action. The punishment could be break in service. On my part, I promised to make all efforts to ensure that the arrears of the allowances were paid early.

There was a lot of pressure from the HQ to punish these guards with a break in service since they had disrupted traffic. I flatly refused to do that to anyone. The following Monday there was a video conference with the GM.

I told the GM that the Division needed ₹40 crore urgently to pay for the long pending arrears of staff. This was crucial, since one day's earning of the Division was ₹24 crore and any strike may result in a loss of earning which would be difficult to make up. It would therefore be fitting that this small amount of ₹40 crore, which I had promised to the staff, was arranged. This was readily accepted by the GM. It is a different matter altogether that it took more than four months to make these payments as a lot of paperwork had to be done. The staff was tremendously satisfied to get their legitimate money.

Bomb Blasts

Almost 12 bomb blasts took place on tracks during 23 months of my tenure at Dhanbad. In about 50 per cent of the cases, I had personally visited the site on the day of the bomb blast itself. The first bomb blast took place near Parasnath. It was at around 2 a.m. I spoke to the Chief Secretary and the DGP Jharkhand and requested them to provide police assistance for early site clearance. Unless the local police gave clearance, restoration work could not start.

This happened to be the first bomb blast on tracks in my tenure. I went to the accident site in an ART. S.P. Dhan, the Superintendent of Police, Dhanbad, was directed by the DGP to accompany me, along with a police force to ensure faster clearance. Both the main lines on Grand Chord were involved, disrupting movement on the Delhi–Howrah route. We reached the site at 4.30 a.m. with adequate police force in the ART. Police force from Gomoh, near Parasnath, was already present at the site.

Both Up and Down line tracks had been blown apart due to the massive bomb blast. There were two banner flags placed on both sides of the track, owning responsibility. Since the SP Dhanbad, was with me in the ART, restoration work started immediately. By 8 a.m. both the tracks were made fit and traffic restored. It was done in the shortest possible time. Even Viney Mittal, the Chairman was amazed at the pace at which the traffic had been restored.

I remember that the bomb blast sites used to be handled only after sunrise. This was the culture prevailing. I wanted to change that. While we were going to the site of the blast by ART, close to the site, we heard a blast. Clearly, the Naxalites had attacked our train. There was panic inside the train. There was a murmur that the practice of approaching the site of blast only after sunrise was the right practice. This implied that the DRM had not taken the right decision of going to the site in the night. Once the train came to a halt, it became clear that the blast was due to the bursting of a detonator on the track. This would have presumably been put on the track by the guard of the preceding train to alert the driver of the following train. The atmosphere became normal. As soon as the train started again and we reached the site, the restoration work was started.

It takes time to change the culture. You have to be at the forefront of change all the time and every time.

This was the first time ever a Superintendent of Police had travelled in an ART. This was the result of a good personal relationship with G.S. Rath, the then DGP and S.P. Dhan, Superintendent of Police, Dhanbad. There was complete support from the State police and the civil administration because I used to frequently visit and pay my regards to the Chief Secretary and the DGP at Ranchi. In fact, Rath invited me to his daughter's wedding, which I attended.

Driver Taken Hostage by Naxalites

I remember another incident of CIC section wherein some Naxalites stopped the train mid-section and asked the loco Driver to climb to the roof of the locomotive. The Driver was made to climb to the roof to remove the metallised carbon strip from the pantograph and hand it over to them. The strip was made of graphite. Graphite was used for lubricating the barrel of guns. Fortunately, the Driver had taken the precaution of shutting down the locomotive before climbing to the roof. He had lowered the pantograph. In the intervening period, Control got to know about this incident and a patrol party reached the site. The Maoists ran away. The life of the Driver was saved just because of his alertness.

Next day there was a big agitation and train operations came to a grinding halt. Drivers demanded police escort during night journeys. The DGP (Railways) was the wife of the Chief Secretary. I spoke to both of them and informed them about the seriousness of the incident which could have resulted in the loss of life of our staff due to electrocution. A letter was written and sent per bearer to DGP (Railways), Chief Secretary and the DGP. The letter was also shared with the Drivers in all the Lobbies.

The State administration promised that the culprits would be apprehended soon. This assurance was quite important for the staff to be convinced about my earnestness. Train operations resumed and continued smoothly.

My letter conveyed my concern and feelings to the DGP (Railways). Within 48 hours, the culprits were apprehended. This was made known to all the Drivers through the Lobbies, in the entire Division.

The staff was quite satisfied. The DGP (Railways) personally informed me about the culprits being caught. Concern and care for the staff was at the forefront of all my endeavours. Fighting against these Naxalite activities was on my agenda too. Train operations continued with high spirits. National interest was supreme.

Hehegara Station Blown

In one of the incidents of bomb blasts on June 29, 2012, the Hehegara station building was completely damaged and all the station records burnt. I reached the station the next day. Rajendra Prasad, Cabin Master, Hehegara station, met me and explained how he lost his

₹20,465 kept in the almirah at the station. This money did not belong to him as he had received it on behalf of one of the retired railway employees – Pashupati Prasad, ex-Cabin-man. Hehegara is a Halt station in the CIC section of Dhanbad Division, in Latehar district (26 km from Latehar) of the Indian state of Jharkhand, 19 km from Barwadih. The population of Hehegara is about 1,575.

The man was in tears as he would have to bear this loss from his own pocket for no fault of his. I talked to the Unions and decided to pay this money from the Staff Benefit Fund, ensuring that the money was paid to the bona fide retired employee, Pashupati Prasad, in the presence of all concerned. This was a small gesture which brought a feel-good factor amongst the staff and motivated them. They were all working in the most hostile environment, especially in the CIC section.

There were occasions when I was not allowed to inspect a section because the SPs of the concerned districts did not grant permission, especially in the CIC section, for any of my official visits. Our visits used to be kept secret to a large extent.

Meeting Supervisors

I used to hold regular meetings with the Senior Supervisors of all the disciplines in a structured manner at least once in three months. These meetings were generally held on Saturdays. I wanted to hear them out and resolve their problems as much as I could. This would keep them motivated. It served two purposes – direct communication of my priority areas, and their articulating the issues that might not come to my notice otherwise. Above all, it used to energise and galvanise them.

Lightning Strike

One night, around 3.30 a.m., I was informed that the ghat section between Gurpa and Gujhandi had been closed due to a lightning strike in the stormy weather and the trains were suffering serious detention. It was a 22 km long section and extremely vital, on the Delhi–Howrah route. I decided to go to the site within 15 minutes of getting the information. I had given standing instructions to the staff maintaining my inspection carriage that I could leave Dhanbad any time in the day or night, in the event of any eventuality, failure, or accident. By 3.45 a.m. we left Dhanbad.

We reached Dilwa station in the ghat section around 5.15 a.m. and saw that many relays had burnt. The Station Master informed me that he had received electric shock during the lightning strike. The signalling system had been completely damaged.

On-the-spot inquiry revealed that there was poor earthing in the entire ghat section because of the hilly terrain. Dilwa station had a radio communication tower which was 90 m high. The mean sea level of the station was 300–320 m, which effectively meant that the top of the tower was 410 m high above mean sea level. This tower did not have adequate earthing.

The Eiffel Tower in Paris has a height of around 324 m above the ground, and we have never heard about an incidence of shock to anybody due to lightning. A robust design has ensured safety of tourists even in bad weather conditions. Why couldn't we ensure the safety of our installation?

Then and there, it was decided that the entire ghat section of 22 km required improved earthing. Lightning surges in bad weather had often resulted in signal failure and consequently disruption to traffic. A special work was sanctioned for earthing of various important locations and provision of Surge Protection Devices. Over 6–8 months, earthing protection was done at 900 locations in mission mode on the entire Grand Chord section between Dhanbad and Manpur. This action eliminated the problems experienced under bad weather conditions. The Relay rooms were upgraded and provided with air conditioners and earthing to improve the reliability of relays.

This was possible as the root cause analysis was done well, right at the time of the occurrence of the problem. There is no other way out to resolve such issues, except to go beyond the call of duty to make major changes.

Speed Enhanced: 100 years

I vividly remember my first foot plate inspection of the ghat section along with my officers just after I took charge of the Division. I had observed that the Driver drove at a speed of 65 kmph in the ghat section and at 30 kmph inside the three tunnels. Why were the speeds so low when the track looked fine?

I got the answer – it had not been permitted to go beyond the speed of 65 kmph ever since the section was opened in 1906 because it had been categorised as a 'ghat' section.

Lord Minto, the Viceroy and Governor General of India, had inaugurated the Asansol–Gaya section, called Grand Chord, on December 6, 1906, which reduced the distance between Kolkata and Delhi by 80 km.

As regards the tunnel, I was told that the steel sleepers had been damaged and needed replacement before the speed inside the tunnel could be increased.

A two-pronged strategy was worked out – shallow depth concrete sleepers needed to be developed by the private sector to replace steel sleepers, and we needed to do calculations to find out the maximum speed that could be permitted on the ghat section as per design.

I went through the calculations and found that the speeds could go up to 100 kmph. We raised the speed of the section from 65 to 80 kmph in the first phase on November 22, 2012. To enthuse the staff and all officers and to remember this great day, a plaque made of stone was installed at Gujhandi station. It was placed next to the plaque installed to commemorate the centenary celebrations of this section on December 6, 2006. The speed of trains in the section was subsequently raised to 100 kmph.

What a thrill the officers experienced! It took more than 100 years to think and raise the speed of the ghat section from 65 kmph to 100 kmph. The speed inside the three tunnels, also built in 1906, was similarly raised to 65 kmph after one long year of work. It took time to get the shallow depth sleepers. Lights were also provided inside the tunnel for ease of inspection and safety.

We generally do not question the status quo.

Management by Walking

I travelled almost 28,000 km in 23 months of my stay, which comes to 40 km per day. I must have visited each of the 112 stations around 8–10 times. It allowed me to personally connect with the staff and supervisors and motivate them to go beyond the call of duty to perform under the most difficult circumstances.

I remember having undertaken a 11 km foot inspection from Pradhankhanta station to Dhanbad station to diagnose the reasons for trains getting stalled at the Home Signal near Dhanbad and between the two stations, causing serious disruption to train movement. We found that about 2.5 km of track had worn out much ahead of the codal life and the signal needed to be shifted by about 65–70 m towards the Dhanbad station. The rail line was replaced and the signal was shifted, and the problem almost vanished. This became a big motivating story of the time as the problem of stalling at Home Signal of Dhanbad had persisted for a long time.

Officers got so enthused that they started doing foot patrol inspection, especially the Traction Distribution and Civil Engineering officers. So much so, it started getting reported as one of the KPIs by these officers. Asset reliability improved. Officers were happy reporting problems they found during such visits. I remember Bhardwaj Chaudhary, in-charge of Traction Distribution, reporting foot patrolling by his team of four officers of about 600 km in a month. This reduced the incidence of panto-entanglement substantially and the officers felt confident due to their accomplishments.

Similarly, there were frequent train stalling cases between Parasnath and Chegro during rainy weather. Trains used to suffer detention for hours at a time. One day we walked through this 7 km long section. As a result, we introduced the system of keeping a permanent Banker locomotive at Parasnath and encouraged drivers to seek the Banker at Parasnath if they had doubts about clearing this section without stalling. This helped in reducing the detentions on this account drastically. Operations improved.

In yet another incidence, we went to the Gurpa–Gujhandi ghat section where there were cases of frequent uncoupling of freight trains, especially the trains going towards Gaya. It was a down gradient of 1 in 80. A few cases of derailments had also taken place. The location of such incidents was known. I took along with me the wagon maintenance in-charge, Vivek Kumar, to the site.

It was early morning. We stopped at one location in the section and watched a few trains that were crossing there. We found that loose rail joints were causing the rattling and the up-and-down movement of wagons at this place. Because of the dynamic forces under such conditions, there was a possibility of some CBC disengaging from their counterpart wagon. These joints were fish plated and held in place by four bolts. These bolts had become loose. These were supposed to be tightened by the Key Man who inspects 4 km of track daily, early in the morning. This was obviously not getting done. When we spoke to a few Key Men, we noticed that the Key Men were just checking the health of the track for fractures and presence of these four bolts but didn't check for their tightness. It was a case of lack of training and supervision by senior officers. They were urgently counselled by concerned officers and supervisors. We required some 60,000 bolts to replace the defective ones and ensured their tightness on a regular basis. Also, emphasis was laid on the health of CBC. It took time but the situation improved as the cause had been identified.

Hundred Million Tonnes Threshold Crossed

The next year, 2012-13, we were able to load 102 million tonnes of freight traffic, generating a revenue earning of ₹8,500 crore. It was an increase of about ₹3,000 crore of revenue earning in two years. As regards freight volumes, it had increased by 18 million tonnes over this period.

It was quite a satisfactory achievement. One of the important projects languishing for ten years was the commissioning of RRI of the Dhanbad yard. This was accomplished in record time, which substantially improved train operations in the Division.

Route Relay Interlocking

As I mentioned earlier, this work was pending completion for ten years. I had realised early on that RRI would improve safety and reduce the time taken to handle arrival and departure of a train at Dhanbad station. This, in turn, would improve our capacity to handle more trains. My regular visits to Dhanbad station and the Dhanbad yard only affirmed my commitment to get this work completed as early as possible as the health of the track and signalling gear was poor.

Since this work had been pending for a long time, the track material required for this work had already been consumed for regular maintenance activities. The yard plans were not getting finalised as the traffic requirements had undergone a sea change over the past ten years. We had a number of meetings with construction officers, who were the custodian of the project, to reach a consensus. It was difficult to break the logjam.

I started owning this project to bring Divisional Officers on board and find a way out to take this project forward. After many rounds of discussions, the drawing for the yard was finalised. Ved Prakash played a very positive role all along. Headquarters was now requested to divert track material from other projects. I wrote a personal letter to the Principal Chief Engineer to help the Division. I followed it up with a personal telephone call with him to persuade him as this was crucial for completing the project. After sustained efforts, he agreed to the request of the Division.

The RRI at Patna had been badly handled by another team 6–8 months earlier. There were serious operational constraints experienced post commissioning of Patna RRI. Even a few accidents had taken place while the work of RRI Patna was going on. Senior officers from the Railway Board had to camp at Patna to handle that crisis. I was therefore conscious that I should take all possible care while completing this work.

It took almost an year to do the preparatory work for yard remodelling and associated railway electrification. The very fact that it took one year to do the preparatory work shows the quantum of work involved to complete RRI at Dhanbad. This was probably the reason it was procrastinated by successive DRMs.

We had strategised to do all the modification work beforehand. Normally most of the yard modification work is undertaken during switchover period. This was a new way of working and was in fact the Dhanbad Model of doing RRI work. Once we were ready with all the preliminary and preparatory work to undertake final commissioning, the Railway Board and Headquarters were approached to accord a go-ahead. They were reluctant to grant permission because of the lurking doubt that the whole work may not be completed in six days with compliance to safety.

During the period of switchover (from manual interlocking to automatic), most of the mail express trains were cancelled, and the freight operation was reduced to a bare minimum. We were advised to plan cancellation of trains after the financial year 2012-13 was over on March 31. April is a very hot month in the Dhanbad Region. Permission was granted to start pre-noninterlocking with effect from April 14 and to complete the interlocking on April 19, 2013.

When this work is undertaken, all fail-safe features that the system provides to ensure safety do not exist during the period of switchover from the manual system to the automatic system. This is the most crucial time and everything needs to be handled with utmost care. During this period, a lot of manual work is done. The whole yard is divided into small zones, each managed by a set of well-trained staff and officers controlled from a temporary *Goomti*. Goomti is a small, covered shelter with staff, walkie-talkie, magneto phone, padlocks and other necessary tools to clamp a point for safe passage of a train.

Our assessment was that about 600 additional men were required from other adjoining Divisions. The yard was to be divided into 17 Goomties. We had to arrange for their stay and food. Hotels were booked and caterers were arranged. The number was large and these staff members had to stay for at least seven days at Dhanbad. They were coming from other Divisions. Work had to be completed in six days.

After the D-day was fixed, public notification was issued for the cancellation of various trains. I decided to visit the yard exactly during that time of the day when the staff would be working under the sun – from 9 a.m. to 5 p.m. I had a team of officers with me. It was terribly hot. We walked for about 5–6 km from one end to the other end of the yard. Some of the officers had almost collapsed due to the scorching sun. We then decided to start the work from 6.30 a.m. instead of 9 a.m. We also decided to get a good quality cap for everyone to provide some protection from the sun. Dhanbad didn't have the large stock of caps we needed. These had to be arranged from Kolkata. Also, king sized water containers were arranged in large numbers to take care of drinking water.

A Women's Welfare Organisation was also contacted. They arranged a water cooler and also proactively agreed to supply *sattu* and lemon daily to each of the Goomties and to all the 600 staff. We decided to keep a medical team on site round the clock. Arrangements were made to provide breakfast to the staff at 8 a.m. at the site itself to ensure uninterrupted work in the morning hours before the sun was overhead and became too hot. Lunch used to be served in hygienic conditions near the yard at 4-5 places in a makeshift tent. All the officers were expected to take lunch with the staff only. I also had lunch with them. I came to the yard at 6 a.m. sharp and went on a round of the yard. This generally took 2-3 hours. After that I would go to the office and be back by 11 a.m., and again go on a round. It would be lunch time by then. After lunch I returned to my office. At 5 p.m., I went to the site to take stock of the day's work. We used to finish our work at 8 p.m. daily. This continued for five days. The RRI was commissioned one-and-a half days ahead of the target date of April 18, around 12.30 p.m. Viney Mittal, CRB, congratulated me over the phone. It was really a moment to rejoice.

After the work was completed, we decided to monitor the next week's performance. My Additional Divisional Railway Manager, Rajesh Mohan, used to prepare a one-page report indicating the failures observed and reasons identified to remedy these, along with the traffic handled during the past 24 hours. This report went to the GM, East Central Railway every day at 10 p.m., signed by me. This gave everyone the confidence that the work has been well done and the operation has stabilised.

When we released the outstation staff, we gave them each a Certificate of Appreciation for the job well done in recognition of their contribution towards completing this mega work. The RRI was well commissioned. Now all the control staff was asked to go and inspect the RRI building and understand the ease in receipt and dispatch of a train. It turned out that there was a reduction of about 5-6 minutes in dwell time (time taken to complete the process of reception of one train) at Dhanbad station. Dhanbad station handled about 90-100 trains daily. This was simply great.

Life became very simple for most of the traffic staff engaged in this duty. Their work became less stressful. Now everyone realised the importance of RRI. All the old Cabins which were there in the yard became redundant. Most of the supervisors and staff were feeling that this work should have been done long time ago. But earlier no one had the conviction about the comfort and ease the RRI will bring in their working.

Safety improved, flexibility to take trains on different platforms improved, dwell time reduced, yard drainage improved, and the yard became spick-and-span. People used to enjoy walking in the yard for inspection. There were countless gains.

During the preparatory process we had provided seven high masts in the yard for lighting. We had also removed some 600–700 truckload of debris from the yard which had been lying for decades. The Mail Express Drivers were very happy as they were able to see the track ahead the moment they entered the Dhanbad yard because of improved illumination. Even the common people of Dhanbad were very happy about it. I then wrote a concept paper and circulated it to HQ as to how RRI work should be completed in future – 'Dhanbad Model of RRI'. RRI is generally known from the number of routes it caters to. This RRI, a big one, catered to 332 routes. The estimated cost of this work was ₹28 crore at that time. It was completed on April 18, 2013.

This was a game changer, indeed, for the Dhanbad Division.

Reward for Work

Various infrastructure improvement and staff welfare measures were also undertaken which led to overall improvement of the Division. Everyone worked with a positive frame of mind. In both the years of my stay, the Division was adjudged the best Division of East Central Railway and most of the shields were given to the Division. During these two years, 15 of my officers, supervisors and staff were bestowed with the highest National Awards at the level of the Minister of Railways. Once I sent my officers by air to receive an award at Mumbai. It was a big morale booster for them as the work of RRI was to commence from April 14 and conclude on April 19, while the Award Ceremony was to be held on April 16. The result was that the RRI work at Dhanbad was completed 1½ days ahead of the approved schedule of six days. It was an amazing performance.

Bus for Children

I would also like to narrate some of the staff welfare measures taken during my tenure. Whenever I used to visit Gujhandi, the first station on Gujhandi–Gurpa section of 22 km, quite a few staff members used to meet me with a request to look into their transport needs between Gujhandi and Koderma (10 km), especially the school-going children. There were no suitable trains for school children. The majority of them were studying at Koderma. Gujhandi was an important ghat station from the point of view of train safety. There was a Running

Room also at Gujhandi, mainly for Banker drivers. Children play a key role in the well-being of an employee. This problem of the children's difficulties in going to school had persisted for a long time, without a solution.

In consultation with the Staff Unions and Women's Welfare Organisation, we arranged a new school bus that cost around ₹15 lakh. This would be run on a no-profit-no-loss basis and the wards of the employees used to contribute for its running expenses. Assistant Engineer, Gujhandi, was nominated the nodal officer to look after its upkeep and safe parking at the station. This was well-received by the employees and the Staff Unions. Such actions improve staff loyalty towards the organisation.

Staff Welfare: Work Environment

The Running Rooms and Lobbies for the Drivers and Guards needed improvement. The Running Staff played a crucial role in enhanced loading of the Division. To begin with, we replaced all the linen, improved toilets, improved kitchen and executed other infrastructure related works. A massive facelift was given. Drivers and Guards were highly motivated. Care and attention by the administration was loud and clear. In fact, a few new Running Rooms were added without any objection from the Running Staff. It was in the interest of operation of the Division. A motivated staff enhanced loading.

A new facilitation centre was sanctioned to provide a place of stay to the staff coming to Dhanbad from all over. A respectable shelter with all facilities like toilets, bathrooms and cloak rooms was a must. Officers and staff were also posted at this centre to investigate staff grievances. Similarly, Gang Huts, a place of shelter for trackmen (also called gangmen), were upgraded and provided with solar lights and hand pumps.

The Control Office at Dhanbad was fully renovated by shifting it to a new location. It took about four months to shift from the existing place. It was a big risk. A fully air-conditioned Control Office became the centre of attraction for everyone because of its good aesthetics, quality furniture and an overall good ambience. Illumination level had improved tremendously. Inspiring slogans were put up at various places.

The Control Office is the heart of any Division and must be the best-kept place in the Division. This could motivate people and make them comfortable to take decision in realtime as these of the staff work under the most trying circumstances. They must deal with all the unusual occurrences as the point of first contact with the Drivers, Guards, station staff or even passengers whenever there is an emergency. They should therefore be motivated to work and provide the best assistance to the field and keep officers informed on realtime basis. They should feel pride in their place of work.

The Division has a similarly critical job of monsoon and winter patrolling, a very difficult exercise undertaken during rainy weather and winter months. This Division is situated on a hilly terrain with high mean sea levels and there are far too many cases of landslides during rains.

I made it a practice to meet these trackmen regularly (about 80 gangs) engaged in patrolling duty. They were provided with a kit which had all the facilities required to undertake night patrolling during rains and during winter. These men were also provided with a mobile handset and a SIM which could help them communicate with the Control Office on realtime basis. This was the biggest enabler for discharging their duty. They used to feel safe due to availability of communication with the Control Office. Mobile phones and a SIM could not be sanctioned officially, so I sanctioned awards to each of the Patrol Party and bought the handset and SIM with the award money.

The Division did not have even one case of landslide which resulted in an accident. Gurpa Gujhandi had a hilly terrain and loose soil, but alertness of the employees averted any such situation. This performance was unprecedented. The staff was highly motivated because of this small gesture. Their needs used to be looked after at my level.

Similarly, all the Traffic Inspectors of the Division were asked to stay for 48 hours continuously at each of their allotted stations to ensure that they live the life of an Assistant Station Master and understand their difficulties. This enabled them to suggest measures and find the solutions to improve their working conditions.

The observations of these Inspectors were personally monitored by my cell for fast-track attention and resolution. The staff at the stations felt highly encouraged because most of their grievances never came to the notice of the DRM. These were now being looked after by the Inspectors concerned and resolved in a specified time frame. There were stations where there was no hand pump for water. It was provided on priority. Stations had broken chairs and tables. These were repaired. The Station Masters of 84 stations were given a cash imprest of ₹3,000 to ₹5,000 each for procurement of small stationery items and items for cleanliness and other daily needs. The Station Master could buy petty items without waiting for regular store supply. This imprest could be replenished at regular intervals. It was empowering. This helped in addressing the concerns of the staff and they, in turn, took adequate care of safety on the Division.

Safety consciousness really seeped into the psyche of the train passing staff which tremendously helped in containing derailment and accidents. It started becoming a part of the culture.

I found that Dhanbad, being the biggest Division on East Central Railway, was receiving almost ₹1 crore from the Staff Benefit Fund. But the amount was not getting utilised in time. I ensured that this money was spent on all the specified activities as mandated. The funds would be allotted to the Division sometime in April/May and disbursed by October. This was mostly used for meeting children's school or higher education needs, serious ailments of employees, physical disabilities of wards of employees, and women empowerment.

The funds for the disabled were generally going unutilised and returned to the HQ. So I decided to act on that.

Parents love their children the most. Care for their children generates tremendous loyalty. In consultation with the Ali Yaver Jung National Institute of Speech and Hearing disability, Kolkata, the Women's Welfare Organisation assessed the hearing disabilities of the wards of the employees and correctly diagnosed the instruments required. These instruments were procured and distributed to these needy wards in a function organised at the General Manager's level. It changed the lives of those children. It was a big moment of satisfaction. Thereafter, all the divyangs who came forward to seek such assistance, were helped. All this got done based on the suggestions of my wife.

The women empowerment funds were utilised by the Women's Welfare Organisation for training the girls in computer application. Thereafter, laptops were distributed to them by the Women's Welfare Organisation. It was something unheard of in the Railways.

Study Centres were opened at four places in the Division to provide free access to the wards of railway employees to prepare for competitive examinations. All books were made available at the Centres – be it for engineering, medicine or law. New editions of books were available. These Centres had water and furniture besides 24x7 electricity. This was well patronised. A token admission fee of ₹10 was charged per ward. The Centre was funded through the Staff Benefit Fund to ensure sustainable operation of these Centres. The Head of Personnel Department of the Division was the nodal officer who had ensured their success.

Ashutosh Chaurasia

Ashutosh Chaurasia, was a young and energetic officer, working as an Assistant Engineer at Gomoh. He had hardly put in one year of

Acres of Diamonds: Transforming Coal

service. On a fateful day, he was on a Push Trolley inspection between Chaudhary Bandh and Chichaki stations of Dhanbad–Koderma section of Dhanbad Division.

A Push Trolley is a four-wheeled trolley that runs on rail track and is made of iron and wood. It weighs around 200 kg. It has an umbrella and a red flag atop. It is used to inspect the rail track. It is pushed by two people of the staff at a time while inspecting officials sit on a wooden bench, fixed on the platform of the trolley. The Push Trolley can be removed from the track by four staff members who accompany the inspecting officials.

The section being inspected had many sharp curves and gradients. Caution boards are provided at the approach of each curve to alert the drivers. Drivers are supposed to continuously whistle while negotiating such sections.

Suddenly, a train approached the location of Chaurasia's trolley. Either the driver did not whistle, or it was not heard. Ashutosh's trolley was hit by a locomotive of Neelanchal Express. This fateful day was Wednesday, November 30, 2011.

Most of the staff on the trolley somehow managed to jump off and save themselves, but Ashutosh, along with Neelkantha, a staff member, kept trying to remove the trolley from the track to avert the accident. In the process, both were severely hurt when the locomotive hit the trolley. Ashutosh had multiple fractures in his knee. Neelkanth also suffered injuries.

As soon as the news came to the Control Office, arrangements were made to shift the injured from the site of the accident to the Railway Hospital, Dhanbad. A locomotive was arranged to transport them to Dhanbad. A doctor accompanied them from Gomoh. While they were being shifted, Dr Mishra of Railway Hospital, Gomoh, administered glucose and certain other medicines to keep them sedated and ensured first-aid treatment. Experts were consulted to provide best possible treatment at Dhanbad. Neelkanth's condition stabilised.

But Ashutosh's condition deteriorated and he needed to be shifted immediately to Mission Hospital, Durgapur, for a radical surgery. There was danger to his life and the limb as some of the nerves had been badly damaged.

The hospital demanded an advance payment of ₹5 lakh. Action was needed to be taken immediately. His wife was in Jhansi. DRM had no powers to sanction payment of an advance for this treatment.

Ved Prakash was Secretary of the Officers Club. I consulted my officers and decided to pay this money from the Officers Club to save Ashutosh's life. The money was paid, and the surgery was performed the same day. After three weeks of hospitalisation, the officer was discharged. It took 4–5 months for him to be back on duty.

This money could not be sanctioned and thus the expense regularised for at least 6–8 months due to various procedural delays. I used to speak to the HQ and Railway Board officers for the sanction of the amount and for the empanelment of this hospital for Dhanbad Division. This hospital was already an empanelled hospital of CLW. Despite this, the hospital was not empanelled by Railway Board throughout my stay at Dhanbad. Officers of the Division were a little upset that I had used the Club's money for this treatment which in fact had saved Ashutosh's life. One day I even offered to reimburse the money from my pocket if it was not sanctioned. Finally, the money was sanctioned, and the Club got its money back. I thought life was more precious than money. Ashutosh was back to normal and in 2020 he was working as Deputy Chief Engineer at Hazaribagh, looking after the assignment of construction of rail line.

Since I knew the institutional callousness in such cases, when I was head of the Transformation Cell in Railway Board, it was ensured that DRMs were empowered to sanction ₹5 lakh to deal with such emergencies. Also, DRMs were empowered to empanel super specialty hospitals to provide better healthcare to employees.

Compassionate Appointment

In another unfortunate incident, Badri Nath Dutta, Master Craftsman of Carriage and Wagon Department, was run over by a shunting train in the yard and died on January 31, 2013. This was the day of his retirement. He had already completed 60 years of age before January 31, as his date of birth was January 9, 1953. Dutta was having quite a disturbed life as none of his children were gainfully employed. The officers had briefed me about him. He was a sincere worker. There were some murmurs about his committing suicide due to grave family circumstances. The way he was run over also appeared a little intriguing. The death of Dutta further aggravated the family's problems. I was conscious of the feelings one has while retiring from service. I did not pay heed to any of these rumours, as the fact of the matter was that he had died. The rule for compassionate appointment provided for the appointment of the wife or the ward of the deceased upon death of an employee while in service. There was a view that since he had already attained the age of 60 years there was no need to consider such compassionate appointment. I, however, had a view that even if the employee had died after attaining 60 years of age, he was still in active service at the time of death and therefore his family deserved this compassion from the administration. We provided compassionate appointment to his son Gopal Kumar Dutta on April 1, 2013, as Trains Clerk. It was out of a deep sense of compassion for my employees. Manoj Kumar was the head of Personnel Department at Dhanbad. He was an encyclopaedia on establishment rules. He went out of his way to get all the credentials of Gopal Kumar verified and did everything to fast-track the process and issue the offer of appointment. Manoj was one of the most super-efficient Personnel Officer I had seen in my career. He loved to do such non routine work. I was extremely happy as the compassionate appointment was made for the greater good of the family.

The two years of my stay at Dhanbad were quite fulfilling as the period saw an all-round development on the Division with the highest ever loading and the best ever safety record. It was time for me to depart.

Time to Depart

The Railway Magistrate, along with his senior judge – Districts and Sessions Judge S.K. Singh – and other Judges of the District Court organised a farewell function for me just before I left Dhanbad. Mr S.K. Singh belonged to Kanpur where I had spent ten years. We got along well. I had got the office of the Railway Magistrate renovated. It had needed improvement. I had inspected his office during one of my visits and had promised to have it improved, which I did. I even got a Railway house allotted to him as it was in accordance with the rules. As Railway Magistrate, he was very helpful in the ticket-checking drive.

All India Railwaymen's Federation (AIRF) and National Federation of Indian Railwaymen (NFIR), the two labour unions, also organised a farewell function.

A regular farewell, usually organised by the Officers Club, was arranged. It was heartening to hear the feelings of fellow officers who had worked with me for two years. The new DRM, B.B. Singh, joined. A large group of employees gathered from all over the Division and saw me off when I left Dhanbad to return to Delhi by Rajdhani Express on September 14, 2013. Some of the employees had come from as far off as Chopan and CIC area. There were thousands of people at the station to bid me goodbye. I was very worried, as it might have resulted in a stampede. It was undoubtedly an emotional moment. What a satisfying experience I had by the time my tenure came to an end. I will always cherish the memories of Dhanbad.

23

Actions Change Destiny: Varanasi and Diesel Sheds

I was DRM Dhanbad, during 2011–2013. This Division was formed on November 5, 1951. It is the highest revenue earning Division in Indian Railways at present (in 2020) and is also the number one Division in coal loading. The Division has two major loco sheds – Patratu, established in 1964 for maintaining diesel locos and Gomoh, established in 1965 for maintaining electric locos.

The Patratu Diesel Shed is situated on CIC section of the Division, while Gomoh Shed is situated on Grand Chord (GC) line connecting Asansol to Gaya. Patratu has an 840 MW thermal power plant. It is a town under the Ramgarh district of the Indian state of Jharkhand and has a population of about 33,000.

The CIC section is fully electrified, but the Diesel Shed exists in the midst of the CIC section as it was established long ago. Most of the coal loading of Dhanbad Division takes place in the CIC section.

The Patratu Shed is slowly losing its utility since most train operations are shifting to electric traction. But the Shed has very rich resources in terms of motivated manpower and physical assets. A training school is attached to the Shed.

Since I had travelled extensively in the Division, I must have visited the two Sheds at least 8–10 times. Whenever I visited Patratu, I thought of this Shed maintaining electric locos. Many electric locos used to be hauled dead due to failures in CIC section since there was no facility to troubleshoot these failures. The failed electric locos used to be taken to the Gomoh Shed for repair. It was a severe pain for operations.

However, there were no takers for this idea as the organisation was completely siloed. No electrical engineer wanted electric locos to be maintained by mechanical engineers, but mechanical engineers wanted to maintain electric locos. Mechanical engineers wanted to upgrade their skills, but they would also not part with the assets of diesel sheds. Mechanical engineers did not allow electrical engineers

Actions Change Destiny: Varanasi and Diesel Sheds

to take control of diesel sheds. This was a typical problem reflecting poorly on the health of the organisation. There was a need for a major organisational transformation.

I was working as Advisor (Rolling Stock) in Railway Board since January 2016. In fact, prior to this assignment, I was working as Executive Director (Development), looking after major projects like Madhepura Factory, Train Sets and 9,000 HP locomotive.

Keeping in view the growth of traffic and the speeds at which Indian Railways had been running freight and passenger trains, I had no doubt in my mind that the right powering of trains was the fastest way forward to increase not only the throughput but also the speeds. That could easily happen by employing multiple locos (two) at the head of the train, be it freight or passenger. After a protracted debate, it was settled that we needed to employ 2 HP per tonne of trailing load if we were to run freight trains at 100 kmph on a tangent track. Similarly, 8–10 HP per tonne was needed to run passenger trains at 130 kmph.

The Mobility Directorate in the Railway Board had done a good job by issuing these directives, which I had been pursuing for more than a decade. The problem now was shortage of locos.

'Mission Electrification', to electrify 100 per cent of Railways track, had already been declared as the stated policy of the Government of India. The focus was to reduce dependence on imported fossil fuel.

Indian Railways consumes about 2.5 billion litres of diesel oil (about 1.5 per cent of the country's total diesel consumption) per annum to run trains with diesel locomotives. Indian Railways similarly consumes 18 billion units of electricity per year (1.2 per cent of the country's electricity consumption) to run trains with electric locos. Diesel fuel costs around ₹22,000 crore annually while cost of electricity is around ₹10,000 crore annually (in 2020). The share of traffic on electric traction is close to 66 per cent of the total freight and passenger traffic. The economics are clearly in favour of electric traction.

In this situation, it was only natural that the production of electric locos was required to be substantially ramped up to match not only the pace of electrification, but also to improve the speed of trains in Indian Railways.

DLW, which had been manufacturing diesel locomotives since inception, was therefore required to switch over the manufacture from diesel to electric locos. Politically, it was a difficult decision.

The political environment may not have allowed any experiment with DLW. I suggested to the CRB that unless this initiative was taken, Railways interest might not be well served. As Chairman, he was to balance between industrial relations on the one hand and the need of the hour on the other.

I kept persuading the CRB that manufacture of electric locos at DLW would be seen as a progressive step by the labour unions and the staff would also feel motivated by being re-skilled in electric loco technology. Manufacture of electric locos would also give the staff a new and modern product that would become their mainstay for a long time to come. Progressive electrification of railway tracks would keep DLW relevant for eternity. Diesel traction was in any case a sunset technology.

The CRB finally agreed to permit the manufacture of two electric locos at DLW in 2016-17, with a clear understanding that I would do everything possible to have a smooth transition for the manufacture of these two electric locomotives, ensuring that there was no industrial unrest. I assured him of my full support. After all, this was my brainchild.

No doubt, it was a challenge as Varanasi was the Prime Minister's constituency. No sooner were the orders issued for manufacture of two electric locos at DLW, than I went to CLW to tie up and ensure that two completely knocked down loco kits were handed over in all respects to DLW. Support of competent staff and supervisors from CLW was also required. They would guide the DLW staff to assemble these kits. DLW did not have any facility to test the locomotive at 25 KV as there was no railway electrification there. It was, therefore, decided to test the electric locos at the Mughalsarai Electric Shed.

I remember that initially electric locos manufactured by CLW also used to be tested at Asansol loco shed, as CLW also did not have 25 KV power supply for some time.

The Unions at CLW were quite agitated as they feared that the transfer of two loco kits could mean a reduction in manufacture of electric locos progressively, in future, at CLW. I had a long discussion with the Chief Electrical Engineer CLW, and the staff wherein I assured the staff that the requirement of locos for Railways was such that even if both the Production Units (CLW, DLW) manufactured electric locos to their full capacity, it would not be possible to meet the requirement of electric locos of Railways for over 6-8 years.

Another problem highlighted at CLW was that the production programme was not being issued in time by the Railway Board. The Production Units were conveyed the annual production plan target as late as in December, while the financial year started in April. This was a genuine problem.

I promised that the production plan for three financial years would be conveyed within the next two weeks. This would mitigate the problems faced by the Production Unit during procurement. This would also put to rest the apprehension of reduced annual production targets for CLW. Within a week, I ensured that the production programmes were conveyed to CLW.

The CRB directed me to visit CLW every fortnight. During my next visit, it was settled that two locomotive shells and a complete kit for its manufacture would be transported without any difficulty as the staff was satisfied about the production targets of CLW. The team responsible for manufacture at DLW also visited CLW for training. It took about three months to assemble and test the first electric locomotive and turn out the same in January 2017. The second locomotive was also turned out in quick succession, in March 2017. Suneet Sharma was the Principal Chief Mechanical Engineer at DLW. He was very passionate about doing something new. Here was an opportunity to produce a new locomotive. He became the champion of this cause.

There was in general a good feeling at DLW as the manufacture of electric locos gave a new product to DLW, something that would survive for decades to come.

In April 2017, it was decided that DLW should manufacture 25 locomotives in 2017-18 and all the material would be procured and arranged by CLW. Simultaneously, it was also decided that from 2018-19, the material would be procured by DLW and the number of locos to be produced would also be ramped up to 75.

This was the beginning of a new era for DLW. The factory manufacturing diesel locos since its beginning in the 1960s was progressively migrating to manufacture a new product. Keeping in view the overall circumstances, DLW was fully empowered to procure material and manufacture electric locos. The plan for electrification of DLW at 25 KV was also finalised. It ensured hassle free working at DLW.

With the pace of electrification and decision to electrify 100 per cent of the railway track, it was decided that from 2019-20 onwards no diesel locomotive would be manufactured at DLW, Varanasi.

If the decision to start manufacturing electric locos had not been taken in 2016, we would have suffered a serious shortage of electric locos. In three years, from 2016 to 2019, the systems at DLW had been fully stabilised to manufacture electric locos.

Aptly enough, the name of Diesel Loco Works, Varanasi was changed to Banaras Loco Works (BLW), Varanasi.

While I was sure that Railways required massive inputs in terms of electric locos with 100 per cent electrification, I was certain that the maintenance of these locos had to be done in the existing diesel sheds, since the business of diesel traction would slowly reduce.

The manpower engaged in the operation and maintenance of diesel locos needed to be re-skilled and productively employed for the maintenance of electric locos. The departmental fight between the two disciplines – electric and diesel – had to be given a burial.

I, therefore, requested Vivek Kumar, Executive Director Mechanical Engineering (EDME) Diesel Traction, to draft a policy in the overall interest of the Railways, to which I would simply agree.

It took almost two months for Vivek Kumar to prepare a draft policy indicating his desire to retain the mechanical officers in-charge of the diesel sheds and bringing in a junior scale electrical officer to assist them to maintain electric locos.

I agreed to the first draft and signed the letter that was to be issued jointly with EDME (Traction). He was taken by surprise as I made no changes in the draft policy he had prepared. This was subsequently approved by Member Traction, Member Rolling Stock and the Chairman Railway Board. This was conveyed to the Zonal Railways.

The General Manager of North Eastern Railway was about to superannuate. Electrification of North Eastern Railway, connecting Lucknow to Barabanki via Zafarabad, Varanasi, was in full swing and the North Eastern Railway management wanted Gonda Diesel Shed to home electric locos.

I asked Ajay Goswami, my Director (Rolling Stock), to visit Gonda. After he reached there, he rang me up and informed me about the festivities planned for the homing of electric locos and inauguration of the facility by the GM during his visit to Gonda before superannuation.

My concern for the safety of manpower engaged in maintenance of electric loco was known to the Director (Rolling Stock). After ascertaining that this aspect would be duly taken care of, he requested me to allow the transfer of ten electric locos from Kanpur Shed to Gonda Shed.

This was done on the same day while the Director (Rolling Stock) was present at the Gonda Shed. Everyone in the management of the Gonda Shed was overwhelmed with this decision. Ten more locos were allotted to Gonda Shed later. The holding of the Shed had reached to about 40. This was the beginning of the maintenance of electric locos in diesel sheds, with suitable safety measures.

Subsequently, I visited Barauni Diesel Shed which was an upcoming shed.

Barauni is an industrial town situated on the bank of river Ganges in the Indian state of Bihar. It has a population of about 72,000. It has a big oil refinery of Indian Oil, set up in collaboration with the Soviet Union in 1969 at a cost of ₹50 crore. It is 125 km from Patna.

I was sure that this diesel shed should maintain electric and diesel locos both, right from inception. GM, ECR was accordingly advised to plan some additional works to enable proper upkeep of electric locos there. A separate project of setting up of Electric Loco Shed at Barauni was hence dropped.

As of 2020, 12 diesel sheds are maintaining electric locos. This has helped Railways in two ways – one, as the electrification progresses, around 44 diesel sheds will eventually get converted into electric sheds, utilising the same manpower after proper training of staff, and two, the infrastructure that would have been rendered surplus because of phasing out of diesel locos would be gainfully utilised for the maintenance of electric locos.

I had been thinking about the maintenance of electric locos in diesel sheds ever since I was DRM at Dhanbad. In fact, I had mooted a proposal in 2014-15 to allow the Patratu Diesel Shed to maintain electric locos. Naveen Tandon and Hemant Kumar, the two Members of Railway Board looking after electrical and mechanical disciplines respectively, had not agreed to it. It was only after I, without questions, agreed to Vivek Kumar's proposal to let the mechanical officers look after electric locos, did they agree.

The two initiatives – manufacture of electric locos in DLW and maintenance of electric locos in diesel sheds, will go a long way in bringing synergy between the electrical and mechanical departments, and will result in gainful utilisation of the huge assets of DLW and the 44 diesel sheds.

Stakeholder Mismanagement: Some Lessons from Train Sets

Mumbai, earlier known as Bombay (until 1995), is the capital of the Indian state of Maharashtra. It is the second most populous city after Delhi, in India. Mumbai is home to three UNESCO World Heritage Sites – the Elephanta Caves, Chhatrapati Shivaji Maharaj Terminus and ensembles of Victoria and Art Deco buildings. Art Deco is a style of visual arts, architecture and design that first appeared in France before World War I. Mumbai is the financial capital of India and generates about 6 per cent of India's total GDP.

EMUs were first introduced in India long ago, on February 3, 1925, in Mumbai, between Victoria Terminus and Kurla. These EMUs were imported from Cammell-Laird and Uerdingenwagonfabrik, Germany. A similar service was started between Churchgate and Borivali on January 5, 1928. The coaches of the EMUs are called Trailer Coaches and Motor Coaches. Trailer Coaches do not have motors while Motor Coaches, as the name suggests, have motors on their axles. About 2,400 train services are run daily in Mumbai area carrying about 7.5 million commuters every day over the 390 km suburban rail network (as in early 2020).

Mumbai suburban railway was built by British East India Company. The first train had run over 34 km between Bori Bunder (now Chhatrapati Shivaji Maharaj Terminus) and Thane on April 16, 1853, at 3.35 p.m. It was a 14-coach train carrying 400 passengers and took 1.25 hours with a halt at Sion to refill the train's water tanks. Three steam locomotives hauled this train – they were named Sahib, Sindh and Sultan. This was the Great Indian Peninsular Railway (GIPR) on broad gauge, that is, 1,676 mm (5 ft 6 inches).

EMU trains operated on 1,500 volt Direct Current (DC) traction. The entire Mumbai rail network got converted from 1,500 volt DC to 25 KV 50 Hz AC traction in 2016. EMU trains, unlike loco hauled trains, have distributed power throughout the length of the train; there is no train engine or locomotive. The coaches have motors provided on their axles, which drive them. These trains do not require detachment and reversal of locomotive when the direction of the train is changed. The amount of horsepower in the train may be 33 per cent, 50 per cent, 66 per cent or even 100 per cent, depending on the type of service and the speed that we want to attain – which essentially means that a third, half, two-third or all the coaches can have motors underneath. EMUs are generally utilised in suburban areas as the coaches of these trains have wider body of 3,360 mm (11 feet) which enables them to carry more people.

EMUs which work on the main line have a slightly narrower coach body of 3,250 mm (10 feet 8 inches) and are therefore called Mainline Electrical Multiple Units (MEMU).

Train Sets are nothing but EMUs that work on main line. Indian Railways has been debating about the induction of Train Sets on main line for more than a decade but the difference of opinions between the officers of the two modes of traction– Electric and Diesel – controlled by two different Members at the apex level of the Railway Board has led to slow proliferation of Train Sets in India.

All the metro systems of the world have EMUs working at different voltage levels. They have a higher acceleration and deceleration. A normal train which is hauled by a locomotive may have an acceleration between 0.25 to 0.35 m/s^2, but the EMU, MEMU and Train Sets have an acceleration ranging between 0.45 to 1.0 m/s^2.

In order to improve decision making, Ministry of Railways decided to bring electric and diesel locomotives under one Member, re-designated as Member Traction and all coaches – including EMU, MEMU and Train Sets and Wagons – under another Member, re-designated as Member Rolling Stock. This rationalisation was done in August 2016. This paved the way for the manufacture of the first Train Set, called Train-18 (Vande Bharat) by Integral Coach Factory (ICF) which entered into commercial operation in February 2019. It was inaugurated by the Prime Minister of India. This could not have been even imagined prior to rationalisation of the two modes of traction.

But this led to claims and counter claims. Earlier, electrical engineers supported Train Sets and opposed loco hauled trains for the right reasons, and mechanical engineers opposed them. In the new scenario, mechanical engineers began supporting Train Sets and electrical engineers started opposing them. This is not the most professional behaviour.

Before the Rail Budget 2015-16 was to be presented to the Indian Parliament, I persuaded A.K. Mital, CRB, to include some reasonable quantities of Train Set coaches for procurement, following the Madhepura model. This would benefit the country and modernise rail operations. A sum of ₹2,800 crore was sanctioned for the induction of 15 Train Sets comprising 315 coaches for running Rajdhani and Shatabdi type of services, with sitting and sleeping accommodation.

As Executive Director (Development) Railway Board, I handled this project right from shortlisting of bidders against Request for Qualification (RFQ) to the receipt of financial bids at Request for Proposal (RFP) stage, following International Competitive Bidding (ICB).

The world's best five companies were shortlisted at the RFQ stage in 2015: Bombardier-CAF, Alstom-BEML, Siemens, Hitachi-Ansaldo and Kawasaki Heavy Industry-Toshiba-BHEL.

The whole project was structured on the lines of Madhepura model to ensure Make-in-India, with comprehensive maintenance to ensure optimal life cycle cost (LCC).

None of the five bidders submitted the financial bids against the RFP. The project finally failed in November 2015. This was a setback. The bidders demanded larger quantities of these Train Set coaches (close to 750-1,000) instead of 315 to make their investment remunerative. I repeatedly tried to get the quantities enhanced, but it could not be done.

It was then decided to allow Integral Coach Factory (ICF) Chennai to manufacture two electric Train Sets to showcase the capabilities of the Production Units and bring an end to the controversy raging between the two disciplines of Railways as to which technology was superior, Train Set or locomotive hauled trains.

The first Vande Express (Train-18) that started running from February 2019 between Delhi and Varanasi was the culmination of the rationalisation of the traction discipline. It allowed the new service to be experienced by the people of this country, something which one of the disciplines in the Railways was not allowing to happen.

The second Vande Express train was introduced between Delhi and Vaishno Devi on October 3, 2019, reducing journey time to 8 hours from the existing 12 hours (reduction by 33 per cent).

Vaishno Devi Temple is a holy shrine of Shri Mata Vaishno Devi, at a height of 5,200 ft. It is 12 km from Shri Mata Vaishno Devi Katra railway station in the state of Jammu Kashmir and is 577 km from Delhi. This station is located on the Jammu-Udhampur-Srinagar-Baramulla Railway Link.

The shrine cave was discovered many centuries ago but its foundation was laid by Maharaja Gulab Singh in 1846. Maharaja Gulab Singh was the first Maharaja of the princely state of Jammu and Kashmir, the second-largest princely state in British India.

All the documentation was handed over to Sushil Vavre, Chief Electrical Engineer ICF, to facilitate fast-tracking of the Train Set project. I was satisfied that the Train Set had brought down the journey time due to better acceleration and deceleration. It received public applause. Delhi to Kanpur (444 km) can be covered in 4 hours, which regular Shatabdi Express with LHB (Linke Hofmann Busch) coaches and WAP 7 loco takes 4.30 hours.

As I reflect on what happened, I find that despite the elapse of more than a year between the inauguration of the first train by the Prime Minister and now (middle of 2021), regular production of T-18 Train Sets has not commenced as yet at ICF Chennai in earnest. The regular production of a new variant of T-18 has started at ICF Chennai now (October 2021), and the first prototype train is expected to be delivered in April/May 2022. This is due to the typical lack of alignment between different disciplines of the organisation., There is a crying need either to unify different services or to find an amicable alternative in order to bring synergy for the greater good of the Railways.

Unless there is a change in mindsets across the board, any new initiative will see a similar response and behaviour. We will lose precious time in resolving disputes. It is all the more important we have the right people for the right job; once alignment is assured, silos will evaporate; fight for fiefdom will probably come to an end.

But this is easier said than done. Let the merit of officers take precedence over seniority, at least for top 100 posts of DRMs, GMs and beyond, in the Board.

25

Pygmalion at Play: Empowering People – A Patiala Story

Patiala State was established in 1763 by Ala Singh, the first Maharaja of the princely state of Patiala. It is situated in the Indian state of Punjab. The city of Patiala was designed and developed according to a plan akin to temple architecture. The city is home to Netaji Subhas National Institute of Sports (NIS), Asia's largest Sports Institute, founded in 1961.

It was May 2017. I was looking after two assignments – Advisor (Rolling Stock) and Advisor (Transformation) Railway Board. The policy of right powering to enhance the average speed of freight trains in the Railways had already been issued in August 2016. This required protracted convincing and interaction with Naveen Shukla, head of Mobility Directorate in the Railway Board.

This policy necessitated provision of 12,000 HP locomotives (2 x 6,000 HP) for running coal loaded freight trains weighing 6,000 tonnes (two HP per tonne of train load).

A zero-based planning exercise was done on South Eastern, South East Central, South Central and East Coast Railway. A minimum of 350 additional locos requirement emerged in this circuit for running freight trains with 2 HP per tonne to improve the average speeds of freight trains. This would then improve the line capacity.

It also meant that empty rakes needed to be run with multi (two locos) freight locos. Naturally, the loco production had to be enhanced. Simultaneously, Mission Electrification – to electrify 100 per cent rail track – became one of the priorities of the Government of India to ensure import substitution of diesel oil.

Ghanshyam Singh, Member Railway Board, asked me to visit Diesel Modernisation Works (DMW) Patiala to explore the possibility of manufacturing electric locos at Patiala. Ajay Goswami, my Director looking after Rolling Stock, and I went to Ambala by the morning

Shatabdi Express. Someone had come from DMW to Ambala to escort us to Patiala by road. It is a 55 km journey and took around one hour. I was conducted around the workshop by senior officers.

DMW was established in 1981 to extend the life of diesel locomotives of the Railways. It was an awesome feeling, as I had not seen this beautiful place earlier. The work culture was superb. The place was neat and clean. I flagged off one recently rehabilitated diesel locomotive. The wheel repair section was extremely well maintained. The Roller bearing section was spick-and-span. The shop was rendering excellent service to diesel sheds.

After the shop visit, I met all the senior officers in the conference room. The bonhomie between executive, finance and stores officers was unbelievable. That must be the reason for the excellent work culture.

I asked the officers whether they could repair and even manufacture an electric locomotive there. The response was an instant 'Yes'. Although, they were sceptical about the fate of diesel locos, there was a desire to do well.

I was more than sure that a new product – the electric loco – could be given to this workshop and they would do their best to keep their pride in place.

After visiting DMW, I suggested that electric locos could be repaired and manufactured there. Regular manufacture of electric locos started at DMW Patiala in 2020. DMW is manufacturing about 60 electric locos per annum (2020-21). My assessment had been right. It is a great feeling to see things materialising. Not an easy task!

Change Architecture I: Inside-Out Transformation – An Indian Story

At the initiative of the Prime Minister Shri Narendra Modi, an unprecedented mega exercise involving the entire organisation took place. The Ministry of Railways organised *Rail Vikas Shivir* (conclave) at Suraj Kund, near New Delhi, from November 18 to 20, 2016. The purpose was to generate innovative yet practical ideas across most critical areas of railway operations. This was the first such event in the 163-year history of Railways. Brainstorming exercises with multi-stage and multi-dimensional dialogues took place, involving all Railways employees, from Gangman to Chairman, cutting across hierarchy. The Prime Minister himself inaugurated the Shivir, visited Suraj Kund and met the participants on November 20, 2016. It was very motivating and thought provoking.

Arrangements for our stay were made at hotel Park Plaza, Faridabad. I shared a room with V.K. Agrawal, Additional Member Electrical. He was a year senior to me. I had taken over from him at Tundla and at Kanpur. We were good friends, so we willingly stayed together for two nights and three days.

Without any regard to hierarchy, everyone was accommodated in some hotel or the other. Participation was by invitation. Getting an invitation as a delegate or as a presenter was an honour. I happily participated as a delegate. Even if you belonged to Delhi, you were not allowed to go back home at the end of the day. Around 600 people participated. All participants ate, stayed and thought together. For two long days, presentations were made to various expert committees. There was an exhibition showcasing what should be our dream journey. The PM has special love and affection for Railways because his childhood days were spent around Railways.

As soon as we checked into the hotel, a welcome kit was given, which had a yoga mat, a cotton shirt, a coffee mug and a coir bag.

Change Architecture I: Inside-Out Transformation

Anticipated fervour for this Shivir had started two months earlier. The Prime Minister had a desire that Railways hold a *Chintan Shivir* (brainstorming conclave) and identify areas that could trigger Railways to become:

The engine for India's economic growth and development by being safe, financially viable, environmentally friendly and caring for its customers and employees.

More than 100,000 ideas got generated at various mini-Shivirs that were organised in the field by DRMs and GMs. Of these, 600 ideas were shortlisted and presented before an Expert Committee. Ideas were broadly categorised under following eight themes:

1. Zero Fatality – Indian Railways will provide safe travel by achieving a Near Zero Fatality performance.
2. Infrastructure Upgrade – Indian Railways aspires to add 1.5 per cent to India's GDP by building infrastructure to support 40 per cent modal freight share of India's freight basket.
3. Preferred Freight Carrier – Indian Railways will develop integrated business solutions to capture new traffic and become the freight carrier of choice.
4. Passenger Experience – Indian Railways will provide temperature-controlled services for long distance travel to all segments of passengers in India. Indian Railways shall aspire to become the epitome of Swachh Bharat.
5. Cost Focus – Indian Railways will value-engineer its processes to ensure transparency, cost effectiveness and expeditious decision making.
6. Organisation Culture – Indian Railways will imbibe a culture which fosters team work, innovation, accountability and encourages proactive initiative taking.
7. Leveraging Technology – Indian Railways is committed to the latest technology, employee training and infrastructure upgrade on stations and trains to increase customer satisfaction.
8. Sustainability – Indian Railways will take a proactive approach to ensure sustainability, especially environmental, in its pursuits.

After the Shivir, a plan of action was drawn and around 100 strategic initiatives were identified to be taken forward in mission mode.

Unfortunately, a major rail accident happened on Jhansi Division on November 20, 2016. The Indore–Patna Express had derailed at 3 a.m. on November 20. Fourteen coaches had derailed and 152 people died. Such a major accident on the final day of the Shivir gravely dampened everyone's mood.

Another major accident took place in December 2016. Sealdah–Ajmer Express derailed near Kanpur wherein 15 coaches derailed but there was no casualty; 6 people had grievous injuries and 62 simple injuries. The spate of accidents and derailments diverted the attention of the top decision making in the Railway Board.

Sometime in January 2017, the PM asked the Railway Minister if any action had been taken on any of the Shivir's recommendations. The Shivir was an ideation exercise, but concrete plans ought to be drawn, not only for necessary approvals and sanction but also for their execution.

As a follow up, it was decided on January 10, 2017 to set up a Transformation Cell. I was appointed to head the multi-disciplinary Cell under the Chairman, comprising Executive Directors from all the eight Services of Indian Railways.

On January 10, I was at Secunderabad. I had planned to visit Vijayawada Training School, the next day. On the evening of January 10, Member Electrical informed me that I had been transferred from Advisor Rolling Stock to Advisor Transformation. I had just completed a year as Advisor Rolling Stock. I had plans to bring about many changes in maintenance philosophy of Rolling Stock, such as maintenance of electric locos in diesel sheds and manufacture of electric locos in DLW Varanasi. These initiatives had just been taken but were yet to stabilise. The maintenance of any loco anywhere in the Railways was yet to get acceptance. I didn't know what exactly the expectations from the Transformation Cell were. I had not been intimately associated with Rail Vikas Shivir. These thoughts crossed my mind.

The next day, I was at Training School, Vijayawada. I had to address many Loco Pilots and Loco Inspectors on safety as the safety environment was scary.

Hanish Yadav, Officer on Special Duty (OSD) to the Minister called, congratulated me and requested me to meet him as soon as I was back. On arrival, I met the Chairman. Neither of us had any idea as to where to begin, where to go and how to navigate the transformation journey. I also met Hanish and told him that the Transformation Cell needed space and a good office environment in the Rail Bhavan only, otherwise the initiative would remain stillborn.

The clear mandate, however, was to set up a very frugal office. The place for setting up the office was to be identified. The Chairman told me to have one floor in the DFCCIL building at Pragati Maidan. I countered him saying that even if the whole building was allocated for this purpose, the Transformation Office could not be set up there. He was taken by surprise.

The optics of sitting far away from the Railway Board would not allow even the germination of the Transformation Cell. I was forthright that the new Transformation Cell had to be established in the Rail Bhavan, in the proximity of the Board Members. I was clear in my mind that the office must be modern, like a corporate office. It must look awesome. We were to create a new work culture and unless the Cell itself looked transformative, it would not be possible to enthuse officers working in the Cell to think differently. I heard sarcastic comments and scepticism about the whole initiative. We were aspiring to transform this mammoth organisation while even the senior management in Railway Board was unwilling to change, and even support such an initiative. Can the onerous task of bringing about a change be contemplated? But that was good enough reason to change.

After a week, it was almost certain that the space in Pragati Maidan would only be a stop-gap arrangement. I was asked to look for a space in Rail Bhavan. We identified a 125 square metre open space on the third floor, in front of the canteen, for constructing the office. An estimate of ₹1.2 crore was prepared and sanctioned.

It was decided to construct a prefabricated temporary office. I had seen the site office at Madhepura. It was a beautifully constructed office. Arun Arora, DRM Delhi, was requested to invite tenders and award the work. Arun was an old friend of mine. We had stayed together for two months in 1992 in Chicago during our Illinois Institute of Technology training. Since then, we had good relations. We had successfully worked together on Cadre Review in 2003. I was sure he would do his best to get this office ready early. I spoke to him. He promised to award the tender quickly.

Tenders were awarded in May and the work started in June 2017. Tushar Pandey was my Executive Director and an expert in civil engineering. He was the man who identified the design for a temporary structure and got the building ready. Both of us used to be on site every day to assess the work done and make any changes that would be needed to suit the working. Progress was slow initially but the moment the design was clear, it picked momentum.

One day we discovered that the glass chambers would only be covered up to 6 feet. Since the office staff was also supposed to work from the same place, it occurred to me that this place would become a fish market. We were getting 8 chambers for 8 officers and 18 workstations. The glass partitions were ready, but the work had to be stopped. The agency was requested to ensure full partitions right up to the roof to ensure a peaceful and serene atmosphere that would provide privacy. The whole building was air-conditioned. We got an independent conference room for meeting within the cell. I thought that this would give complete independence and empowerment to officers working here.

Spot purchase was done to procure the furniture. All my transformation officers selected the quality and the type of furniture that would suit and enthuse them. The office became ready on September 3, 2017. Credit largely went to Arun Arora, Tushar, Chandra, Jeetendra and Sanjeeb.

I continued to look after both the works – Rolling Stock and Transformation – for quite some time. But around end June, I told the Chairman that the Transformation work was likely to pick up momentum and therefore there was a need to have an independent Advisor for Rolling Stock. From June 29, I started working only for Transformation.

We identified 55 strategic initiatives. Hanish was on board. We were to develop business plans. But the senior management was not very enthused and therefore the job was quite difficult.

It was very important to legislate and notify the roles, responsibilities and the decision-making protocols to be followed by the Transformation Cell to take various initiatives forward. Since I had handled one of the biggest Make-in-India PPP projects of setting up the Loco Factory at Madhepura, I was clear about the process of decision making in Railway Board.

Accordingly, the Office Memorandum was prepared. It took many rounds of iterations to come to a common understanding within the officers of the Cell. I was sure of what I should *not* do. All the routine jobs like Right to Information (RTI), matters related to Parliament such as Parliament Questions and Parliamentary Standing Committee on Railways, were not to be handled by the Transformation Cell.

I wanted to concentrate on big change initiatives to bring a visible impact. So, the constitution of the Cell had to clearly define what was excluded from its purview. It was also needed to empower the Cell through this roles and responsibility exercise. Once the draft defining roles, responsibility and the functions was ready, I thought of having it approved by the full Board.

I requested the CRB to allocate time for a presentation by the Transformation Cell to the full Board. The presentation was made on February 21, 2017. High priority 55 initiatives and the mechanism for approval through roles, responsibilities and functions of the Cell were approved. In addition, the issue of the high cost of ₹1.2 crore for the office of the Cell was also raised by the Secretary, Railway Board. I made it clear that without this, the big initiatives may not fructify. There was a silence. The Chairman looked at me and then said, 'Go ahead.' I had by now established the way I would function and the strategic initiatives that we would focus on. A few Board Members were supportive. Change was a must. Unless the top management was fully aligned, transformation would be arduous and might even hit a dead end.

The minutes of the meeting were issued on March 9, 2017. During discussion with the full Board, I also mentioned that a Management Consultant needed to be appointed for at least six months to develop business plans and to provide other necessary support, including capacity and capability building within the Cell and support for holding Workshops in Zonal Railways to disseminate the idea of transformation for a broad-based alignment amongst the stakeholders across the Railways. The Board agreed with the proposal.

The Consultants were selected through RITES and were in place in the first week of July 2017. The construction of the office started in June. The office was ready on September 3, 2017, along with office furniture. We shifted to the new office on September 4, 2017.

By this time, we had conducted one Workshop for capability building for the officers of the Transformation Cell. There was active participation from the Minister's Cell.

We had two meetings with the Railway Minister Shri Suresh Prabhu, and two meetings with the Minister of State Railways Shri Rajen Gohen, in July and August 2017. The focus was very clear. The entire initiative was driven by the Prime Minister.

Between November 2016 and August 2017, a few major rail accidents, resulting in loss of human lives, took place and created a major upheaval. These accidents were:

- November 20, 2016, Indore–Patna Express on Jhansi Division, 152 people died.
- December 28, 2016, Sealdah–Ajmer Express on Allahabad Division, 6 grievously injured, 62 simple injuries.
- August 19, 2017, Puri–Haridwar Express on Delhi Division, 25 people died.

The accident on the Delhi Division at Khatauli was a blatant disregard for safety by the staff, and a reflection of the utter chaos in which the concerned Member Railway Board, GM, and DRM were asked to proceed on leave Such actions are few and far between.

In less than a week, A.K. Mital, CRB, also resigned. The new CRB, Ashwini Lohani, was appointed on August 24, 2017. The very same day I met Lohani and apprised him about the Cell. On August 26, Transformation Cell made its first presentation to the new Chairman.

I had known Lohani since a very long time. He used to be my next-door neighbour in Delhi. The first time I met him was when he was Director, Rail Museum, Chanakyapuri. I had handed over the first AC electric locomotive of Indian Railways christened 'Jagjivan Ram' bearing number 'WAM 1 20202' to the Rail Museum in 1996. This was the first AC locomotive of Indian Railways and had been decommissioned by me as in-charge of Kanpur Loco Shed after 39 years of service.

Lohani saw only a few slides of my visual presentation. Whatever I explained, just did not go well with him. It was a little intriguing. He said that the 55 items list was a wish list, and rightly so, as we were going for Big Bang initiatives.

There was a complete U-turn. I thought of listening to him and aligning with him. My officers were upset. I changed my course. But an agreement was reached that the 55 items that we had been pursuing may continue.

Lohani was clear and focussed on the process, structure and cultural reforms as the top priority. He also inspected the new Cell which had come up and commented, 'Modern office with a motivating environment and good ambience'.

We made a course-correction in our strategy for the transformation journey. It was no doubt a difficult task, as we had just started and hardly been able to stabilise. Even to reach this stage, we had worked hard to have the initiatives approved at the highest level.

On September 16, I was in office. It was a Saturday. I was suddenly called by Lohani to attend a video conference that he was having with the General Managers. All the General Managers were vehemently demanding substantial delegation of powers.

Every GM was saying, '*A lot of time is getting wasted in pushing files from Division to Zone and to Railway Board with usual Finance objections without tangible gains.*'

The GMs were feeling helpless. Negativity was all encompassing due to the number of train accidents. All powers were concentrated in the Board.

The GMs were advised to send their proposals to me within a week's time. By the end of the day itself, a formal letter was issued to all GMs in this regard. It sent a very positive message – we meant business.

As luck would have it, there was yet another major tragedy at Elphinstone Road bridge in Mumbai on September 29, 2017, in which 29 persons died. The incident happened due to stampede on the foot overbridge which connected Parel Station on Central Railway to Elphinstone Road Station on Western Railway. Four trains had arrived simultaneously at the station, and it had been raining. This was the morning rush hour.

Elphinstone Road Station was named after Lord Elphinstone, the Governor General of Bombay from 1853 to 1860. The name of the station was changed to Prabhadevi on December 16, 2016.

Railways came under severe criticism since the replacement bridge sanctioned a year earlier was nowhere in sight due to procedural delays.

Shri Piyush Goyal had taken over as Minister on September 5, 2018. The day following the Elphinstone Road bridge tragedy, the Minister held a Safety Review Meeting with both the GMs of Central Railway and Western Railway along with the Chairman and other Board Members. The situation was really grave.

A plethora of requests for delegation of powers and empowerment were put forth before the Minister. The sense of disenchantment the senior officers had with the system of vetting and the circuitous process of approvals was loudly conveyed. **The Minister directed that all demands for delegations and empowerment must be met by October 15, 2017. So, there was a deadline.**

The Chairman told me that the exercise of delegation based on the GM's proposals must be fast tracked.

I thought of having a pan India schedule of power for DRMs and GMs from the Railway Board that would bring all Divisions and Zones on a common base to improve decision making. This had never happened in the past. No one had thought about it.

My experience as DRM about delegation of powers was quite bad. My interactions with adjoining DRMs used to reveal that all the DRMs did not have similar powers. For example, the Bilaspur Division could hire a data entry operator at ₹3,000 per month for office work from the imprest of ₹30,000 per officer, while others could not do it. Similarly, in Dhanbad Division, I could sanction work of ₹1 crore for repair to private sidings whereas Bilaspur Division had powers up to ₹10 crore. There was a world of difference. These differences were demotivating.

Earlier, Railways, especially in the eastern part of the country, had delegated limited powers to the DRMs, while western and northern parts had quite liberal delegations.

All the GMs and DRMs started responding. All the officers in the Transformation Cell were working overtime to shortlist top priority items that could be taken up in the first phase for approval by the full Board.

On October 10, I gave a shortlist of 100 items and a Model Schedule of Powers (SOP) to the CRB, for approval. The CRB was going for an inspection of Jammu station in Northern Railway. He returned on October 12. At around 8 p.m. on October 12, Rakesh Chaudhary, Director Coordination, informed me to make a presentation to the full Board at 12.00 noon the next day.

A lanky, young and energetic person, Rakesh was like a disciplined soldier of Lohani. He would do exactly what his boss wanted. He generally accompanied Lohani on tours and had a good rapport with young as well as senior officers.

I had no time to prepare, but I agreed. I conveyed the message to all my officers and told them not to worry at all. The presentation was made to the full Board by all the officers of the Transformation Cell.

The Board was proactive in considering and approving a majority of our suggestions, including a pan India Modal Schedule of Power, based on the template of South Central Railways (SCR).

The draft minutes of the Board's meeting were also prepared and handed over to the Secretary, Railway Board, that day itself. Jeetendra did this job well.

The following Monday, all the officers of the Cell were at Secunderabad to validate the proposal that had been approved in principle by the full Board, although the minutes were yet to be approved. I wanted to be sure of the desirability and practicability of delegations before the orders were issued. This was done in confidence with the active support of GM SCR.

The minutes of the Board meeting were issued on October 17. I returned to Delhi on October 18. Everyone expected to have the final delegation of power issued with respect to around 80 items approved by full Board. A few items that were in this list of 80 were:

- Vehicle to all officers and supervisors to improve mobility.
- For safety, purchase of items of value up to ₹10 lakh, no Finance vetting.
- Software development permitted at Division level.
- Consultancy contracts permitted at Division level.
- Advance payment for medical treatment up to ₹5 lakh at Division level.
- Funds for training enhanced to ₹40,000 at Divisional level and ₹50,000 at Zonal level, per employee per occasion.
- Full powers to Division for repair through OEMs.

Approval of the CRB was obtained on file at 2 p.m. on October 18. The exercise of finalising the letter was completed by 8 p.m. by

Jeetendra. This day was very crucial as the next day was Deepavali, a major festival in India.

The very first copy of the letter was given to Lohani by me. He had no time to even read it. He put it up on GMs and DRMs WhatsApp groups on October 18, 2017.

The response from GMs and DRMs was simply amazing. These were a 'Deepavali of delegations' was the reaction from the officers. No one had ever imagined that it could happen so soon. The CRB called me at around 10 p.m. and conveyed his thanks as people were overjoyed after the issue of enhanced delegations.

The joy was, however, short-lived. The Financial Commissioner (FC) called me at around 11.15 p.m. the same day, and asked me to keep the letter in abeyance, till such time it was re-examined on Monday. He told me that some of the Financial Advisors and Chief Accounts Officers had given him negative feedback. It was a complete anti-climax for me, but I did not share anything with Lohani. I thought it would be better to settle the issue after Deepavali. After all, Deepavali was a big festival.

The next day was Deepavali.

On Deepavali day, at 8 a.m., the FC again called me and asked me to issue a letter withholding the implementation of the delegations. Every time the FC spoke to me, he had a very gentle tone and tenor. He was almost persuading me to do something that would convey 'a hold on everything'.

After a little while Sanjeeb, my Executive Director (Accounts), informed me that the Additional Member Finance had asked him to open the office and issue a letter jointly with Jeetendra, withdrawing the delegation.

Sanjeeb was a very cool and well-read person. He had already done his LLB and was doing MBA from the Faculty of Management Studies (FMS), Delhi. I had an agreement with him in which he would be given adequate support to pursue his MBA. Jeetendra, a sober, energetic and self-motivated person, was not aware of all this. I never wanted to disturb him. He was my main pillar of strength.

Additional Member Finance (AMF) was known to me for more than 25 years. He was a very knowledgeable finance officer. He was a soft spoken and sincere human being. I was not able to understand why such a crisis was getting orchestrated, that too by AMF and FC. Both these officers were well-meaning and had very good relations with me.

I guess some of the finance officers in the field wanted a showdown and convey that they had got everything struck down even on a holiday. It was a fight for fiefdom.

At 9.15 a.m., I called up Lohani and requested for an urgent meeting with him, to which he readily agreed. I met him at 9.45 a.m. on the day of Deepavali and explained him the sequence of events. This was a decisive moment.

I told the CRB that if the letter was withdrawn, the Transformation Cell must be closed. He thought over it. He was forthright and told FC that the letter shall not be withdrawn. By 10.30 a.m., the matter was put to rest. I conveyed the same to AMF. Sanjeeb was also briefed. He was very happy. No one else in the Cell knew anything.

This was the start of a real journey of transformation as Finance was asked by the CRB to work in close coordination with the executives to achieve the overall goals of the organisation.

The following week, the environment was full of apprehensions. The Finance wing was very unhappy with me. It was subsequently decided that except for three items – sanction of laptop at ₹1 lakh, spot purchase of material and full powers to GMs for Consultancy contract – nothing else would be changed. This was approved by CRB.

A week later, the Modal Schedule of Power was also issued, on September 26, 2017. This replaced 27 such schedules of power in place in the different Zonal Railways and Production Units.

I then met both AMF and FC separately to remove any misunderstandings, if any, they might have. The environment improved. They had no grudges left. Three items had been reversed.

The Modal Schedule of Power brought all DRMs, GMs and SAG and HAG officers at par across Indian Railways in one go. It gave me a big sense of satisfaction. It was a major initiative taken for the first time in the history of Railways. This changed the way Railways had been working for decades.

The journey of the Transformation Cell continued. We consciously decided to consider any and every proposal emanating from a Branch Officer, DRM or any other senior officer of the Railways, even if it was not approved by the GM. The only condition was that the proposal should be sound.

We did not look at the hierarchy as otherwise it would not have been possible to source a large number of ideas in a short time and grant approval as the job at hand was simply mammoth. There were occasions when the CRB phoned me from the field and expected me to issue the orders the same day. Approval used to be accorded by the CRB on WhatsApp, and orders issued the same day. There was utmost trust. He would approve on file the following day.

With the active support of Board Members, especially Financial Commissioner, Director General (Store) and Member Engineering, many delegations were made to the field units, helping them in a big way. The idea was that the officers must have complete autonomy in the areas of their responsibilities with reduced inter-dependencies in order to ultimately improve delivery.

It was a conscious decision that the levels of decision making must be brought down substantially and a majority of the powers vested in the Board must go to Zones and those vested in the Zones must be delegated to the Divisions. In fact, many committees of the Railways had been suggesting enhanced delegation of powers to the field to improve decision making and improving service delivery. But this had not happened.

Now we had the mechanism of a Transformation Cell. The Chairman was at the forefront of change. This was reinforced with the strong political will of the Railway Minister Shri Piyush Goyal. There was a big risk of accidents and subsequent perceptible public anger. If we had not improved and changed then, maybe we would have reached a point of no return.

The pace of actions taken by the Transformation Cell could be adjudged by a simple fact that one policy letter regarding the reform either empowering the field units or simplifying the decision making process, was issued every second or third day. This was conveyed to me by one of the officers of SCR while we were deliberating the extent of further delegations to the field officers.

It was also a conscious call to simplify the process of registering a vigilance case to mitigate its fear perception. It was mandated that a vigilance case could not be registered unless the vigilance angle had been endorsed by the Principal Head of Department (PHOD) concerned. This came as a big relief to the officers who genuinely wanted to take proactive action and go beyond the rule book to ensure that work was done.

There was no department which had not been touched, to the extent it was required, for empowerment and delegation, be it Railway Protection Force, Establishment, Commercial, Store, Works, Services, Medical, Mechanical, Revenue Earning or any other. The only guiding principle we followed was not to breach the General Financial Rules, and we used to take the FC on board every time.

Every action was taken after due diligence as the Cell had representation from all the disciplines, except Medical and RPF. This energised the field units in an unprecedented manner.

The DRMs and GMs had no blocks/ impedance to produce results and therefore improve safety and service delivery.

Since all the policy letters were issued with the approval of the FC and CRB, the finance officers in the field had very little to raise any objection. After all, this was done to improve the rail operations and serve our valued customers better than before.

We issued more than 260 policy letters, including a revised Model Schedule of Powers (second time in July 2018). A compendium of instructions containing all the policy letters was also issued in December 2018. Everything was put in public domain. Even a person from the media could go to the Transformation Cell website and download any policy letter. That was the way we worked. This was to enhance credibility and for faster and wider dissemination.

While the process of simplification of rules was in progress, the Consultants were working on preparing business plans for the 55 identified initiatives.

Six workshops were held to disseminate the transformation agenda in different Zones with the assistance of AT Kearney, covering various aspects of leadership, alignment and the transformation which Railways had embarked upon. I went to the Zones to address large numbers of officers and get their feedback.

At the instance of the Minister, *Sampark, Samanvay, Samvaad* (contact, coordinate, converse) was also organised on December 16, 2017 inviting all GMs and PHODs to identify key strategic initiatives that could become a part of the transformation journey to improve delivery. This was a Town Hall engagement. All participants were under one roof and discussed freely. The major policy decisions taken collectively were:

- Right powering of freight and coaching trains to improve average speeds.
- Point-of-sale (POS) machines for Travelling Ticket Examiners.
- Rate contracts for coaches and locomotive items by Production Units.
- Reduced negative list of powers of GMs.
- Introducing dynamic pricing.
- Improvements in hospitals and railway colonies.
- Improved project monitoring to reduce cost and time over-run.

The Minister addressed DRMs and GMs on many occasions to drive reforms and change. Many initiatives allocated to the Cell by the Minister on his Dashboard were also completed during this period. Consequently, a few projects were sanctioned in the Budget 2018-19. The most important were:

- Track machines for maintenance for ₹6,000 crore.
- Simulators for drivers for ₹350 crore.
- Decision Support System for Crew Booking for ₹25 crore.

During the course of 18 months, I had the occasion to visit and address a large number of officers and supervisors in all the training schools including National Academy of Indian Railways and various Divisions and Zonal Headquarters.

I travelled almost 60,000 km during 2018, disseminating the intent behind the unprecedented empowerment and delegation which every railwayman had been yearning for a long time, and the expectations of the top management from the field. The intent was to trust the field units for delivery and let them take a quantum leap in performance. There was a need to change the mindset and reduce red-tapism in decision making, create a culture of collaboration and fearlessness in decision making at the grassroot level. These thoughts were drilled into the minds of junior officers.

While we were engaged in hardcore processes and structural reforms, we also looked at the softer side of human behaviour and organised Transformation Lecture Series inviting eminent speakers to address the officers and supervisors to motivate them. Inner Engineering and Leadership Programme at Isha Foundation, and Emotional Intelligence Workshops for all DRMs and GMs and other officers to improve overall personal well-being were organised.

Ashwani Lohani, CRB, superannuated on December 31, 2018 and V.K. Yadav, GM SCR, took over as the new CRB on January 1, 2019.

The focus shifted slightly to bringing new technology, modernising Production Units and Workshops and fast-tracking project execution, since adequate empowerment had been done.

Some of the officers who had completed their five-year tenure in the Board were transferred out – Tushar Pandey and Neeraj Sahay. The posts of Executive Directors of Signalling, Personnel and Electrical were moved to the field. Posts of Mechanical, Accounts and Stores were utilised for other jobs and even shared with other initiatives. As a matter of fact, there was no Cell in the same form that existed in January 2017. However, the journey had been even more exciting as the focus shifted to major reforms.

Quite a few proposals were still pouring in from the Zonal Units, requesting further delegation and simplification, some of which were taken up and approved, such as air-conditioning of the Relay Room at the stations to improve their reliability, pan India approval of Central Government Health Scheme (CGHS) empanelled speciality hospitals for Railways, as well as to improve healthcare, etc.

There was no change of Government after the 2019 Lok Sabha elections and we had the same Minister continuing. We tried to consolidate the gains of empowerment and delegation already effected over the previous 18 months, from October 2018 to May 2019. The pace of action with respect to empowerment reduced. The top management thought that enough had been done and we should therefore consolidate before the next wave of reform could begin.

From May 2019 onwards, with the same Bhartiya Janata Party (BJP) Government at the Centre, the *100 days agenda* became the new focus area of the Ministry of Railways, and therefore the Transformation Cell got engaged in big-ticket reforms such as:

- Opening up the rail sector for operation of private passenger trains on Indian Railways.
- Organisational reforms to bring in customer centricity.
- Focus on e-governance across the Railways.

The Transformation Cell, in consultation with Niti Aayog and Ministry of Finance, developed a business model to enable the private sector to invest and bring in state-of-the-art technology to run premium trains in the Indian Railways network. It was planned to run 100 pairs of trains, employing 150 Train Sets with an estimated private investment of about ₹30,000 crore. A Committee of Secretaries was constituted in October 2019 by the Ministry of Railways. It was headed by the CEO, Niti Aayog, with the CRB and Secretaries from the Department of Economic Affairs and Urban Development as its members. I was made the Member Secretary of the Committee. In about a year's time we were able to finalise the bidding framework, the draft Concession Agreement and obtain the necessary approvals of Public Private Partnership Appraisal Committee (PPPAC), the apex body that enabled private investment. Request for Qualification (RFQ) could therefore be brought out on July 1, 2020. This changed the market sentiment for investment despite the Covid-19 pandemic. This was slated as the biggest reform ever in the 157-year history of Railways in India. Partha Reddy, Executive Director Transformation, was the main driver of this initiative. However, there are still a lot of challenges to overcome and many unanswered questions to be resolved before this initiative can move forward.

To effect organisational reforms, a consensus was built during the *Parivartan Sangoshthi* (Seminar for Change) organised on December 7 and 8, 2019, which has been detailed in another chapter of this book. As a result, a single Indian Railway Management Service (IRMS) replacing the existing eight services and a Functional Board, was approved by the Union Cabinet on December 24, 2019. This would bring customer focus and focus on the next generation technologies for Railways along with accelerating network creation with better synergy at the apex level to take Railways away from silo working.

Concerted efforts were put in to roll out 'e-office' throughout Indian Railways with more than 50,000 users covering all Zonal Railways, Production Units, RDSO, CITs and all the Divisions. This was the result of the empowerment of RailTel. This enabled it to undertake the whole project on a turnkey basis with powers delegated to the CMD RailTel to sanction an estimate which otherwise used to be done by the Railway Board. This project had been languishing for more than five years as Centre for Railway Information Systems (CRIS) was not able to resolve the issue of technology. Introduction of technology led to reduced movement of physical files from one place to another by about 40–50 per cent. It really helped in the Covid-19 pandemic situation.

Another very exciting initiative undertaken by the Cell was the digitisation of medical cards of the employees through SCR and CRIS. The project was named Unified Medical Identity Cards (UMID). This has been proliferated very well in Indian Railways. In this system, an employee can himself or herself generate their UMID card which helps them get easy access to Railways medical facility anywhere in the Indian Railways healthcare system. It is a significant employee welfare scheme. This initiative was successfully handled by Umesh Balonda, Executive Director, Signal Transformation.

Heading the Transformation Cell of the Ministry of Railways has been a hugely satisfying journey personally and professionally to me as a railwayman.

Change Architecture II: Driving Culture of Empowerment

The very thought of transforming an organisation requires an in-depth understanding of the processes, structures and the culture of the organisation, with a clear understanding of what needs to be transformed, why it needs to be done, how it can be done and what is the timeframe available to undertake this mission. Quite a few frameworks have been advocated by top business schools. However, the recipe for a particular organisation largely depends on the context in which the mindset of transformation germinates.

Railways is a typical government organisation which must meet the twin objectives of looking after the social needs, while running as a corporate entity – a challenging cocktail of expectations.

Over a period, a plethora of rules and regulations get evolved, primarily to ensure standardisation of the protocols to handle any situation globally and uniformly. This makes the whole task of transformation still more demanding. It is also a fact that an input to the system largely governs the output; yet it is not definite that one would achieve the desired output even when the intended input is given to the system.

But without an input, output cannot be expected at all. After the culmination of Rail Vikas Shivir which was more like a Chintan Shivir, the expectations were sky high. More than a hundred thousand ideas had emerged, and it was therefore a natural expectation that at least 10 or 20 of them should find implementation in real-life situations. That was why the Transformation Cell was set up. In all the transformations that I have driven, upon reflection, I noted that the John Kotter model comes closest to how the transformations got driven. But by no means is the model adequate or fully representative.

It is important to establish high urgency across the organisation to build the momentum for change. This will ensure cooperation from all the stakeholders. Unless everyone feels concerned about the impending crisis, the momentum may be lost. More often than not, people remain in denial of a problem due to lower benchmarks of Key Performance Indicators (KPI) and this creates complacency. They remain blissfully unaware of the reality that the standards that have been set for them to achieve are low. Moreover, the path of least resistance is a natural choice to follow. People rarely like to question the status quo. In a large organisation, most of the processes are well regimented to ensure uniform understanding and implementation. Even if these processes have been laid down ages ago, no one likes to attempt or think of modifying such processes not only because of the inertia of the system but also because of the amount of efforts required to make this change happen. Larger the organisation, more the inertia. This naturally requires going the extra mile to accomplish the task. Being conservative and taking the business-as-usual approach will derail the whole initiative. The organisation needs a well aligned and dedicated group of 10–15 per cent of the staff to look at things with a new lens if the organisation is to be established afresh to achieve higher KPIs. Alongside, at least two-thirds of the management must align itself and acknowledge the sense of urgency, as without the support of the overwhelming majority, the actual transformation will not take off.

The day the Prime Minister personally came to Surajkund and addressed the participating delegates at the Rail Vikas Shivir on November 20, 2016, a major rail accident near Jhansi caused a loss of 152 lives. In yet another accident at Khatauli, near Delhi, on August 19, 2017, 25 people died due to gross human error. This led to the transfer of even the GM, Northern Railway. Chairman, Railway Board, had to resign. After some days, in September 2017, even the Minister resigned. The new Minister and the new Chairman were just about 3–4 weeks into the organisation that a stampede at the Elphinstone Road Station foot overbridge caused the death of 29 people. The poor public perception about hygiene, food, punctuality and slow pace of creating infrastructure had placed enough pressure on the railway administration for change. The threat was definitely like a tornado hitting the organisation.

Having established the urgency that the Railways cannot run in a business-as-usual mode, it was important to have credible and proven leaders with management and leadership skills to work in mission mode to drive the change. These change-leaders needed to have a team comprising individuals with no ego and no mistrust amongst them. Trust fosters teamwork. The burning desire to make the organisation perform at the highest level, transcending parochial interest, with a common shared goal that was sensible and sensitive, was desired utmost by every member of the team. Individuals, no matter how charismatic or competent, never have all the assets needed to overcome the tradition and inertia, especially in a huge organisation like the Railways. A guiding coalition is the only way forward for a change.

The Transformation Cell was constituted in Railways with individuals who were high achievers and had extensive experience not only in the Railways but also in other Ministries and PSUs. To top it all, the new Chairman Railway Board took charge of the organisation in August 2017. Ashwani Lohani had worked as Chairman and Managing Director in Air India, Indian Tourism Development Corporation and Madhya Pradesh Tourism. He had also worked as DRM Delhi. Roles, responsibilities and functions of the Transformation Cell were framed accordingly. The Cell was totally empowered. WhatsApp groups were formed with the top management and included all GMs and DRMs which helped in realtime dissemination of information and receipt of feedback with fearless reporting of the pain points in the field units to dramatically improve service delivery.

The Executive Directors of the Transformation Cell were allocated 68 Divisions in October 2018 to shorten the time between feedback from the field and decision from the Ministry of Railways. Each of the 8 Executive Directors, were allocated 6–10 Divisions (total 68 Divisions) to act as a single point of contact between the Division and the Ministry. The whole set-up thus created a perfect guiding coalition for undertaking transformation.

Setting a clear Vision – and a Strategy to achieve the Vision – is the bedrock of the journey of change. If one is not sure of what is to be achieved, there cannot be a strategy to achieve that. Setting an effective vision which is imaginable, desirable, feasible, focussed, flexible and which can be communicated in less than five minutes is what is required to be set out. Vision tells you about the future and motivates people to take the right direction and allows a coordinated action among people. It has got to be grand and mystical, but doable. The job of leadership is to set out a clear vision and strategy while the management has to draw out timelines, plans and allocate budget. Railways rightly set out its Vision:

Railways to be the engine of India's economic growth and development by being safe, financially viable, environment friendly and caring for its customers and employees.

Railways also took upon itself to be the epitome of Swachh Bharat. In order to meet this vision, we had focussed on improving the work culture with improved workplaces. The whole strategy was laid out focussing on safety as the first priority followed by development of infrastructure, induction of new technology for signalling, rolling stock, and redevelopment of railway stations.

During the journey of transformation, one must use every possible way to communicate the new vision and strategy. The guiding team must present the 'role model of behaviour' that employees will observe and emulate. The urgency for a change requires effective communication which should be simple, avoiding jargons at multiple places, exemplary behaviour, with two-way communication between the listener and the speaker. It also requires giving employees more discretion to do the right things, and throwing away the rule book so to say, empowering the front-line employees by de-bureaucratisation. All these have to be communicated through well-chosen words that would make the message more memorable.

The Transformation Cell conducted regular workshops in the Zones and Divisions and made regular visits to all the Centralised Training Institutes for communicating the paradigm of change. I travelled 60,000 km in about one year. Regular meetings were convened at the level of the Chairman even with the juniormost officers from the Divisions. CRB made sure that he was in the field every week to talk to a large number of officers and staff to communicate the overall priority of the Railways and stressing upon delivery and giving 100 per cent to the cause of the organisation. All the protocols were given a go-by – no bouquet, no one to receive at airports, etc. Meeting the frontline supervisors like Travelling Ticket Examiners, Station Masters, RPF Inspectors and a plethora of other supervisors was the new normal. Communication with the media was direct at the level of the Chairman and others including the Transformation Cell and through the Chief Public Relation Officers to create the right atmosphere and communicate the extent of efforts put in by the organisation to see that the ultimate service delivery improved, and we serve the customer with grace.

No transformation journey can be successful if we do not get rid of obstacles and change systems, structures and behaviours that undermine the change vision. The frontline officers and supervisors need to be encouraged to take risk and adopt non-traditional ideas. We must think out-of-the-box. There is a need to impart training to acquire the right skills and attitude that would make officers and supervisors more empowered. Undoubtedly, alignment among the stakeholders is to be struck. The troublesome supervisors and officers have to be confronted as otherwise they will undermine the whole initiative. It is well established that nothing dis-empowers the people more than a bad boss.

Unprecedented delegation, not seen over three decades, and empowerment was done directly by the Railway Board to DRMs, GMs and other officers, in the form of a Model Schedule of Powers (SOP) which was applicable pan India, replacing the existing 27 such SOPs. This really brought a paradigm shift across the board bringing in uniformity with enhanced financial and administrative powers.

A capacity building exercise was also done by organising various leadership workshops such as:
- Inner Engineering and Leadership by Isha Foundation, Coimbatore – a five-day programme for officers of transformation cell and others which included meditation and yoga for inner wellbeing; and
- Emotional Intelligence for DRMs and GMs at National Academy of Indian Railway – a three-day programme for sustainable success for top leadership.

Programmes like:
- *Saksham* for staff – one week on the job training for all staff; and
- *Satya Nishtha* – workshop on ethics, integrity and honesty at work, coupled with transparency became the defining enabling mechanisms to enthuse and motivate the masses and inculcate a sense of belonging to the organisation.

Principal Heads of the Departments were empowered, to be a part of decision making for registering a Vigilance case against an officer. This was a big step forward to mitigate the fear perception of Vigilance which was leading to suboptimal delivery. Quite often officers did not take decisions and hid behind the fear of Vigilance. The change removed a lot of misgivings, and any alibi that one could possibly take recourse to.

Misbehaviour of Union office bearers was dealt with an iron hand and the staff at fault was removed under section 14(2) of the Discipline and Appeal Rules wherein under certain circumstances an employee can be removed from service without even conducting an inquiry. This rule was invoked in the case of a misconduct by an office bearer at the Divisional Hospital, Lucknow, and in another case in one of the workshops in Southern Railway Chennai. This helped in navigating the transformation journey and bringing a deeper impact in a vast organisation like the Railways, in a reasonably short time.

For achieving a grand success, small successes are pertinent as the journey for a big win can only be achieved through baby steps. A small success instils confidence amongst the stakeholders involved in the transformation journey and with every passing day, we need to consolidate these small wins into a comprehensive victory. This needs to be backed up with recognition and reward to those who make these small wins possible. A major success takes a lot of time and is not possible without short and incremental successes. Without short wins, the transformation journey runs the risk of getting short closed due to scepticism. These small wins not only provide evidence that the sacrifices are worthwhile by a pat on the back of change agents, but also undermine cynics and self-serving resisters, keep bosses on board and build momentum for successful transformation. All this builds pressure, and more pressure is not all that bad.

The DRMs and General Managers were duly awarded. As Change Agents, four DRMs (for being at the forefront to suggest practical changes) and as Change Leaders, two General Managers (to implement changed delegations at a fast pace) were given awards in the Railway Week function at the level of the Minister of Railways in April 2018. The entire Board was completely committed to the direction that the Ministry had set out for the transformation, with the CRB standing rock solid in the forefront. This could be inferred from the fact that every two or three days there was one policy circular issued which was either to simplify a process or to delegate powers to give autonomy to the field.

By May 2019 almost 230 policy circulars had been issued. The Transformation Cell did not look at the hierarchy of the origin of the idea necessitating Board's approval. It took time for all the processes to be modified and structures changed over a period of 16–18 months over the entire network of the Indian Railways. Changes were visible in healthcare where the Northern Railway Central hospital underwent a sea change for the benefit of the railway employees. The Central Hospital, Northern Railway got a separate Outpatient Department with all the facilities, the Operation Theatre improved, the role of Hospital Administrator was introduced, and an independent Purchase Officer was posted for Central Hospital.

Stations wore a new look with the introduction of a Station Director with an imprest of ₹1 lakh, rest houses for officers and staff had improved, the control centres looked like corporate offices and above all the DRMs and GMs were overwhelmed by the faith and trust reposed by the top management in them.

This was the first time in the history of Railways that the delegation and empowerment was done trusting the people rather than the sense of mistrust and apprehensions that used to be the paradigm earlier whenever delegation used to be considered for empowering the frontline officers. I had completed my 37 years of service in Railways, but I had not seen such enthusiasm and galvanisation of workforce in my career. The result is visible – no casualty due to rail accidents in 2019-20, a record of sorts. As on June 30, 2020, about 260 policy change directions have been issued which are in public domain on the Transformation Cell website of the Ministry of Railways.

It is important to promote and develop people, reinvigorate the process with new projects, themes and change agents to keep the momentum of change intact. Whenever you let up before the job is done, crucial momentum is lost, and regression may follow. It is, therefore, important that a large number of people help to effect more change, involving leadership from senior management with reduced interdependencies.

Delegations and empowerment led to reduced and unwanted interdependencies and therefore, the demand for further delegations and empowerment rose, which was viewed positively. In this way the process continued. Field Units developed confidence in approaching the Board to get processes simplified further and empowerment done. Supervisors felt more enabled to perform their jobs with Special Utility Vehicles (SUVs) provided to them. As a measure of their delegation, they have even been enabled to phase out or condemn their old equipment or tools to improve their work environment, something which never existed for them earlier. There was a feel-good factor all around which was changing the public perception about Railways.

Some of these items were:

- Divisions empowered to handle contracts of ₹100 crore for cleanliness to ensure long-term contracts for better delivery; earlier such powers vested in the Minister of Railways.
- Divisions empowered to handle contracts of ₹50 crore for works to improve the pace of execution of infrastructure works; earlier such powers were vested in the Headquarters.
- Divisions empowered to handle contracts of ₹10 crore for store to improve availability of material in Sheds and Depots for better maintenance and improved safety.
- Full powers given to Divisions for earning contracts to improve Railways earning and reduce time for decision making.
- Full powers to Zones for healthcare to improve the health of employees, enhance satisfaction and save lives of people in emergencies.
- Full power to Zones for safety works to fast-track execution and sanction of safety works.
- Full powers for inter-Division and inter-Zone transfers to Divisions to improve employee satisfaction.
- Full powers for training and capacity building to Zones to enhance motivation and improve work culture.
- Every supervisor to have a SUV to enhance the mobility of staff to go to the work sites with material at short notice and therefore improve operational efficiency. This gave a major

boost, and even if we take 20-25 SUVs per Division, it meant only 1,400-1,800 vehicles for 68 Divisions.

Culture refers to norms of behaviour and shared values among a group of people. It is important to establish a link between new behaviour and organisational success. It is equally important to gauge the performance through productivity-oriented behaviour with better leadership and effective management. The organisation has to ensure development of leadership and right succession at key positions. Norms of behaviour manifest through the quick response of employees to customers, involvement of lower-level employees in decision making and managers working at least one hour post the official close on each day. The shared values are reflected through the managers taking care of customers and the employees being concerned more with quality than quantity. It also needs to be understood that human beings are emotional creatures; we ignore this reality at our own peril. We need to take care of our men in this crucial journey.

In the context of Railways, leadership development was ensured through workshops on Inner Engineering and Emotional Intelligence. There were regular vendor meets organised for commercial issues, stores procurement and for various works matters. A Sampark, Samanvay, Samvaad conclave was organised at the level of the Minister of Railways with all PHODs and General Managers to send a loud and clear message that delivery is important.

Proactive roles have been played by frontline staff – Station Masters, RPF, Travelling Ticket Examiners – in helping distressed passengers.

Resolution of employee grievances has been given a high priority.

All this has led to the evolution of a new culture of collaboration, customer care, care for the men engaged in Railways business and, above all, a craving for doing something good for the organisation.

A good rule of thumb is that 'changing the culture' comes last and not the first and depends on results, requires a lot of talk and change of key people. Decision on succession is very crucial to ensure that the journey of transformation, requiring sustained efforts for a sufficiently long period, continues.

Organisation of the 21st Century

A non-bureaucratic organisation, limited to fewer levels of leadership by the top management, and management by the lower level with minimal interdependencies is the new defining structure of the present century.

A performance information system, widely disseminated with management training at multiple levels, defines the system of this new century.

A culture of empowerment, quick decision making, and more risk tolerance with openness is what is required in the 21st century.

We removed most of the red tape, ensured sufficient empowerment and encouraged fearlessness in decision making. There was collaboration amongst internal stakeholders. We removed the hierarchy, enhanced training at various levels, introduced transparency in decision making, reduced levels of decision making, reduced levels of protocol, inculcated risk-taking behaviour and ultimately ensured that the frontline managers had complete autonomy in the area of their operation to improve the ultimate service delivery to the customers.

When the powers rested with the Railway Board, any decision would have to traverse nine levels before it was finally taken. The same decision requires just three levels now. Files going to Zone from Division reduced by 60 per cent as the majority of powers had been delegated to the Divisions. The time to finalise tenders for import of material reduced from three months to one month. Tenders in the field got finalised in as short a period as three days. No case was referred to the Railway Board for medical advances and this saved precious human lives. RPF was fully empowered with a special Schedule of Powers. *Bara Khana* (community lunch for the force, with highest to junior-most rank) for RPF, which is an annual event and organising funds for which used to be quite stressful, could now be organised by the Division with full powers with the DRM. In fact, arranging funds became a non-issue. All posts and outposts of RPF were given two- or four-wheelers, which had not existed earlier.

The baseline for transformation has been set. It needs to be pursued with vigour and sustained over 3–5 years for a new culture to settle down and become the DNA of Railways.

Clarion Call: Building Consensus for Major Reforms – Parivartan Sangoshthi

Rail Vikas Shivir (camp for rail development) was held at Surajkund, near Faridabad, from November 18 to 20, 2016. Prime Minister Shri Narendra Modi inaugurated the Shivir on November 18 and personally attended the Shivir on November 20, 2016.

Surajkund is an ancient reservoir of the 10th century, located in the Aravalli Range (mountains that run through Delhi–Haryana–Gujarat, for around 700 km) in Faridabad city. It is about 8 km from South Delhi and is an artificial lake with an amphitheatre-shaped embankment constructed in a semi-circular shape.

The purpose behind organising the Shivir was to energise the entire organisation, crowd source ideas from a cross-section of officers and the staff, brainstorm, build momentum to execute and finalise a roadmap for the modernisation of the Railways. It was the first such exercise in the 163-year-long history of the Railways. It was the culmination of a two-month long preparation wherein 76,000 officers and staff had submitted 1,10,000 ideas.

The roadmap drawn was taken forward for implementation through a fully empowered Transformation Cell, set up on January 10, 2017. The Cell was put under the direct charge of the Chairman, Railway Board. I was appointed to head the Cell. It was a multi-disciplinary group with the representation of all the eight services of the Railways.

A.K. Mital was the CRB in 2017. After his untimely departure, Ashwini Lohani took over the charge on August 24, 2017. Lohani superannuated in December 2018. A lot of reforms were undertaken during Lohani's tenure.

Vinod Yadav, whom I know since my first work assignment in 1985, took over as the new CRB on January 1, 2019. I was quite thrilled.

Vinod Yadav was a man who had always talked of building a leadership pipeline for modernising the great Indian Railways. You need the right people for the right job – something which was not happening in the organisation, and the 'date of birth' and the 'date of joining' the organisation had been the sole criteria for selection. Date of birth decided the fate of the individuals and the great Indian Railways. It was tragic.

Vinod Yadav had been the General Manager of SCR prior to his appointment as CRB. He was truly a Change Leader providing wholehearted support to my transformation initiatives that I had been driving for two years.

SCR became the Transformation Laboratory for testing any and every process reform. Yadav extended unqualified and unforgettable support. But for the proactive assistance from SCR, the transformation journey would have been quite difficult. To cite a few examples:

- The Model Schedule of Powers which replaced 27 independent schedules of powers existing in different Zonal Railways and production units was thoroughly examined by SCR before being issued for the first time by the Railway Board.
- The protective gear for trackmen who patrol the track at night got finalised on this Railway and had an immensely positive impact on the morale of the trackmen.
- Powers for procurement of material for safety category items was enhanced from ₹2 lakh to ₹10 lakh without concurrence of Finance; this originated from this railway.

I was therefore thinking of the second phase of reforms – the big-ticket organisational reforms, wherein the appointment of officers to top leadership positions would be made through a 'positive act of selection' and the organisation became less bureaucratic and more collaborative, agile and customer centric, and everyone worked towards achieving the mission of the Railways rather than trying to build an empire for a department. Let Railways become the 'engine of growth' in the real sense. A rupee spent in Railways has a multiplier effect and results in an increase of about ₹5 in the Gross Domestic Product (GDP) of the country due to forward and backward linkages.

The very first discussion I had with the new Chairman was about working towards building the leadership pipeline to bring a paradigm shift in the selection of DRMs and GMs, to create a new cadre called the General Management Cadre that would enable the Railways to navigate the journey of modernisation and expansion. It would bring in a cultural change, far removed from siloed working that has been department centric. There are 68 DRMs, 27 GMs and 9 Board Members. This makes the top management of the Railways, comprising 104 officers across the 8 departments.

We reached an agreement. Within a fortnight, I was ready with the first draft for this new policy change that we needed to consider for selection of DRMs and GMs and the way the Railway Board should be re-oriented on functional lines rather than the existing departmental ones.

Many iterations followed thereafter. An agreed-upon draft was ready by March 2019. Time was running out as the General Elections were round the corner, but this was one reform which was most needed, and I was pretty sure that this would bring a strategic shift to the overall working of Railways.

The 60,000 km I had travelled in 2018 across the length and breadth of Railways, meeting many officers and supervisors, had given me an idea of what the organisation needed for a major change. Officers from the Railway Board normally go on inspection once in two months and therefore may travel 6,000 to 10,000 km in a year. Lohani wanted me to travel extensively all over to communicate with railwaymen to the extent possible and spread how we wanted the Railways to change. The massive rapport with the people in the organisation also gave me an understanding of how a sustainable cultural change could be brought about in the organisation.

We were looking for a culture of collaboration, fearlessness, empowerment, transparency and trust in the field units, and the highest standards of honesty and integrity. I always emphasised that the massive empowerment and delegation had been done keeping trust in the institution of DRM and therefore it was important that this was not breached. It was everyone's responsibility.

Unprecedented empowerment, delegations and the process reforms that had been brought about during 2017-18, motivated the officers. There was a sea change perceptible in the way service was delivered in the field. DRMs were quite excited, but there was something that was holding some people back within their silos. I was able to sense some irritants during the informal interactions on field visits. These related to the organisational structure. Some departments felt more important than the others.

The organisation was upbeat, motivated and galvanised as the cutting edge of management had major empowerment effected during a very short span of time, much to the dismay of others. Policy changes were happening every other day. In fact, this statistic was worked out and conveyed to me once by a vigilance officer of SCR while I was having a brainstorming session there. I was quite surprised that people had developed such high expectations and respect for the Transformation Cell.

Everyone in the field used to eagerly check out the Transformation website daily for issuance of a new policy that would ease their work. All that they were doing was discharging their legitimate duty. Even for doing a legitimate duty one was quite strangulated in the processes and levels of hierarchy, far more than what a normal business enterprise should allow.

General Elections to Lok Sabha were round the corner as a new Government was to be elected before May 2019. All the efforts that I had put in for building a leadership pipeline had not borne fruit by that time.

While the elections were in progress, each Ministry was preparing an action plan that could be rolled out as soon as the election results were announced.

One day in May 2019, the Chairman asked me to accompany him to CEO Niti Aayog to discuss the action plan which could be finalised in a week or so.

My expectations rose high and along with Niti Aayog, I prepared an action plan which included some of the big-ticket organisational reforms such as:

- Restructuring of Railway Board on functional lines to improve customer focus and bring synergy.
- Single service named IRMS through UPSC against the eight services at present to circumvent the siloed working in the organisation and bring focus on organisational goals rather than departmental ones.
- Opening the rail sector for private investment for passenger train operations to bring efficiency and world's best technology in the shortest time and make Railways future ready.
- Redevelopment of stations to improve passenger experience.
- Allotment of 5 MHz frequency in 700 MHz range for Long Term Evolution (LTE) communication to improve signalling and therefore safety.
- Corporatisation of Production Units of Railways to make Railways PU the global hub of manufacture.
- Modern signalling system to improve the speed of train operations and safety.
- Speed of 160 kmph for the entire Golden Quadrilateral and its Diagonal to reduce travel time and thereby improve line capacity.

This was considered by the full Railway Board in the fourth week of May 2019. In the meanwhile, I also had a chance to meet Rajiv Kumar, Vice Chairman, Niti Aayog, during a meeting with the Chairman and the Member Traffic wherein the initiative of Private Train Operation was discussed. He was also quite excited about bringing new technology to run modern trains like those operating in Europe and Japan.

No sooner was the new government in place on May 30, 2019, than some of these items found a place in the **100 days agenda** of the Government, duly approved by the Group of Ministers and conveyed through the Cabinet Secretary to the Chairman, early in July 2019.

Shri Piyush Goyal continued as the Minister with the charge of Railways, along with Commerce and Industry. This ensured continuity in decision making.

I thought the job of creating the leadership pipeline would become a little easier. No reform of this magnitude could ever happen so soon. But I am an overly optimistic individual. You need to think big and question the status quo if the best is to be brought out; opportunities are to be harvested.

The journey was in the right direction for this level of reform – slow but steady.

Let me take you a little deeper into what kind of structure Railways has for a better insight and understanding, and what change I was striving for.

Indian Railways is typically organised into eight functional departments – Civil Engineering, Mechanical Engineering, Electrical Engineering, Signal and Telecommunication, Traffic Transportation, Personnel, Accounts, and Material Management. This has been there for decades. While in theory such a structure promotes functional specialisation since each department is manned by an independent cadre, this structure leads to lack of unity and strategic coherence.

From recruitment to retirement, officers spend their entire lifetime in the same department and therefore get deeply steeped into departmental thinking and silo-based fiefdom, barring a limited exposure in general management cadre as Additional DRM, DRM and GM, where the focus is broad based, strategically aligned, and objectives integrated.

The recruitment to various departments is done through Union Public Service Commission (UPSC). There are eight different services (one service for each department) and two different examinations – Combined Engineering Services and Civil Services.

It is only natural that an individual recruited for a particular service will have wholehearted allegiance for the well-being of that service, and therefore a great deal of organisational energy is expended in inter-departmental rivalry, competition for resources, viz., more funds for new lines, electrification and diesel locos. But every department, in its own area of specialisation and influence, does try to bring in the best for successful outcomes of the department. Often, there is a lack of coherence in achieving the goal of the organisation. The fact is that carrying passenger and freight transportation at optimal cost with the highest standards of safety, and the best value for money for the customers, is often lost sight of.

A large number of committees over three decades had looked into the railway organisation and suggested organisational reforms in some form or the other. They had adversely commented upon the departmental biases and rivalries in the functioning of the Railways. Even the Board Members focussed on departments rather than on integrated rail business or the customer.

Historically, Indian Railways started as an integrator of activities to be successful, and therefore provide *cradle-to-grave care* for its employees to produce everything from *wheels to meals* to operate the railway system. Today, Indian Railways runs hospitals, schools, catering, manufacturing and real estate. Railways also undertake all of the operation and maintenance, infrastructure creation, manpower training and research and development.

This makes life more complex than it should be. It is high time that the organisation focussed on business and customers with a rationalised management cadre for Railways for a unified line of command and decision making.

This is intended to mitigate the departmental orientation and bring undisputed focus on ultimate service delivery, making Railways the engine of growth. This was one of the major transformative agendas of the Government to build Railways for the **New India @75** which would serve both passenger and freight customers and be the preferred mode of transport.

Due to the over-differentiated organisational structure with separate verticals (one for each service), there is a lack of coherence. The decision making at the highest level of the Railway Board typically comprised the policy making, regulation and rail operation These decisions are centralised at the apex level.

The organisation also confronts with the duality of roles – commercial as well as social – without clear demarcation resulting in bureaucratic decision making and lack of customer orientation. The present set-up has led to inadequate investment in technology development and attracting private investment. The overall organisational structure with functional Board Members (one Member for each of the eight Services) and recruitment through two different sources (Civil Services and Combined Engineering Services), has existed for decades. There has been a craving amongst most of the middle and senior management level officers to bring a change that would serve the needs of New India and therefore build a New Railways.

After 2018, almost a year elapsed but nothing tangible happened to bring about organisational reforms. Vinod Yadav was to superannuate in December 2019. The task of bringing this change was no doubt daunting.

The Minister of Railways Shri Piyush Goyal, in one of the video conference meetings in November 2019 with DRMs and GMs, had asked the officers to submit ideas for the next phase of reforms.

It was Monday afternoon on December 2, 2019, when I was asked to convene a big Town Hall of the magnitude I had conducted in December 2017 (Sampark, Samanvay, Samvaad) at Hotel Ashoka.

We had to invite all DRMs, GMs and the young officers who had submitted their suggestions as a follow up of the MR's call. The conclave was to be organised on December 7 and 8, 2019. There was hardly any time to prepare. Fixing the venue was a big issue as Ashoka was already booked for holding a conference for doctors for three days during that week.

A.K. Chandra, my Executive Director, was somehow able to arrange Pravasi Bhartiya Kendra to hold this conclave on December 7 and 8, 2019. We decided to name this event as *Parivartan Sangoshthi* to create the right environment and connect with the next level of reforms. It was to convey that this meet is for a change. Chandra was a perfect event manager. He loved to conduct such events and had been doing that for a long time. When I was DRM Dhanbad, all the annual functions at Patna used to be organised by him.

Two days before the conclave, 400 suggestions were received from officers of different seniority. Minister of Railways decided to actively participate in the Sangoshthi, thus indicating the seriousness of the reforms.

All the 27 GMs, 68 DRMs and 60 young officers were formally invited from the field to participate in the Sangoshthi. All the officers of the Railways up to the level of Principal Executive Directors were also invited.

We spontaneously formed 12 heterogenous groups of GMs, with each team having 10–12 senior officers of the level of DRMs, Principal Heads of Departments and other GMs to get quality ideas.

The following eight strategic shift items were identified based on the 400 suggestions:
- DRM, GM selection, inter-se seniority, security under DRM, workshops merged with Production Units, Personnel and Finance under Executive;
- Cost cutting / expenditure control;
- Throughput/Mobility /Capacity enhancement;
- Earning enhancement;
- Productivity enhancement;
- System/process improvement to improve delivery and safety;
- Customer orientation;
- HR/Culture improvement.

The 8 strategic items given to 12 groups were not known to them in advance and therefore whatever was presented by the groups, evolved during the brainstorming session only.

Each group was allocated two or three major strategic shift items, but organisational reforms was allocated to every group. This was one of the most debated reforms agendas. It was a marathon two-day brainstorming session. Each group was asked to present its recommendations in front of both the Minister and the full Board. All the participants were present all the time. It was a gathering of about 450 officers in the hall. There was absolute freedom to express views.

This was live telecast across all the 68 Divisions, 17 Zones and 6 Production Units. A live chat was visible to all the participants which reflected the views of participants present in the hall.

The most popular recommendations that emerged in the end were:
- Restructure Railway Board on functional lines and reduce the size of the Railway Board from eight Members to five Members, including Chairman, Railway Board. It was a historical decision as the Board Members could be selected without any tag of a department from any of the erstwhile cadres. It was an amazing alignment. It meant there was a willingness to change for a better Railways.
- All the eight services recruited through two different exams – Civil Services and Engineering Services – need to be merged into a common Indian Railway Management Service (IRMS).

The group overwhelmingly felt that this change would bring in the right synergy and facilitate the development and modernisation of the Railways and also eliminate the biases associated with the growth of a particular service. The focus would be on the organisation.

No sooner was the majority decision of the house sensed on the second day of the Sangoshthi on December 8, 2019, than an emergency Board meeting was convened at the Pravasi Bhartiya Kendra itself. It was quite unprecedented. This was done to take a final call to ensure that the right steps were taken urgently to freeze most of the decisions.

Two days later, a Committee of Secretaries was formed, headed by the Cabinet Secretary with Chairman, Railway Board; Secretary, Department of Personnel and Training; Secretary, Expenditure, Secretary, Law; and the CEO, Niti Aayog, to work out the modalities and to evolve the decision points for approaching the Cabinet in the shortest possible time This was to obviate the need for inter-ministerial consultation which normally takes 4–6 weeks.

CRB was to superannuate on December 31, 2019. Superannuation was the key driver.

After 2-3 meetings chaired by the Cabinet Secretary, it was decided to approach the Cabinet. On December 24, 2019, the Cabinet approved restructuring of the Railway Board on functional lines with four functional Board Members designated as Member Infrastructure, Member Operation and Business Development, Member Traction Rolling Stock and Member Finance. Chairman Railway Board was re-designated as Chairman Railway Board and Chief Executive Officer to give him over-riding power over any matter and over any Board Member including Member Finance. Except for CRB, generally no other Board Member has a helicopter view of the organisation.

Late evening on December 24, 2019, I got a call from CRB informing me that the decisions taken in the Parivartan Sangoshthi on two major issues – Restructuring the Board and Single Service (Indian Railway Management Service) – had been approved by the Cabinet that day. This quick action was completely unexpected. It took merely 16 days after Parivartan Sangoshthi. I was very happy. CRB also thanked me for my contributions in organising the Parivartan Sangoshthi on a short notice that could forge a consensus for such a major organisational reforms.

It was no doubt a great moment for me as these ideas had persisted with me for a very long time as the next level of reforms for the organisation. These reforms were most needed for a strategic shift in thinking and to meet the aspirations of New India@ 75.

The reforms are moving forwards, in spite of the focus on fight against Covid – 19.

This is a defining moment in the history of Railways. The fast-track execution of projects, identification of new technologies as accelerator of modernisation, the highest level of performance and creating a new culture of collaboration can take place only if big-ticket organisational reforms are implemented. After all, the Minister had witnessed the mood in the hall.

We must build the Railways at least as much over the next 10 to 20 years as had been built over the preceding 160 years if Railways has to play a pivotal role in the Indian economy. A Herculean task indeed!

Postscript

It is, however, the management of this change which will decide the success of these unprecedented decisions. Only time will tell how well we navigate these major organisational reforms.

I am quite satisfied that I could contribute to this major strategic shift. The Union Cabinet has accorded its approval. There is nothing beyond this that could have been aspired for. CRB got an extension for one year, beyond December 31, 2019. This will provide continuity in implementation. In October 2020, the policy decision regarding redesignating Chairman Railway Board as Chairman and Chief Executive Officer (Chairman & CEO) and reorganisation of the Railway Board was implemented. The strength of the Railway Board was reduced from eight members to four members. However, GMs could not be placed in the apex grade of Secretary to GOI. It was a pathbreaking development in the reform of the Indian Railways.

The Future Is, Unforgivingly, Now! Private Passenger Trains

The country's first passenger train ran between Mumbai's (then Bombay's) Bori Bunder station and Thane on April 16, 1853. The 14 carriages were hauled by three steam locomotives – Sahib, Sindh and Sultan – on broad gauge (1676 mm). It travelled 34 km and carried 400 passengers. This was the Great Indian Peninsular Railway (GIPR).

In eastern India, the passenger train operations started on August 15, 1854, between Howrah and Hooghly (39) km. This was the East Indian Railway (EIR) Company.

Lights in passenger coaches were introduced in 1897. First air-cooled coaches were introduced in 1934 in the Frontier Mail. The Frontier Mail was started in 1928 between Mumbai and Peshawar (now in Pakistan) before the Partition of India. After Partition, this train ran between Mumbai and Amritsar. It was called the Frontier Mail because Peshawar was close to the frontier of British India in those days. This train was named as Golden Temple Mail in 1996.

That was the paradigm in which passenger trains were run in India and with such rudimentary technology. It took 47 years to get lights inside the coach, and 81 years to have air-cooling.

Quality of service is what people are looking for today, and it includes the speed of the train.

Running passenger trains has always been the forte of the Railways before and after Independence, over 167 years of its existence in India. Railways sets up various Production Units for manufacturing coaches and locomotives, and other systems and sub-systems required for its Operation and Maintenance. In fact, quite a few Railways workshops produced a number of strategic goods during World War II.

As of 2020, we run 13,000 passenger trains and carry 23 million passengers every day. Of the total of 8.4 billion passengers carried annually, close to 55 per cent passengers belong to the suburban rail system and only 6–8 per cent of the total passengers carried are in the reserved segment. There is a huge unmet demand in the reserved passenger business. It is, therefore, for the Government to think of innovative solutions to run more reserved passenger trains and provide better travel experience.

Earlier, people were happy spending time to save money; today the concept has changed and people are willing to spend money to save time.

Due to inadequate investment in infrastructure in the Railways, the speed of train operations has been substantially impacted. As of 2020, Indian Railways runs around 7,000 freight trains daily at an average speed of just about 23 or 24 kmph while the average speed of a Mail Express trains is anywhere between 50–55 kmph. Speeds are quite low.

When we talk of rail infrastructure, we mean railway track, signalling, stations, buildings, bridges, tunnels, electrification, communication, freight and passenger terminals, maintenance depots, workshops, factories, coaches, wagons, locomotives, etc.

From 1950 to 2017, route-kilometres of Indian Railways have grown by 26 per cent (from around 53,000 km to around 67,000 km), while passenger-kilometres have grown by 1,629 per cent, and net tonne-kilometres have grown by 1,550 per cent.

The Signalling system has still not developed enough to provide protection from an accident. If a driver commits an error of judgement, technology should come to the rescue of the driver to avert an accident. Stations have not been upgraded to international standards. Rolling stock, especially coaches, have old designs, with technology that is 30 years old.

With heavy investment in development of national highways, and private investment in airports, there is always a preference for air travel vis-a-vis rail due to shorter travel time and quality of service provided by the airline industry. An equally important competitor of Railways is the Roadways, as not only has the road network been progressively improving, new designs of Volvo buses and cars have emerged, tempting people to make choices for road travel, even if they are at a higher cost.

I have travelled overseas quite a lot – USA, UK, France, Germany, Switzerland, Japan – and every time I visited, I made sure that I travelled by High-Speed Trains and also in the driving cabins of the trains. I have talked to the drivers and have had a feel of the network and experienced the speed of operation – at 300 kmph and above. It has been an amazing experience. There has therefore been a nagging question for a long time – why don't such trains run in India for our fellow citizens? Improved stations and fast trains will make a difference in the lives of the people who travel for business, tourism or under emergencies.

Keeping in view these challenges, aspirations and the sustainability of the environment, I have had a burning desire to bring in new technologies that would reduce travel time, improve service delivery and make rail travel akin to air travel over long distances. It would also reduce journey time for short distances. It would then make Indian rail travel world class.

And therefore, if the Railways must invest in infrastructure upgrade and expansion of rail network, the money will be well spent. We need to connect cities and districts in the hinterland through rail lines, as a priority, rather than spend on rolling stock, especially the coaches and locomotives, which can easily be sourced from the OEMs. The return on investment is very high on rolling stock. From day one, the moment it is put into commercial operation, a coach or locomotive starts earning, so OEMs will be keen to work in this manner.

Globally, countries such as the UK and Spain have adopted a business model in which rolling stock companies operate trains while fixed infrastructure is provided by the government.

I have always believed that the industry where the high-end rail technology resides (such as train sets, coaches, locomotives), must be brought in as the dominant stakeholder in the business of running railways in a more efficient manner, with high level of reliability and safety, compared to Indian Railways.

Why should we not enable private sector to invest in running private passenger trains? These trains will have high-end technology and reduce journey time by about 30 per cent between same origin-destination pairs, with value added services like high quality catering, first mile–last mile connectivity and infotainment.

We need to bring in three to four new technologies simultaneously, to make a visible impact pan India. Transfer of technology models have long gestation periods to imbibe, ramp up and proliferate – something our country can ill-afford, not only in the new paradigm but also in the 21st century.

With this intent in mind, it was proposed to run at least 5 per cent of the trains in the premium segment (out of 2,800 rakes operated in

Indian Railways, 5 per cent means 140) with the private sector fully enabled to bring in technology of their choice and be responsible for comprehensive maintenance. This essentially means that capex and opex belong to the private sector; and it is only reasonable that they have full freedom in selection of technology.

While doing so, the investor will have absolute freedom to fix the fare to be charged from the passengers for the journey and the services that they offer. I had suggested this as one of the items for the next level of reform and it was included in the 100-day agenda of the new Government.

It was therefore decided to initiate action for private investment of about ₹30,000 crores including about 5–10 per cent of this investment to be used for creating maintenance infrastructure for the O&M of these trains. This is a major investment sum, indeed.

This project has evinced global interest. The Covid-19 pandemic has led to some delays.

It is for the first time that a policy decision has been taken to provide access to Railways fixed infrastructure to private operators at a fixed cost, defined as haulage charge for running private trains with drivers and guards belonging to the Railways.

We have identified 100 routes to operate 150 modern private trains on Indian Railways.

The investor will be selected based on international competitive bidding. The investor will share a portion of their revenue with the Railways, which would be the sole bidding criteria for selection.

This concession will run for 35 years as that is the codal life of the rolling stock. It would open up a new era of investment by the private sector with a mandate to encourage Make-in-India. This is a strategic shift in the Railways business to augment its own capacity in passenger segment while concurrently investing in the fixed infrastructure – multi-tracking, electrification, speed raising and freight corridors.

This initiative is expected to bring in three or four private players with different technologies such as Velaro EMU trains of Spain, Germany and UK; or Locomotive hauled TGV trains of France; or Tilting Talgo trains of Spain.

When the private sector starts operating trains all over India, it will usher in a new climate of investment, create a feel-good environment and enable ease-of-living in the true sense. This is first-of-its-kind initiative taken by Railways in independent India and is being tried on a pilot basis to cater to only 5 per cent of the mail express trains that Indian Railways run.

The new system will generate additional capacity for people to book a ticket. Today, about 6 crore passengers remain waitlisted and are not able to travel at the time they desire. Let there be no unmet demand in passenger business. A person should be able to go to a station, buy a ticket, and travel. This should be our long-term goal.

A robust mechanism was evolved to drive this initiative. A Group of Secretaries (GoS) headed by the CEO Niti Aayog with CRB; Secretary Department of Economic Affairs, Ministry of Finance; and Secretary Urban Development, was constituted in October 2019 by the Minister of Railways. The GoS took ten meetings to finalise the contours of the project.

Following these meetings, two meetings of the PPPAC were chaired by Secretary, Department of Economic Affairs, to finalise the whole business plan and the bidding frame on March 29, 2020. The decision making has really been very fast in this project. We needed to go to the market with the RFQ to kickstart the new reform of the Government. Robustness of the process always enhances credibility.

Some of the key and the critical issues that have been resolved are:
- The concession will be awarded for 35 years which is the life of rolling stock.
- Concessionaire will have the freedom to choose the technology.
- There will be freedom to fix market determined fare for the service.
- Tickets will be booked on the IRCTC platform on a pre-determined fee.
- Origin–destination will be fixed but stops will be decided by the concessionaire.
- Complete capex and opex will be by the concessionaire.
- Maintenance intervention will not be before 40,000 km of train run.
- Cleanliness and travel worthiness will be ensured every 7,500 km.
- Key Performance Indices (KPI) – 95 per cent punctuality, 100,000 km per failure reliability, and high level of hygiene.
- Insurance for any accident and any damage to train and loss of life.
- Driver and guard by Railways.
- Safety certification by RDSO, prototype clearance based on international norms set out by International Union of Railways (UIC), Paris.

- Depots on 'as is where is' basis by Railways for any upgrade by concessionaire.
- Concessionaire to pay fixed haulage charge to Railways, indexed to Consumer Price Index (CPI).
- No competing train to run 60 minutes before or after the fixed path on the OD (origin–destination).
- Share of gross revenue as the bidding criteria.

PPPAC is a high-level committee comprising Secretary, Department of Economic Affairs (in the Chair); CEO Niti Aayog; Secretary, Department of Expenditure; Secretary, Department of Legal Affairs; and Secretary of the Sponsoring Department. All projects of the Central Ministries with investment size of ₹500 crore or above are appraised by PPPAC and then processed for the approval of the Minister concerned, but those above ₹1,000 crore are submitted for consideration and approval of the CCEA.

Many rounds of heated discussions took place in the GoS and within the Ministry of Railways, but the clarity that I had enabled me to navigate this journey for more than 10 months after the constitution of GoS, and 18 months after the approval of Group of Ministers.

I remember a discussion when the provision of driver and guard was being debated and the opinion of most in the Group of Secretaries was that the private sector may be allowed to bring their own men. I kept listening for some time, but after the discussion was almost over, I emphatically told everyone that this provision would be a recipe for failure in this great initiative. There was a pin drop silence.

I explained that firstly it would send a wrong signal that even hardcore train operation is being outsourced to the private sector, and secondly the type of talent and experience we need in the drivers and guards to run such premium trains would be impossible to find in the market.

This would force the private sector to either poach such persons from Railways or they would not be able to operate these services. These set of personnel will have to liaise with the station and control staff every day while running trains. There would be a cultural mismatch as they would be considered rank outsiders. Running trains by drivers and guards of Railways was a very emotive issue and could not be overlooked. We would do it at our own peril.

Even during stakeholder consultations, some of the investors had raised this issue. Operationally also, it would not be possible for the private sector to keep a set of spare drivers and guards at different stations all over the network to provide relief and replacement on long distance trains after eight hours of journey – we need to replace the driver and guard after every eight hours of running duty.

Once these arguments were heard, the decision was immediately reversed. It was then agreed that driver and guard will be provided only by Railways. This was the most important make-or-break decision.

Similarly, fixing the haulage charges was quite tricky. This was the fixed charge which the private investor had to pay to Railways for getting access to fixed rail infrastructure. The way we calculated cost of a service on Railways was quite old fashioned. Our overheads were in the range of around 6 per cent. Once we added that in fixing the haulage charges, there would be no business case for such an investment, as the concessionaire would only be paying fixed charges for running the train without earning a return on their investment. Industry standards for overheads could be anywhere between 10–15 per cent.

All the rationality was presented to the GoS. Appa Rao had done a lot of work in firming up this haulage charge, keeping overheads as 25 per cent. Appa Rao was my Executive Director Transformation Cell and had worked outside the Railways in Ministry of Power and Ministry of Civil Aviation. He understood business very well. This proposal was not only accepted by GoS but also by the PPPAC and finally by the Ministry of Railways. A very important parameter had thus been finalised.

With the above issues settled, the project team has to address the issues raised by the prospective investors and resolve them. It is not easy to mobilise investments to the tune of ₹30,000 crore. But the market sentiments are definitely very positive. Lot of homework has yet to be done to take the project forward.

This was my last contribution before superannuation on June 30, 2020. After the RFP is finalised (which has also been processed), another round of approval of PPPAC will be required before placing the project proposal to the CCEA.

I shall wait for the day when I see modern trains run all across the country. I will travel like any other Indian and enjoy the experience of an airline with regards to aesthetics, reduced journey time, good quality food, better first and last mile connectivity and a high level of hygiene.

I expect these trains to run on Indian Railways tracks in the years to come if the challenges that have been posed by the investors are overcome. It is this reform which will bring a paradigm shift in rail travel.

This has been one of my dream projects, similar to Madhepura. I am quite satisfied to have propagated the new idea for a new India. It has resonated well across the Government of India and with the investors. Modalities to implement this idea may vary depending on the market response and the circumstances.

Brief and Intimate Biographies: Some Alchemist Personalities

I have written about these great people without following any order or sequence.

Ashwini Lohani

Khatauli rail accident of Puri–Haridwar Express on August 19, 2017, led to the resignation of A.K. Mital, CRB, on August 23, 2017. DRM Delhi had to proceed on leave. GM Northern Railway was transferred to Southern Railway. In this train accident, 25 people had died due to gross human error.

Earlier, on November 20, 2016, 152 people had died in a train accident of Indore–Patna Express in Jhansi Division. The Prime Minister had come to Surajkund to address the participants of Rail Vikas Shivir on that day.

Ashwani Lohani was appointed as CRB on August 24, 2017. The morale in the organisation was quite low. Public perception about Railways was unfavourable due to the spate of accidents and poor service delivery. Field officers at the cutting edge, as we call the DRMs, felt quite disillusioned. GMs were equally handicapped due to the Railways bureaucracy and the extremely difficult work environment. Everything was centred in the Ministry of Railways and most of the things would require marathon efforts to get past Finance at different stages due to our own policies. Yet, everything was to be delivered by the Zones and Divisions, but without any substantive powers. Over-centralisation of decision making had made the organisation less market oriented and less centric to service delivery. No one was prepared to let go of his powers.

No sooner did Lohani join on August 24, than I met him and introduced my team of officers of the Transformation Cell, which was fully empowered and was multidisciplinary in nature. We had the desire to perform and produce results. That was our mandate. We made a small presentation to him on August 26. He heard us all but changed the course of the journey altogether.

His directions were – let us look at the process, structure and cultural reforms if we want to achieve anything in Railways. If this was done, the 'wish list' as he called what we had been driving at, would also get done. This was the clarity he had, and the new journey began. We never looked back, and corrected our course of action along the way.

The first thing we did was to empower the field officers and make the Railway Board irrelevant for things that did not require any value addition from the Ministry. As a result, we delegated huge number of powers to the Divisions and Zones, to such an extent that even the directorates in Railway Board started feeling threatened. It was a war for retaining their fiefdom. Lohani however did not relent. We succeeded. We brought out a Model Schedule of Powers from the Ministry of Railways for the first time in the history of Railways. Without Lohani's outright support, it would not have been possible.

Fear perception of Vigilance was one of the biggest concern officers had in the field, and most of them would try to hide behind it. We brought out a policy that unless the concerned Principal Head of the Department agreed with the opinion of the Vigilance department, a case would not be registered against an officer. This brought a major shift in the mindset of the Vigilance officers and also the executives. It was hard to drive this policy. Lohani was determined and therefore this was done.

A presentation was to be made to the Railway Minister on December 12, 2017. Various departments had already done it. The Chairman was the boss of the Transformation Cell. The presentation was scheduled at 5 p.m. But due to some exigency, it got delayed and was rescheduled to 8 p.m. Anuj Gupta, OSD to the Minister, accompanied me to inform Lohani. He was supposed to go to Vishakhapatnam to commission a bridge that had taken marathon efforts on the part of the Waltair Division to recommission. He did not stay for the presentation and told Anuj that Sudheer was enough to make a presentation to the Minister.

During the presentation it was decided to hold Sampark, Samanvay, Samvaad as a mega Town Hall with all DRMs, PHODs, GMs, Additional Members and full Board. It was arranged to be on December 16, 2017. I had only two days to plan as officers were supposed to reach Delhi on December 15.

Our presentation was over at 10 p.m. I rang up Lohani and suggested that a programme of this magnitude and at such a short notice required that all officers stay at Ashoka Hotel and all arrangements made by IRCTC. The Chairman's approval was therefore required. His answer was 'Done'. Very decisive indeed.

He returned to office on December 14. The event was conducted on December 16. He did not get into the nitty gritty of the event except that he directed, 'No bouquets and simple food'. For arranging a lecture by Sonam Wangchuk, he said, 'We could spend any amount as it would energise Railwaymen.' The programme was to be telecast live to the whole Railways establishment.

During the event, I requested that the day's deliberations needed to be finalised – what needed to be done and with what timelines. It was done. Clear directions were given in front of the whole house that GM's recommendations will not be reviewed by the officers junior to GMs. The Minister also took note of it. It set the pace for fast-track decision making. Members of the Board also understood it. It laid the foundation of a new paradigm. We had legislated this already in the Transformation Cell's roles, responsibility and functions in February 2017. It was re-emphasised.

It was the first week of January 2018. It was 11.45 p.m. I was going to drop my son to the airport. CRB told me that he was going online for foot patrolling to witness the difficulties that the gangmen face during night patrolling. It was chilling cold.

While Lohani was on foot patrol inspection on railway track, he telephoned and asked me, 'What to do to improve the working conditions of the gangmen?' I suggested to him to form a high-level committee to address the various issues pertaining to gangmen. We made a committee of GMs from South Central, Northern and Central Railway and made Tushar Pandey, my Executive Director, the Member Secretary. We finalised the report that recommended an expense of ₹10,000 per gangman for protective gear. There were 60,000 gangmen. The protective gear would include safety shoes, a good winter jacket, luminous vest, a torch, a helmet and a tool kit. It meant an expenditure of ₹60 crore.

Similarly, a safety device called 'Rakshak' was recommended by the GMs committee for the safety of gangmen. This device was to be worn by the individuals while working on the line. It warned the gangmen about an approaching train and saved them from any untoward incident. Railways was losing about 300 gangmen every year due to accidents online. It was a one-time expenditure of ₹50,000 per route km. The receiver and transmitters were to be provided along the track on the busiest 10,000 route-kilometres of the Golden Quadrilateral and its Diagonal.

Objections were raised by various Members. I was asked to prepare a note and the CRB approved the proposal costing ₹110 crore. This was to ensure the safety of Railwaymen. He did not hesitate for a second.

He recorded, 'File called for and approval accorded'. Thereafter, the file was sent to other concerned Members for their perusal and if they had any suggestions for change. Otherwise, it was deemed to have been approved. This style of decision making was unprecedented.

Most of the time while reading a proposal in a file, CRB recorded approval in the margins against each item of the proposal to make sure he had read it and agreed to it. This conveyed a much stronger commitment of the CRB compared to simply writing 'Approved' at the end of the proposal, as was the practice till then.

Railway Protection Force is very vital to Railways operations but had little empowerment. Director General (DG) RPF had been making efforts, but they were not fructifying. One day, while he was in a meeting with DG RPF, CRB called me for a discussion. Right there in the meeting, it was decided to provide two- and four-wheelers to all 700 RPF posts (main *thana*) and outposts (sub-*thana*). We issued the instructions the same day. A special Schedule of Powers for RPF was also issued, which provided them with numerous powers for procurement of uniforms and gadgets, arranging *Bara Khana* and procuring necessary equipment for their day-to-day functioning. What an empowerment for RPF! It boosted the morale of the force.

In all the courses that Centralised Training Institutes (CTIs) and National Academy of Indian Railways (NAIR) organised, I was told to give the inaugural lecture or else send my officers to disseminate the message that 'delivery is important'. Rules can be overlooked by recording cogent reasons in the interest of delivery. A letter to this effect was written on CRB's behalf. It was amazing.

One day CRB was in Dhanbad. He asked me to delegate powers to DRMs to empanel private super-specialty hospitals for treatment of Railways employees. Earlier, these powers were vested with the Board. A lot of time used to be wasted. By the evening, he approved the proposal on WhatsApp. Orders were issued the same day. The next day he approved the proposal on file.

Generally, he did not get into the nitty-gritty of the proposal, as it was my job to take due care of financial limits and policies of the Government. He had blind faith in me. Whatever the Cell recommended, he approved. I used to participate in most of the meetings convened at his level. This would ensure that there was no confusion. It also used to hasten the pace of decision making. My job, therefore, used to be more onerous – after all, the responsibility was mine.

He liked to meet and seek ideas from young officers. So we called junior officers from the Divisions for meeting with the Transformation Cell and CRB over lunch. Quite a few proposals emerged from such meetings and were approved.

We recommended awards for Change Leaders and Change Agents – for GMs and DRMs respectively. He simply agreed and these were given in April 2018. It was quite motivating for the DRMs and GMs.

Similarly, for leadership development, we wanted to organise three-day workshops for all the 68 DRMs and 27 GMs, that too, in the very busy loading and festival season of October–December 2018. He agreed and attended two workshops at Vadodara. He was concerned about his men.

He trusted his people and therefore wanted the maximum enabling environment in the field. Whatever was within the domain of Board Members, got delegated to DRMs.

On the day of Deepavali, on October 19, 2017, as mentioned earlier in my description about the Transformation journey, I saw him being decisive to the hilt in over-ruling the Finance officers with regard to the decisions already taken in meetings with the full Board present. A typical problem with the Board was that it used to review and re-review its own decisions. He put an end to it.

If files did not reach him, he would call for them and approve. I used this method quite often, otherwise things could remain in limbo for any amount of time, without any accountability.

He had a clear focus that workshops must be held across the Zonal Headquarters to understand what people in the field needed and to tell them what was being done by the Board to improve their working.

For the first time, Indian Railways probationers were sent for overseas training to give them global exposure. An international training just before joining a working post was a big motivator. Training related powers of DRMs and GMs were enhanced ten times over for capability building. Earlier, GMs had powers to sanction expenditure up to ₹10,000 per person to attend any training or workshop, with a limited budget of ₹1 crore per annum. This was enhanced to ₹50,000 per person and ₹10 crore per annum for each GM. This would pay rich dividends in the long run.

We delegated most of the powers to the field staff keeping in view the need, and to reduce the levels of decision making, be it RPF, Publicity, Medical, Store, Commercial, Works or Services, with outright support from, and clarity of CRB to make the Railway Board irrelevant for such things which required the field to act and perform. The Railway Board's job was policy making, perspective planning and regulation. Overall coordination also was required at the Board's level as 17 Zones and 6 Production Units were involved.

His ultimate mantra was, 'Take care of men, simplify processes, reduce protocols, make youngsters fearless to say their point of view, improve workplaces, if rules have to be changed, change them, and do simple things till the house is brought back in order. Things will begin to change.'

He also believed that everyone was equal in competencies and delivery, provided an enabling environment existed. This was something with which I used to respectfully disagree. 'Right person for the right job' was somehow not his belief. He had his likes and dislikes. He sometimes showed a fair degree of anger.

He was a people's man. People came first and the organisation later, was his firm belief. He had high energy levels.

He had an impressive personality. He was fair, tall and of athletic build. He had four engineering degrees to his credit and a Limca Record 2017 for that. He had a place in the Guinness Book of World Records for successfully running Fairy Queen Express, the world's oldest working steam locomotive.

Vinod Kumar Yadav

I have known Vinod Yadav since 1985 when I had an occasion to stay with him as his guest. I had no place to stay in Delhi at that time. I cannot forget the generosity of Vinod and his wife. In fact, his wife relocated herself for those 6–8 days and lived with her parents. Vinod and I stayed at his official residence. She used to come every day and take care of our meals. It was an incredible gesture by any standard. It is so fresh in my memory even now. This was my association with Vinod Yadav. Who knew he would be my boss one day? I have a very high regard for both his wife and him. We have been good friends since that time.

When we were navigating the transformation journey in 2017, Lohani arrived on the scene. We decided to focus on process, structure and cultural reforms, and I decided to seek maximum inputs for delegation and empowerment from Vinod Yadav. He had all the resources and a positive mindset. As GM SCR, he needed empowerment the most, to improve operational efficiency. We were on the same page.

After a careful analysis, the Transformation Cell decided to take the template of South Central Railway to firm up the Model Schedule of Powers (SOP) for all Zonal Railways. I made a presentation to the full Board on October 13, 2017, and said that the SOP of SCR was by far the best and the most liberal. Therefore, all the best practices of various Zonal Railways should be incorporated in the SOP of SCR to make it the Model SOP. We finalised the model SOP and issued it on October 26, 2017. It made history. SOPs had never been issued by the Railway Ministry earlier. Lohani wrote the foreword for this SOP. It brought all officers of the same grade – DRM, CWM, SAG, HAG, GM – at par with one another in one go, in all the Zones. What an incredible work was done!

His support was beyond imagination, all through. Officers of our Cell used to visit SCR as if it was their second home. We used to get a lot of confidence as documents used to be ratified by SCR before issue. This would not have been possible without the support of Vinod Yadav. On other reform processes, he would generally get the homework done before submitting the proposal. I also assigned the highest priority for his items. I kept a good liaison with his team.

I remember an occasion when some of the young doctors of SCR had been selected for the Post Graduate programme, but were not getting relieved. Vinod Yadav narrated to me the story. There were tears in eyes of these youngsters as there was a rule that doctors could be relieved for higher studies only if no relief was demanded by the Zones.

He wanted to help them. Selection in the PG programme was as such very difficult. He wanted a change in the rule and wanted GMs to be empowered to engage Contract Medical Practioner (CMP) against the vacancies of doctors proceeding on study leave. It was quite in order as the engagement of CMP had already been permitted. I briefed Lohani. I knew he would agree in the blink of an eye. That was what happened. These doctors had very little time left to report for their PG programme. We issued the policy in a day. The doctors were relieved.

After Vinod Yadav assumed the charge of Chairman, Railway Board, a few new initiatives, such as opening the rail sector for operation of private trains and corporatisation of Railways Production Units, were allocated to me. Both initiatives were a part of the 100 days programme of the Government. We delivered on them. Request for qualification (RFQ) was finalised and bidders shortlisted in late 2020. The project did not receive good response as Ministry of Railways could not resolve some of the issues raised by the bidders as those were complex issues. This would been the biggest railway reform in independent India. This project required alignment with other ministries. We got that done through a mechanism of Group of Secretaries. Other important initiatives like e-office and Unique Medical Identity Card (UMID) for Railways employees were implemented due to the free hand given by Vinod Yadav, and the trust he had in me. Because of the trust, he made me look after three portfolios in the Railway Board – Transformation, Planning and Railway Electrification.

He focused on sustained communication with the field staff through video conferencing (VC) with DRMs and GMs. He interacted with them every month to remain connected to improve operational efficiency and safety. VCs used to give him the opportunity to connect with 1,500–2,000 senior officers at one go and help him communicate on a sustained basis. He introduced the concept of digital approval of drawings for fast execution of projects called as 'e-DAS' (electronic drawing approval system). This project became functional in June 2020.

Approval of new and single service for Indian Railways – Indian Railway Management Service – replacing eight erstwhile services, approved by the Cabinet, once implemented, will bring a paradigm shift in Railways operations. The organisation will benefit the most due to better alignment amongst fellow officers. This would be one of the biggest contributions of Vinod Yadav.

One important event that I remember about him was when he agreed to visit the Indian School of Business (ISB), Hyderabad, in October 2019, and signed an MOU with ISB. The outcome was a case study written by ISB and published by Harvard Publishing on the Madhepura Project, that is so close to my heart. In June 2020, we were to sign a letter of consent for the use of this case study for classroom purposes. He approved and then I signed the consent letter. The case study was published on June 24, 2020, the first such case study of Indian Railways.

That is Vinod Kumar Yadav – a very cool, calm, soft spoken and a tall person. He trusted his people but took his time to decide to move forward in some of the cases. His dress sense was quite different. He was always in a formal suit and a tie.

Ved Mani Tiwari

He is a genius, of medium build and a handsome person. I have yet to see such a competent officer in the Railways. Once I wrote in his Annual Confidential Report, 'He is more competent than me.'

It was September 2007. I was going to Switzerland with a delegation of eight officers, coming from different educational backgrounds and from different working areas – Ministry of Railways, Zonal Railways and a Project organisation – to study tunnel ventilation, adopted in Lotschberg Base Tunnel (34 km) and Gotthard Base Tunnel (world's longest – 57 km). I was looking for someone who knew tunnel ventilation quite well. We were to lay down a policy for tunnel ventilation in Railways.

I spoke to S.S. Joshi, my batchmate in DMRC. He told me about Ved Mani Tiwari. Till then I did not know him. I talked to him and within half an hour he was with me at the Railway Board. Upon my request to get some guiding principles and methodology followed in DMRC, he sent me three reports, each containing 150–200 pages, within an hour. The reports had been prepared earlier by Ved Mani Tiwari. I was simply overwhelmed. It made my day.

We went to Switzerland and inspected the mesmerising technologies and operations at 250 kmph in the Lotschberg Base Tunnel, which had become operational, and Gottahard Base Tunnel, which was under construction. Ved Mani's memory remained with me.

In December 2007, I was asked to lead the Madhepura project. After looking at the contours, I realised that it was going to be a long haul and a very big initiative. This was where my heart was when I was a Director in the year 2000. But I was all alone. I wanted one more officer of the level of a Director.

Ved Mani was still in my memory. Again, I checked up with S.S. Joshi about him. He said that Ved Mani had already resigned and would be joining Veolia Transport, a French multinational.

Even then I wanted to talk to him. I got Ved's number and spoke to him. He told me the same thing. Despite that I asked him to come and meet me. He did come and met me. When I requested him to work with me on this mega project – setting up of loco factory in PPP, about which I also had no clear idea, he agreed.

Thereafter, I ensured his resignation was withdrawn and he was posted in my directorate. He joined me on January 14, 2008. I was confident I would be able to complete my project. That was my opinion about Ved Mani.

What has gone in the making of this project is history, as the 12,000 HP locos are running well in Indian Railways. He would often be seen working till 2 a.m. in his office. Once I left office at 8 p.m. and asked him to leave, too. Somehow, I had an inkling that he would not go home till late night, as a lot of work was yet to be done. That night I had gone to India Gate for some reason, and it was around 11.30 pm. I thought of going and seeing whether he was still in his chambers; and to my surprise he was still working with thousands of insects all around him. I was flabbergasted. I persuaded him to leave and go home. That's Ved Mani for you.

I am convinced that 'first who, then what' only works. His capabilities were beyond imagination. He would take over everyone's workload and deliver the results as well. Together, we created a framework for setting up the Kanchrapara and Dankuni factories. We settled all the issues related to Madhepura and took the proposal to the Cabinet for approval, four times. Without Ved Mani, it would have been impossible. At Kanchrapara, we wanted to set up a separate factory to manufacture EMUs that would have replaced slow-moving loco hauled passenger trains to improve line capacity. Similarly, at Dankuni, we set up a factory to manufacture locomotives to enhance loco production. A centre of excellence was also to be established after the induction of 9,000 HP locomotives for the Western DFC. This initiative did not move forward in a manner as it was conceived.

In October 2011, I went to Dhanbad. Ved Mani was left alone to defend the Madhepura project. He did this with amazing skills. Unbelievable performance! He used to take good care of his staff.

In June 2013, he was appointed as Director Systems in the Kochi Metro in Kerala He established a new system – Common Mobility Card – that became a common access card for Metro and city bus transport services and could be used for some other general purposes also. At that time, he was the youngest Director in any PSU. He finalised contracts for Rolling Stock and other systems for Kochi Metro, at least cost, at that time.

Thereafter, he sought voluntary retirement from Railways and worked as CEO of Sterlite Transmission. He completed the J&K transmission line project using Heli Cranes (helicopter cranes) in record time – six months ahead of target. He won several contracts in Brazil for Sterlite. Later, he moved to the Welspur group as Managing Director. After his tenure with Kochi Metro, he also worked as Managing Director of Sun Edison, a US based company.

During the time, I was DRM Dhanbad, luckily, he became my neighbour and helped my family like a younger brother. I lived alone at Dhanbad. My wife lived alone in Delhi. He is a kind hearted, simple and helping person, and at the same time a super-competent human being with outstanding leadership qualities. He helped me deliver Madhepura; all the credit goes to him.

A.K. Mital

I met him first on August 2, 2014, after the superannuation of Kul Bhushan, Member, Railway Board. He was Member Staff, Railway Board, looking after Member Electrical's duties as well. He had only heard about me, not known me. Madhepura, Kanchrapara and Dankuni projects were known to everyone due to their size and uniqueness. I was handling all these projects.

I had put up a file containing 53 pages, pertaining to 9,000 HP locomotive for Western DFC. He asked me, 'Do you want me to read such a long proposal?' I said, 'Yes.' He went through the proposal while I was sitting and was simultaneously responding to his queries. He read all the pages. He complimented me for the professional clarity with which the proposal had been made and approved it.

Sometime in the second week of August 2014, he had a long debate on the business model of Madhepura. This created a strong bond of trust as he was able to see the clarity with which policies were being conceived, and how these policies would impact the organisation positively and help in improving the financial health of Indian Railways. The level of transparency and professional honesty was at its best, and this was very much liked by Mital. He remained Member Electrical for about five months.

He was appointed CRB on January 1, 2015. He trusted me, and consequently provided all the support for successfully getting awarded with the Madhepura project in November 2015. As he came from Store service, his support for the project enhanced the credibility of the Madhepura model, and therefore I got full support from the Store Directorate. Mital was the Chairman at a very critical stage of the Madhepura project. The tender committee finalised its recommendations within 15–20 days for a ₹25,000 crore project. It was phenomenal. Mital had understood the whole business model and he was completely supportive of the idea. He was able to see the future of PPP in India and the role of new technology of 12,000 HP in the freight operations of the Railways.

After the project had been awarded in November 2015, a key decision was to be taken for the release of ₹119 crore for payment to the villagers who had lost their lands through the State Government of Bihar. The Ministry of Finance had imposed a cut in Gross Budgetary Support. He intervened and the money was released to East Central Railway for payment to the District Magistrate, Madhepura. The villagers were paid and the project was successful. I developed a good relations with him, and I was delighted when he got two years extension of service.

After the Madhepura project was awarded in November 2015, I was posted as Executive Director Rolling Stock on January 1, 2016. For the longest time, the Minister of State for Railways Shri Manoj Sinha, had been talking about finding a new product for Diesel Locomotive Works Varanasi (DLW). Varanasi was the parliamentary constituency of the Prime Minister Shri Narendra Modi. I used to feel quite excited about DLW. This was the place I had spent one month in December 1983 during my probation period. This was the best place to live during probation.

Somewhere around September-October 2016, I suggested to Mital to approve manufacture of electric locomotives at DLW. He was a little displeased and asked me, 'Will you not let me work as Chairman?' He hinted the importance of the PM's constituency. I explained what the Minister of State Shri Manoj Sinha had been saying, and also told him that the electric loco manufacture at DLW would be seen as a sign of progress. He was still not convinced. After a few days, I again broached the subject of the manufacture of Train Sets at DLW, as a new product. Finally, he agreed to manufacture two electric locos. But he cautioned me to handle this with care. I assured him of my full support, especially from the point of view of Staff Unions.

I went to CLW a number of times to convince the staff and supervisors that two sets of loco kits would be taken from CLW to DLW to start manufacturing electric locos at DLW. We were able to manufacture two locos in 2016-17. A new beginning was made. Since 2020, we are manufacturing only electric locos at DLW without any industrial relations problem. This was all thanks to Mital. DLW was rightly re-named as Banaras Locomotive Works (BLW) in 2019-20.

After the Rail Vikas Shivir (a conclave of railwaymen to ideate), he selected me to head the Transformation Cell and let me have the Cell based in Rail Bhavan. I drafted the constitution of the Cell such that it enabled us to drive major reforms in the Railways. The credit for this too goes to Mital. He had given me full freedom to do what I wanted to do in my role.

Mital is a simple, kind-hearted, and a well-meaning person. He followed rules in true letter and spirit, and generally did not like to deviate. Once he was convinced, he gave full support. He generally did not like to change the smoothly running system. That is what A.K. Mital was like.

Transformation Team

Rail Vikas Shivir was held from November 18 to 20, 2016. The Prime Minister had addressed this conclave on November 20, 2016. More than a lakh idea had been generated by about 70,000 staff members and officers. The Transformation Cell was constituted to drive and execute some of the strategic initiatives identified during the Rail Shivir.

The orders were issued on January 10, 2017, and I was appointed to head this Cell. It was placed directly under the CRB. Jeetendra Singh (Electrical), A.K. Chandra (Mechanical), Tushar Pandey (Civil), V. Arun Kumar (Store), Rajesh Gupta (Signal), Niraj Sahay (Traffic),

Sanjiv Narain Mathur (Finance) and Ravindra Kumar (Personnel) were initially posted to the Cell. They represented all the eight services in Railways.

Sanjiv Mathur went on deputation to Department of Personnel and Training in about three months time and was replaced by Sanjeeb Kumar. V. Arun Kumar went on study leave to UK to pursue LLM and was replaced by Ashok Kumar. Dr Anand Khati was posted to represent the Personnel discipline, as the Personnel officer initially posted worked only for a few weeks. Umesh Balonda replaced Rajesh Kumar and Ashok Kumar was replaced by Appa Rao.

There was no convenient place to work from. A temporary office was set up in DFCCIL building at Pragati Maidan, New Delhi. It was the most inhospitable place from the point of view of location and environment. On the very first day, I had told the CRB that the Cell would not be able to function from Pragati Maidan. A modern office set-up in Rail Bhawan was agreed upon. Tushar was asked to take full care, prepare an estimate and get the office constructed in the shortest possible time. Tushar was at his best as a Civil Engineer and had the passion to get the best possible layout. DRM Delhi would have the office constructed.

We went to see the Invest India office in Vigyan Bhawan. This was one of the finest buildings I had seen in the government. Invest India is a JV company set up by Department of Industrial Policy and Promotion, Ministry of Commerce, and Industry (35 per cent equity), FICCI (51 per cent equity) and State Governments of India (0.5 per cent each). The core mandate of Invest India is investment promotion and facilitation. Our desire was to have an office of this kind. After the visit, Tushar got clear ideas as to what to do and how. I gave him a free hand.

It was a challenge to engage a management consultant for at least six months to develop business models for the strategic initiatives that had been approved, as mentioned earlier. Jeetendra and I concentrated on finalising the Terms of Reference (TOR) for engagement of the consultant. We finalised the TOR and handed it over to RITES to take the bidding process forward. As soon as RITES was able to float the tender and arrange a pre-bid conference, I went to the RITES office along with my team and addressed the prospective bidders to make everyone clear about what we expected from the consultant we proposed to engage. Jeetendra handled this subject very proficiently and wherever he needed my help, it was available. We got the consultants engaged by the first week of July 2017. In the meantime, we also prepared a policy to hire young professionals (YP) like Niti Aayog did. This was approved by the Board but the hiring did not come to fruition as we wanted to do it through Niti

Aayog. This was Jeetendra's charge, as he had come from Niti Aayog and had a good touch and feel of the YPs in Niti Aayog. We did not pursue this further as there was no personnel officer for some time.

In the meantime, Jeetendra proposed to organise an Inner Engineering and Leadership programme for all the Transformation Cell officers at Isha Foundation, Coimbatore. He had attended the programme a year earlier while he was in Niti Aayog. I thought that staying together while attending this programme would create a good bonding and provide everyone an opportunity to reflect. What Jeetendra had briefed me about Isha Foundation was wonderful. Isha foundation is run by volunteers and aims to bring about physical, mental and spiritual well-being for everyone.

We decided to organise a special programme for Railways for a group of about 50 officers, participating on voluntary basis, from all Zones. CRB approved it after a lot of effort put in by Jeetendra. We went to Coimbatore in June 2017 for five days with all the officers of the Cell except Sanjeeb, who had to appear for an exam. I consider this as the most memorable event of my life as it changed my life. My wife had accompanied me. I started practicing *Shambhavi Mahamudra*. It is a meditation exercise for 21 minutes, preceded by yoga exercises. It is experiential in nature. It gives me much peace of mind. My food habits have also undergone a sea change – more fruits and salads. I thank Jeetendra for this inner cleansing journey that all of us started in the Cell. In fact, everyone liked the contents of the programme and the beautiful and serene surroundings. What I still remember is the frozen mercury kept in a big container at the centre of the bathing pond (unique, as mercury is in liquid state at room temperature; some special techniques were followed to freeze it at room temperature) and the *dhyan kendra*. It truly did foster a bonding and brought us closer than we had been prior to the visit.

This ashram is situated at the foothills of Velliangiri Mountains, 40 km from the city of Coimbatore. A 112-feet statue of Adi Yogi Shiva is located here. It was inaugurated by Prime Minister Shri Narendra Modi on Mahashivaratri on February 24, 2017.

The journey continued, and everyone was working on his identified initiatives, from amongst the 55 initiatives approved by the full Board in February 2017. Jeetendra was much ahead of others. He organised an international conference on 'Simulators for Drivers'. All the leading manufactures in the world – Lander Spain, Sydac Australia and CORYS France – participated. I had visited Spain a little while earlier and had seen Lander make simulators in Barcelona. Long back in 1992, I had gone to the USA to acquire simulator technology. This was the most exciting initiative taken by Jeetendra. We proposed a pan India sanction of this project for about ₹600 crore, but ₹350 crore were sanctioned to procure and provide these simulators in all training schools in Indian Railways.

Similarly, Tushar worked on mechanisation of track maintenance and got track machines worth ₹6,000 crore sanctioned, the most exciting of which was track videography – one machine for each of the 16 Zones. It was unprecedented.

We organised an inspirational transformation lecture series. Lectures were delivered by Shiv Khera, a motivational speaker and author; Pramath Raj Sinha, founding Dean, ISB Hyderabad; O.P. Bhatt, ex-Chairman, State Bank of India (SBI); M. Damodaran, ex-Chairman, Securities and Exchange Board of India (SEBI); and Suresh Narain, Chairman and MD, Nestle India. All this was slowly and steadily building alignment amongst all the stakeholders and sending a clear message that 'change is the crying need of the hour and the only thing constant' under the prevailing circumstances, and most needed in the Railways. Status quo would not serve us any more.

AT Kearney, our consultants, organised two workshops on leadership – one at the Railway Board itself for capability building of our own officers and the other at North Frontier Railway HQ, Guwahati. Each officer of the Cell was to organise one workshop each, in coordination with AT Kearny and the Zone of his choice. Everyone did it. I attended five of these workshops.

After Lohani arrived on the scene in August 2017, the pattern of working changed. While all of us continued working on the 55 identified initiatives, empowerment and delegation became the central theme and major efforts were directed towards process, structure and cultural reforms.

Jeetendra was extremely good at drafting and making cogent notes. He took care of the rules and regulations, and coordination with SCR. He worked on all items where no dedicated officer was available, such as RPF or Personnel. Jeetendra also did excellent work in identifying locations to build short-stay homes for vulnerable and runaway children in need of care and protection at stations, as well as homes in Delhi, Guwahati, Danapur, Samastipur and Ahmedabad to accommodate 25 children each as transit accommodation to restore the children to their families. This was in accordance with Juvenile Justice Act. This was for a noble cause, and it took time for us to draft the policy.

A.K. Chandra was brilliant at organising Town Hall events like Sampark, Samanvay, Samvaad and Parivartan Sangoshthi and was very good at coordinating with external agencies. He was also well versed with public relations, service contracts and workshop related matters.

Tushar was good at works contracts, rail track maintenance, issues relating to gangmen and Vigilance related items. He was pursuing MBA from FMS Delhi, with my permission. He liaised with Divisions and construction wings in Railways and Central Public Works Department (CPWD) to understand how to ease processes and how to bring in best practices in Railways.

Initially, medical matters were handled by Rajesh and later by Umesh Balonda. Rajesh wore his Vigilance hat and brought out factors which could compromise public interest and give his critical appreciation of the various proposals, and I valued this the most.

Balonda was an all-rounder. He could dive deep, understand any issue and come up with a suitable proposal. I assisted him wherever he needed my help. The word 'No' was not there in his dictionary. Except for one occasion in relation to CGHS Card for Railway Board officials, I do not remember he ever had any difficulty in deciding upon a matter.

Arun Kumar was like a professor and therefore put up forceful arguments with regard to Store matters. We did the maximum delegation on Store matters. The DG Store was very supportive of his ideas and wherever there was difficulty, I resolved it after dialogue with DG Store.

After Arun's departure to UK, Ashok Kumar played an extremely positive role. He had come from Central Vigilance Commission (CVC) where he had spent five years, and I had heard K.V. Chaudhary, Central Vigilance Commissioner, speak very highly of him in one of the workshops organised by Railways. He organised a very thought-provoking workshop on Store matters in Pune and it benefited the Railways as a follow up – the most important being the enhanced pace of computerisation of Stores Department in the Divisions.

Niraj was very knowledgeable in his field – Traffic and Commercial – but was very cautious. He was generally not happy with the overall system. He had worked in the Ministry of External Affairs. He had a good command over language and was well read. His mother was not keeping well at Chandigarh and therefore he was genuinely concerned about her. Once there was an opportunity for him to go to ISB Hyderabad and attend a one-week programme on leadership. He was quite interested, and I immediately approved his visit.

After his return, he briefed me about his experience at ISB. It led to a major initiative on capacity and capability development. A major event was organised by him by convening a meeting of all the Directors and faculty members from CTIs and NAIR. A speaker was also invited for a lecture on Emotional Intelligence (EI). The speaker was Rajeshwar Upadhyaya, the master trainer of EI in India. This was simply awe-inspiring. This event was organised in September 2018.

Meeting Rajeshwar Upadhyaya was the experience of a lifetime, difficult to explain in words. One can only experience and feel.

After this learning, we organised EI programmes for 27 GMs and 68 DRMs at NAIR Vadodara. Lohani agreed to let all GMs and DRMs to attend this programme. I stayed with all of them at Vadodara. I had no idea about EI prior to September 2018.

Thereafter, from the experience and feedback that we received from the DRMs and GMs, we drafted a policy on EI for Railways. In fact, my association with ISB started after Niraj and Upadhyaya introduced me to the ISB faculty. Together with ISB, we were able to write case studies on the Madhepura project. These were published by Harvard Publishing in June 2020. It was an unforgettable experience!

Sanjeeb was a big psychological support in the team and in all our endeavours. Finance has always played a key role in decision making. He had already done his LLB and was pursuing MBA from FMS Delhi. I had an agreement with him that I would do everything possible to ensure that he completed his MBA. On his part, he would do what was right for the organisation, evaluate everything on merit and do the work with the alacrity it deserved. He would clear files even at 9 p.m. if the situation demanded. I had no concern on this account.

All the officers were free to express themselves without any fear or compulsion whatsoever. Sanjeeb was entitled to agree or not to agree with the proposals. Similarly, others could also do the same. I had my own views which I expressed independently and that would obviously be the view of the Transformation Cell. However, I briefed everyone about it. It was transparency at its best.

There were occasions when I prepared a draft on certain subjects and gave it to the officers to discuss amongst themselves and either reach a consensus or convey their reservations or dissensions. I conveyed my views from my perspective. Usually, we came to a common understanding. But there were a few occasions when I initiated the proposal myself either due to the reservations of my officers, or as a final note that Lohani would approve based on observations of other Board Members. Such a note was always put up by me. I loved to do it.

Once an issue emerged in the Cell in the early days. Some officers wanted my signature on the policy letters. I told them that they should bear the signature of the officer who had initiated the proposal, as that would be most appropriate. Generally, the policy letters were signed by Directors or Executive Directors in the Railway Board. Also, since these policies would be in place for times to come, the person would feel happy as the signatory whenever someone attributed the change to him. It would also give the person a sense of ownership. The matter was settled but some of the officers still wanted my signature on the office copy, to which I complied without batting an eyelid as it assured my confidence in them and made them feel secure. It was a confidence building measure.

As passed, we decided to bring out a compendium of all these policy letters. I hadn't envisaged the kind of thrill I saw amongst the officers. Everyone was counting how many letters had been issued by him. It was then that they realised the impact of my decision and thanked me for what I had decided more than a year ago. In fact, each time a policy letter was issued, field officers used to generally thank the officer who had signed the letter. It became a sentimental issue later. If an officer concerned was not present and the file had been received duly approved, we used to wait for the concerned officer to return, and then issue the letter.

In the whole journey, one officer who played a vital role as an interface between Lohani and the Cell, and between field units and the Cell, was Rakesh Chaudhary. He was Director Coordination, attached to Lohani. He was an amazing character – a tall, quiet and supremely competent person who first took the inputs from the Divisions, discussed them with me, understood my opinion on the subject, and then formally forwarded new proposals to the Cell. Quite a number of officers in the Cell initially disagreed with him. These disagreements were about those ideas whose time had not arrived but were important for the field. Rakesh Chaudhary would generally be in sync with me. Crowd sourcing ideas from the field, firming them up and sending them to the Cell required a marathon effort on his part. I really thank him for the proactive role he played in our journey of transformation.

Partha Reddy and Appa Rao played an important role in putting together a framework for Private Train Operators which has been brought out in detail in earlier chapters. Both Partha Reddy and Appa Rao are electrical engineers by education and had worked in other Central Government ministries. They had a good understanding of Public Private Partnership framework. While Partha had earlier worked in the NITI Aayog, Appa Rao had worked in the Ministry of Civil Aviation. Both had done what an average officer would not have even understood. The most important part of the framework was fixing the haulage charges at ₹518 per km for a 16-car train with overheads limited to 25 per cent, as against 66 per cent considered by Railways for internal calculations. Appa Rao and Partha Reddy did amazing work in getting the contours of the projects finalised after ten meetings of the Group of Secretaries and two meetings of PPPAC, Ministry of Finance. My support and thoughts were always there.

Chandra put together the framework for corporatisation of Production Units and we were able to finalise the draft Cabinet Note for consideration.

The role played by my staff and two Deputy Directors – Niraj Kumar and Satish Solanki – was simply brilliant. They would work with minimal resources every time and all the time.

My Senior Principal Private Secretary Veda Thakur and earlier Principal Private Secretary Seema Khanna were very respectful, well-meaning, and always willing to support. All the approvals for the tour programmes and leave of the officers used to be done without any delays. In fact, I never looked at where the officers were going on tour or when they were taking leave. I only questioned if they were not travelling by air, as it would take more time and waste their productive time in transit. This kept the team of my executive directors supremely motivated. Sometimes I entertained them at the Civil Services Officers Club for lunch.

It was a very warm and cordial working environment without any tension or worries and everyone had his say in decision making without any pressure. Each one was fully empowered to do what he thought was going to improve ultimate service delivery.

This journey came to an end on June 30, 2020, when I superannuated from service. I'll cherish my journey of 42 months in the Transformation Cell all my life.

Dr Phil Zerrillo

During my entire career of 37 years, I did not get many opportunities of attending training institutes in India. I did get several opportunities to go overseas for training. Whenever some training opportunity arose in India, my bosses did not relieve me due to some urgent situation or the other. I therefore could not even go to ISB. Those who visited this campus were quite appreciative of the infrastructure and the ambience.

Sometime in June 2019 (I do not remember the exact date), someone called me on WhatsApp. I did not respond as the number was not on my contact list. Immediately thereafter, there was a very humble message. When I read it, I returned the call immediately. The caller gave the reference of Rajeshwar Upadhyaya, whom I knew quite well. She also told me about her plan to collaborate with Railways for writing case studies. She asked me if I was willing to do that.

I instantly agreed. Rather, I said I would be only too happy to see it happen. The caller was Mamtha Reddy, Head, Government and Public Sector, at ISB Hyderabad.

On June 5, 2019, she connected me to Dr Deepa Mani for some data about suburban rail operations in Mumbai. On June 12, 2019, she introduced me to Dr Phil Zerrillo, Deputy Dean, ISB, through email. A week later, Dr Phil and Mamtha flew down to Delhi. I met them at the Civil Services Officers Institute over a working lunch. For a long time, I had been thinking of writing case studies on Madhepura and Transformation.

Dr Z, as Phil loves to be addressed, then heard the story and got quite interested in both the cases. Thereafter, Geetika accompanied Dr Z and visited my office. Geetika is a very humble and soft-spoken professional, working in ISB. She holds an MBA degree and is quite proficient in handling executive education; writing of case studies forms a part of her portfolio. I also decided to go to ISB and give a full 3-4 hour-long brief to all those who wanted to understand and write the case study on Madhepura along with Dr Z. After that several interactions took place, and Dr Z finalised the two cases. The Covid-19 pandemic did lead to delays. The two cases were finally published by Harvard Publishing on June 24, 2020. I am grateful to Dr Z and the ISB team.

Fair, tall and handsome, Dr Z is an amazing professor who is so motivating and convincing that you will do exactly what he tells you. He mesmerises his listeners with his intellectual insights. He once hosted dinner for me and my son in Hotel Maurya.

I requested Vinod Yadav to visit ISB to engage with them in a more structured manner. We were having lunch with Dr Raj Srivastava, Dean ISB and Dr Z along with other professors. Dr Raj floated an idea of signing an MOU with the Railways. CRB was sitting next to me at the lunch table. He quietly asked me as to what should be done, and within seconds he agreed with the proposal. The deal was closed. Alka Arora Misra, the Executive Director, Head of Training and Manpower Planning, Railway Board, was also sitting next to Vinod Yadav.

On October 30, 2019, the agreement was signed by Dr Raj and Vinod Yadav. Dr Raj flew to Delhi along with his team of professors. Dr Raj is a very renowned professor of international repute. His desire to create a blend of government and academia to bring tacit and explicit knowledge together will help a new India take shape.

The journey of collaboration with ISB started. Mamtha also introduced me to Dr Milind, yet another pleasing and eminent Professor. He did a lot of work on the Private Train Operation Project of the Railways. In April 2020, he started working on Social Impact Assessment and Artificial Intelligence initiatives of the Railways. The engagement of the Railways with ISB continues even now, in June 2021. I hope it benefits both mutually. I am very happy about bringing ISB and Railways together, and I thank Mamtha for this. I am also grateful to Rajeshwar who introduced me to ISB.

Rajeshwar Upadhyaya

Niraj Sahay returned from ISB after a week-long leadership development programme. Niraj had high standards in appreciating something or someone. He praised both the ISB and the content of the programme. I was delighted to see Niraj happy. By early September 2018, I had been to several CTIs of Railways as desired by Lohani. All direct recruits get trained and groomed from day one at these CTIs. I requested Lohani to meet all the faculty members and Directors of these CTIs together as I was not very happy to see the infrastructure at these CTIs and the motivation levels of the faculty members who had a great role to play in shaping the destiny of Railways. This was bothering me quite a lot.

Lohani agreed to organise a one-day workshop at the Rail Museum. We decided to invite an inspirational leader and a speaker. I spoke to Pramath Sinha, the founding Dean of ISB. He was in fact at the airport when I called but was kind enough to respond to me and suggested a few names. I then discussed with Niraj and told him to organise the event all by himself. He suggested that we invite Rajeshwar Upadhyaya. He had attended his lectures at ISB, and so I agreed with him. I told Lohani about the decisions.

Rajeshwar Upadhyaya, visiting faculty at ISB, was invited by the Ministry of Railways. He flew from Mumbai. He came to the Rail Museum on that day. I sat near him in the conference hall. He spoke for about an hour or so. He was simply awesome. He talked about Emotional Intelligence and its relevance for sustainable success of the top leadership. Niraj had given me a hint about EI earlier. I was extremely interested in connecting with Rajeshwar Upadhyaya after the session and engaged with him for a longer duration.

We organised separate three-day workshops between October–December 2018 for all the GMs and all the DRMs at NAIR Vadodara. The speaker was Rajeshwar Upadhyaya, and the theme was Emotional Intelligence. I stayed for the duration of all the three workshops with the GMs, DRMs and Rajeshwar Upadhyaya at NAIR Vadodara. A bond was established.

Upadhyaya's depth of knowledge and thoroughness in the subject is impressive. If you listen to him once, you'll want to listen to him many times over. His intellect, his personal conduct and the aura of his personality will mesmerise you. His command over the language and the motivation that comes along due to the depth of his nuanced understanding of the scriptures, spirituality, mythology, philosophy and extensive international experience will make you his staunch follower and admirer.

I benefited immensely from his personal guidance. I revere him as my *guruji* (guru is a teacher, guide, expert, or master of certain knowledge, a reverential figure for students). After my engineering days at Pantnagar, where I had Dr Subir Ray as my role model and teacher, I looked up to Rajeshwar Upadhyaya as my second such teacher.

Dr Subir Ray, besides teaching, had fascinated me with his simplicity and knowledge on a variety of subjects. His talks were quite motivating. He used to be one of the speakers at almost all fora.

Pursuing a Fellow Programme in Management (FPM) at ISB was an important personal decision which I took, inspired by Rajeshwar Upadhyaya and my son. Rajeshwar is a great thinker, motivator and himself a Level 5 leader. He is a perfect teacher and a guide. No wonder, therefore, that he is the Master Trainer for India for EQi, certified by Multi Health Systems, Canada.

I do not have adequate vocabulary to express my feelings for Rajeshwar Upadhyaya. He has taught Emotional Intelligence to MPs, MLAs, doctors, ambassadors, officers from IAS, IFS, IPS, IRS and Railways, entrepreneurs, scientists, academicians, and even monks. The list is unending.

He has been a visiting faculty at ISB for more than 16 years. He has taught at eminent Business Schools around the world such as ESADE Spain; ERAMUS Netherlands; THUNDERBIRD, Arizona USA; SKOLKOVO, Moscow, Russia; KAIT South Korea; and FIA Brazil.

This book you are now reading is due to his inspiration. He is my friend, philosopher, guide and, above all, guruji. I owe everything to him.

I am grateful to God, for bringing me close to him – and his agreeing to guide me!

Piyush Goyal

It was at 8 p.m. on Tuesday, December 12, 2017, when I got an opportunity to meet the Minister of Railways, Shri Piyush Goyal. He had taken charge of this great organisation on September 3, 2017. We, in the Transformation Cell, were probably the last to make a presentation to him. A tall, fair and handsome person, Shri Goyal is a highly intellectual Minister in the Union Cabinet. He had additional charge of Coal Ministry at that time. His mother was elected MLA thrice from Maharashtra. His father was the Union Minister for Shipping in the Vajpayee Government during 2001–2003. He is a qualified Chartered Accountant (CA) who held the second rank in All India CA exam.

He had taken over charge from Shri Suresh Prabhu. Before he took over the Railways portfolio, the CRB had also been changed. The Khatauli rail accident of August 19, 2017, in the Delhi Division had created a lot of furore, leading to the appointment of a new Chairman Railway Board and a new Minister of Railways.

From the word 'Go' we were able to see Shri Goyal's dynamism, leadership and intellectual depth in the variety of subjects we were talking about with reference to Transformation. By now he was in full command and control of Indian Railways. He had been more than three months already as its head. His full office team was with him. Decisions were taken even while we were making the presentation. Some of the key decisions were – Operations Research-based approach to prepare crew and loco links and mechanisation of track maintenance and simulators for drivers. He appreciated the efforts of the Cell in issuing a lot of delegations, especially after the unfortunate incident of Elphinstone Road bridge in Mumbai in which 29 people had died. It was he who told us that delegation of powers to GMs with regards to organ transplant saved the life of one of the members of the Railways family.

In fact, the culture of empowerment started after his deep understanding of the Railways system. Without such strong political support, we would not have been able to do so much, because we were doing something that had not been experienced by Railways over the past four decades. Credit goes to the Minister for his dynamic leadership and the vision.

By the time we came to the end of the presentation, we were told to organise Sampark, Samanvay, Samvaad at Ashoka Hotel with all the GMs, DRMs, all PHODs and the full Board on December 16, 2017. It was 10 p.m. at that time.

We had just two days to prepare as officers were to arrive on December 15 evening. Ashwini Lohani did not attend the meeting as he was to go to Vishakhapatnam to see a rebuilt bridge. As soon as the meeting was over, I spoke to Lohani. Immediately we decided to do everything at Ashoka Hotel, including the stay of the officers. We were also asked to arrange a motivational speaker. Time was short but we arranged Sonam Wangchuk as the speaker for the occasion. The Minister came with his wife to attend the event. His wife, however, left after Sonam Wangchuk's speech was over.

The Minister sat through the conference on both the days. A number of issues were decided, and 14 committees of GMs were formed to submit their recommendations. He was quite happy with the conduct of the meeting. He spoke of about ten commandments for good governance, the most notable being decisive leadership (no shirking away), reduce red tape (reduce paperwork and reduce signatures on files to four or five), do root cause analysis (simple solutions), outcome oriented action (not an ostrich approach), think of innovative financing, deep contact with technology, time bound action, partnership with stakeholders, accountability and monitoring of projects, and transparency in work.

Another such big event that he desired that we organised on December 7 and 8, 2019 was the Parivartan Sangoshthi. The venue this time was Pravasi Bhartiya Kendra in Delhi. Some of the historic decisions taken during the Sangoshthi included a single service 'Indian Railway Management Service' replacing eight services and 'Functional Board'. It was only Shri Piyush Goyal who could take such transformative decisions. The Union Cabinet approved these decisions on December 24, 2019. It was unimaginable that such critical, life-changing decisions could be taken in such a short time.

Some of the major decisions taken by Shri Piyush Goyal as the Minister for Railways were:
- Empowerment of field units in an unprecedented manner.
- 100 per cent electrification of railway tracks.
- Modernisation of railway signalling.
- Stop manufacture of old ICF design coaches and switch over to 100 per cent German design LHB coaches (safer for travel).
- Single service for Railways (IRMS) instead of eight services.
- Restructuring of the Railway Board on Functional lines rather than Department ones.
- Open Rail Sector to run Private Passenger Trains.

On the day of my retirement on June 30, I gave a three-hour long presentation on a variety of subjects as he had given me the charge of three directorates as Additional Member – Planning, Transformation and Railway Electrification. I remember that he had liked my presentation on Social Impact Assessment of Railways Investment as I had suggested to have a Social Impact Measurement Tool (SIMT) developed. We wrote to ISB Hyderabad to work on this project.

He called me over phone once on December 7, 2018, when I was at IGI Airport, waiting to board a flight to Vadodara. He asked about the purpose of my visit. I told him about the workshop on Emotional Intelligence for DRMs.

He wanted me to get SOP for Publicity issued immediately. I assured him I would do so. We did it. In fact, the proposal was prepared on Sunday, December 9, 2018, while we were in Vadodara. My Executive Director Finance was with me that day in Vadodara. It was done within 4–5 days. That was how focused Shri Piyush Goyal was.

I remember another occasion when I presented him a Compendium of Transformation Cell Policies and Circulars in December 2018. He was visibly very happy, and he showed it to all the visitors who came to see him, including one of the Ambassadors.

That is Shri Piyush Goyal – a dynamic and visionary leader, an inspirational speaker, and a person full of energy.

A.K. Jain

He was the DRM Allahabad when I got to know him in January 1993. A tall, soft spoken, well-read person, and someone I consider as my role model. He was responsible for my posting in the Railway Board. After his tenure as DRM, he worked as Chief Electrical Loco Engineer in Delhi while I continued as in-charge of Kanpur Loco Shed. He was a man of very high integrity and was a very humble human being. Whenever he got very angry, he would say, 'It is not acceptable.' It was a pleasure to work under him and learn how to handle complicated matters. He would never get worried and keep his cool. He would be very confident, as he knew his subject well.

I remember an incident in early January or February 1993. He had just joined as DRM Allahabad. Prior to his taking over, an accident had taken place between Kanpur and Etawah wherein Rajdhani Express had collided with derailed wagons of a freight train. The Rajdhani loco had also derailed along with other coaches. The Guard of the freight train had got down after the derailment of his train to protect his train and protect the other line on which the Rajdhani Express had arrived and collided with derailed wagons. There was no time to avoid and avert this accident. This Guard was not traceable for a long time. The Unions were agitating. There were rumours that the Guard had gone into hiding somewhere in his village.

One evening around 6 p.m. A.K. Jain called me and asked me to go to the site of the accident where the derailed locomotive was lying. While all the derailed coaches were handled and were kept away from the rail track, the loco could not be moved due to its heavier weight and a bulldozer was needed to deal with it.

The information that he had received was that some stray dogs were found eating some flesh around the derailed locomotive. This locomotive was deeply embedded in earth and therefore it was difficult to see what was underneath the loco body. He wanted me to go to the site and assess the situation and report. I reached the site at around 9.30 p.m. and tried to go under the body of locomotive by crawling and was able to see a torch, a pair of shoes, a woollen coat and some remains of a skeleton of a human being. It was undoubtedly the body of the Guard who had gone missing. I briefed the DRM from the site about the situation. I stayed at the site whole night. By 7 a.m., the DRM special arrived and a bulldozer was also arranged. Unions were taken into confidence as the information was available in time. The family of the deceased Guard was informed and necessary actions as per the protocol were taken. The bulldozer driver did a good job of removing all the derailed coaches and shift the locomotive to clear any suspicion of any kind. All the body parts were retrieved.

It was 2 p.m. and we were all preparing to leave the site. The DRM was very thankful to me. In the meantime, the bulldozer driver went to repair a broken hydraulic pipe as the oil had been oozing out. Suddenly we found that his hand had been chopped off as he had slipped, and the hand had gone inside the radiator compartment. I was standing next to him. It was a crisis of unsurmountable proportions. I saw the DRM handle the situation with calmness. We shifted the bulldozer driver to Kanpur Hospital and got the amputation done by 10 p.m. that day. The DRM then left for Allahabad. All the Unions and staff were satisfied because of the pre-emptive action by Jain in asking me to go to the site immediately. This satisfied the Unions as he was prompt enough to take action. I learnt a great deal from this event.

A.K. Jain used to prepare well before going for any meeting as Additional Member in Railway Board. I was the Director Rolling Stock then. I used to suggest to him to outsource maintenance of ABB locos. He would ask me to build a consensus.

Some of the major contributions of A.K. Jain were:
- Rehabilitation of Tap Changer through OEM – what I had been pursuing for a long time happened due to his support as Additional Member;
- Establishing the process of condemning old WAM 1 locomotives based on negative camber (camber is the contour of the underframe of a locomotive which should not start sagging downwards over its life of 35 years) of the chassis of the locomotive while he was CELE Northern Railway, which continued while he was Additional Member;
- His significant contribution in finalising the maintenance regime of the Madhepura project while working as a domain expert with Mott McDonald, UK. This enhanced the credibility of the Madhepura project.

He recommended me for a National Award at Minister's level in 1993, which I got. One gets this award only once in a lifetime. That was A.K. Jain.

Other Aspects

Dedicated Freight Corridor

The Indian Railways track linking four metropolitan cities – Delhi, Mumbai, Chennai, and Kolkata – is called the Golden Quadrilateral. The quadrilateral and its two diagonals connecting Delhi–Chennai and Mumbai–Howrah (Kolkata) add up to a total route-length of about 10,122 km. This is 16 per cent of the total route-km of Indian Railways. This network carries more than 52 per cent of the passengers and 58 per cent of the freight traffic of Indian Railways. Delhi–Howrah and Delhi–Mumbai routes are saturated and working at 100 to 150 per cent of the network capacity. Over the past seven decades, Railways has lost its share of freight volumes, which have gone down from 83 per cent in 1950 to 29 per cent in 2018, predominantly due to inadequate infrastructure expansion. To meet the demand of the Indian economy, two corridors – Eastern, and Western – were sanctioned in 2006–2008 and a special purpose vehicle called Dedicated Freight Corridor of India Limited (DFCCIL) was incorporated in 2006.

- The Eastern Dedicated Freight Corridor (EDFC) runs from Ludhiana in Punjab to Sonnagar in Bihar and extended to Dankuni in West Bengal, is over 1,856 km; Sonnagar to Dankuni is 538 km.
- The Western Dedicated Freight Corridor (WDFC) from Dadri in Uttar Pradesh to Jawaharlal Nehru Port (JNPT) in Mumbai runs over 1,504 km.
- Both these corridors add up to 3,360 km and estimated to cost ₹81,500 crore.

Both corridors are under construction and expected to be operational by December 2023 (about 1,000 kms of Eastern and Western DFCs became operational by April 2021). WDFC is partly funded through soft loan from Japan International Cooperation Agency (JICA) – ₹38,000 crore out of ₹51,000 crore. Similarly, EDFC is partly funded by a loan from the World Bank – ₹13,500 crores out of ₹30,500 crores for Ludhiana to Mughalsarai, which is 1,192 km. Sonnagar to Dankuni is estimated to cost ₹15,000 crores and is planned to be constructed on Public Private Partnership mode. Mughalsarai to Sonnagar is 126 km and is fully funded by Railways.

EDFC is projected to carry commodities like coal, fertiliser, cement, limestone and salt of about 160 million tonnes (both directions) in 2021-22. WDFC is projected to carry about 5.3 million TEU containers in 2021-22. Freight trains will run at 100 kmph on these routes against 75 kmph on Indian Railways network. These corridors will operate on 2x25 KV traction system while Railways network operates on 25 KV system. The height of moving dimensions will be 5.1 m on EDFC and 7.1 m on WDFC. Indian Railways has a moving dimension of 4.265 m. These corridors will be capable of carrying freight trains of 13,000 tonnes against Indian Railways trains of 5,000 tonnes. WDFC will run container trains in double stack formation under highrise OHE.

The project is expected to reduce GHG emissions by 2.5 times on EDFC and 6 times on WDFC due to modal shift expected from road to rail. In addition, it will create a capacity to carry 30 per cent more passenger trains on the existing Delhi–Mumbai–Howrah routes.

National High-Speed Rail Corporation

A 508 km distance between Mumbai and Ahmedabad, with 12 stations in between, will be covered in about 2 hours at 320 kmph with two stops at Surat and Vadodara. All other stopping trains take about 3 hours.

This project costs about ₹1,08,000 crore, and is 80 per cent funded through a soft loan from JICA. The states of Gujarat and Maharashtra will each contribute 5 per cent of the equity while Railways will contribute 10 per cent. Aerial Light Detection and Ranging (LiDAR) is being adopted to undertake high accuracy survey (100 mm).

The project is unique as it will be on standard gauge (1.465 mm) and will be mostly (92 per cent) viaduct with 25 km of the route through an underground tunnel. Of the 25 km underground tunnel, 7 km will pass under sea through Thane Creek. This area is a protected sanctuary of flamingos and nearby mangroves. That is the reason that it will pass through the tunnel under water.

The stations will be at Mumbai, Thane, Virar, Boisar, Vapi, Billimora, Surat, Bharuch, Vadodara, Anand, Ahmedabad and Sabarmati.

Maintenance of the train will be done at Sabarmati (major maintenance), Surat and Thane. A Training Centre has been set up at Vadodara. The Operational Control Centre will be at Vadodara. The traction system will be 2x25 KV. Initially 24 trains of 10 cars will operate on the network. There will be one train every 30 minutes and will carry 750 passengers. The train will be of Japanese Shinkansen (Japanese Bullet) design and equipped with a modern signalling system

All India Railwaymen's Federation

The All India Railwaymen's Federation (AIRF) was formed in 1924 during British rule. The British government started negotiating with the Federation from 1928 and biannual meetings were held between AIRF and the Railway Board, which was at that time headed by the Chief Commissioner of Railways. The main aim of the Federation was to improve the service conditions of railwaymen. It was recognised in 1930.

AIRF has a policy of having continuous dialogue between the Organised Labour and the Railways Administration at various levels, which helps in maintaining industrial peace. AIRF is also engaged in social service activities like health check-ups, and blood and eye donation. They also organise seminars on safety. Their belief is that a satisfied workforce will ensure safety and efficient operations, and to achieve that objective they also undertake agitations, dharnas and strikes. They are affiliated to Hind Mazdoor Sabha.

Jayprakash Narayan and George Fernandes have been their past presidents.

National Federation of Indian Railways

The National Federation of Indian Railways (NFIR) was formed on May 16, 1948. It is affiliated to the Indian National Trade Union Congress (INTUC) of Congress party. It also has similar objectives as AIRF as far as staff matters are concerned. It was recognised in 1948.

Both the Unions have played a very constructive role in Railways operations. It was 1974 when all India rail strike was called by the Unions.

I have always considered the Unions as the ears and eyes of administration and have found them playing a positive role. One must have a positive mindset to deal with staff matters.

If we take care of the rightful entitlements of our staff, Unions will support in various other areas. There are however areas of conflicts, especially while trying to outsource certain activities of work or bringing in investment from the private sector to improve technology and improve operational efficiency in Railways, due to limited resources. But these issues also get resolved with dialogues and negotiations.

Key Decision Points for Success of Madhepura Project

- The first and the foremost decision taken by the Board was to transfer the project to Executive Director Electrical (Development) from Executive Director Mechanical (Project). This provided a higher level of understanding and commitment to drive this initiative forward. A passionate team was needed. Ved Mani Tiwari was posted on January 14, 2008. A team cannot be more than seven or less than three (ideal size being 5 or 5±2) for effective control and command. We were two officers and three Senior Supervisors.
- The business model and the project agreement were placed before the Union Cabinet on five occasions. This ensured the highest level of commitment of the Government of the day and enhanced the credibility of the process. Wherever there were departures from General Financial Rules (GFR), the Union Cabinet approved the provisions. As the period of the contract was spread over 19 years for maintenance and 11 years for the supply of locomotives, approval of the Union Cabinet was a big comfort to the prospective investors. It was believed that change of successive governments at the Centre would not lead to any dispute and lack of commitment to the project. Investors were looking for long-term engagement for making an investment in India.
- There was a mechanism available in the form of an Empowered Committee of Secretaries, approved by the Union Cabinet, to make changes in the Agreement to ensure competitive bidding. It would have been impossible to approach the Union Cabinet for making changes in the Agreement arising out of the pre-bid conferences in order to address the concerns of the bidders. Only a Cabinet approved committee could make changes in the documents.
- Risks perceived by the bidders were equitably managed. Whichever party is in the best position to manage the risk, risk must rest with that party. Risk of technology, long-term maintenance and creation of infrastructure for manufacture, maintenance, and training was to be managed by the investor. Risk of inflation, timely payment for the goods and services provided by the investor, provision of land for factory and depot, provision of electricity for the factory, and rail and road connectivity were to be borne by the Government.

- The concept of Learning Curve was introduced. Once indigenous production starts and crosses a threshold, after complete industrialisation, it is expected that productivity will improve. This would lead to a reduction in the price of the locomotive. From the fourth year of production, a reduction of 3 per cent of the price over third year price was introduced. The 3 per cent reduction continued for the rest of the production cycle, each year, till the 11th year of manufacture. This is what we had observed in ABB loco manufacture at CLW. It was one of the global best practices.
- The business model envisaged 26 per cent equity in the JV company by the Government to demonstrate its commitment. While remaining at arms-length from operations, the Government would ensure that the stated objectives of the business were adhered to. The 26 per cent equity enabled veto rights of the Government on certain pre-specified terms of the Agreement. Later, we found that this provided higher level of comfort to lenders. The JV company was provided loan on slightly softer terms due to presence of Government equity.
- The role of RDSO was limited to giving comments on the design documents of the JV company. There was no concept of RDSO approval. But homologation was to be ensured by RDSO. Safety was within the domain of Railways, therefore RDSO had to satisfy itself of the safety of the rolling stock with reference to laid down norms followed for Railways own production.
- Prices of spares were pegged to the price of the whole locomotive to contain maintenance costs.
- Diesel loco manufacturers were also enabled to participate in the bid to ensure higher level of competition. This alarmed Alstom, Bombardier and Siemens. But they had not participated in the bid in February 2009 and therefore their arguments were weak. Finally, diesel loco manufacturers did not participate.
- Impeccable honesty and integrity of the project team was very important.
- RFP opening was video recorded to ensure high level of probity.
- Selection of the right people for the right job is very important for the success of mega projects. Continuity of the decision making, and the people involved from beginning to end will ensure higher chance of success.
- Forfeiture of bid security of ₹40 crore ensured seriousness of bidders and therefore the final decision was taken within 15–20 days for the award of this major project.

Key Decision Points for the Turnaround of Dhanbad Division

- No departmental bias.
- Root cause analysis for every failure, especially accidents, derailments.
- Massive outreach (28,000 km inspection in 23 months) to meet the people and understand their difficulties.
- Management by walking to see things as they were and to take spot decisions.
- All Senior Supervisors met regularly, irrespective of their department, for clear communication directly from DRM.
- Improved work environment – yard lighting, yard cleaning, control office renovation, Station Masters provided with cash imprest to ensure cleanliness, arrange office stationery and petty items which generally demotivates if these are not available in time.
- Direct communication with Control – Staff at the Control Office could talk to me any time in 24 hours. That is what I drilled into their psyche, otherwise they were hesitant.
- Free access to staff to meet the DRM for redressal of grievances.
- Disciplined meetings each Monday with Branch Officers and coaching them in areas not clearly understood by officers.
- Environment of collaboration and commitment and no fear of failure.
- Dissensions handled upfront rather than circumventing them.
- Everyone encouraged to challenge the status quo and relinquish denial.
- No compromise with delivery, but freedom to maintain office time of their choice.
- Empowerment of frontline staff to stop a train if unsafe and spot reward.
- Rewards for outstanding performance across the spectrum – these were very motivating.
- No work was left pending for the next day as far as I was concerned.
- Officers not engaged in DRM's paperwork, especially inspection notes, etc.
- No industry allowed to enter personal space of DRM. Probity in public life given highest importance. Only officers were allowed to visit my residence.

- Annual Confidential Reports written in the presence of each officer.
- Played cricket matches with adjoining Divisions to improve interpersonal relations. Stadium improved with high mast light for night sports.
- Staff amenities and places like running rooms, crew lobbies and RPF barracks well-maintained.
- Took good care of my personal staff – TADK, PS, peons, staff car driver, saloon attendants and bodyguards.
- Lived the life of staff whenever there was an accident or major work like RRI in yard, where long hours and strenuous work was involved, to ensure that they were well taken care of with respect to food and refreshments.
- Met the Rajdhani drivers regularly to give them confidence that they must follow safety first and punctuality later. It took time for them to accept even what the DRM said, that they would not be questioned for slowing the speed of trains if there were cattle on rail track, as even that might cause an accident.
- Setting personal example; unless you have a high energy level and you are willing to go beyond the call of duty, do not expect people under you to do it.
- Excellent rapport with the State Government officers as I needed their support at odd hours in case of bomb blasts and whenever there were law-and-order problems.
- Excellent rapport with MPs and MLAs and Public Representatives of Passenger Amenities and Consultative Committees.
- Compassionate appointment was given highest priority.
- Staff benefit fund of ₹1 crore sanctioned each year, utilised in the same year.
- More than 3,000 new recruits issued appointment letters within a week with all the required activities like bank account, ID cards, medical card, etc., prepared and handed over in the camp, then and there.
- Achieving 100 million tonnes became a slogan which every member of staff, including their families, knew.
- The Women Welfare Organisation ensured no wasteful expenditure.
- Regularly visited Chinnamasta Temple at Rajrappa every 2–3 months or whenever my inner voice called for inner peace.
- Quite often narrated inspirational stories and success stories and listened to the success stories of the officers.

Key Decision Points for Successful Transformation of Railways

- Did not follow any hierarchy for crowd sourcing of ideas that needed consideration for empowerment and simplification of processes.
- Trust in the field officers was a big driver for higher financial and administrative delegation.
- Mitigation of fear perception of Vigilance was very important to bring delivery as the focus and remove any alibi. No one could hide behind Vigilance.
- Reducing the interdependencies was a key driver to cut down bureaucracy in the organization and therefore we drastically cut down the levels of decision making.
- Areas where there was dependence on the industry to do legitimate official work were legally brought out as a policy such as vehicles for all officers and SUV for supervisors in-charge, enhanced budget, and unit rate for arranging snacks, tea–coffee and lunch–dinners.
- Collaborated with Financial Commissioner, Member Engineering, Director General (Store), DG RPF, DG Health and Member Traffic in particular.
- Issue of Model Schedule of Powers on pan India basis that changed the overall environment and ignited trust in the Transformation Cell and therefore a large number of proposals poured in on how to improve further.
- Visit to all CTIs made a big change as the dissemination of change agenda was quite high.
- An ambience of a good, glass office, good furniture and the location in front of the Canteen in the Railway Board made a big impact.
- Roles, responsibilities and the functioning of the Cell were so well defined that no one could detract and drag the Cell officers into day-to-day routine work. Files of Transformation Cell were put up directly to Board Members and not routed through Directorates. What the Cell would not do was clearly defined.
- Workshops on Change Management were organised in different Zonal Railways. This played a big role in aligning people. It was a part of the communication exercise towards Change Management. All communications and delegations issued by the Cell were put on the website and therefore dissemination was very fast.

- Cell officers had full freedom to go on inspection anywhere in India.
- Focus on leadership skills for improving alignment – Inner Engineering and Leadership Programme at Isha Foundation Coimbatore, Emotional Intelligence for GMs and DRMs also played a key role.
- Transformation Lecture series by eminent speakers also brought focus on change to the centre stage.
- Every discipline of the organisation was looked at to improve – SOP was issued for RPF, Publicity and Services. The Medical department was of particular focus as it impacted the masses.
- Everyone believed he could contribute to change and therefore the whole organisation got galvanised in a short time.
- Never be afraid of conflict between the parties. Unless this is discussed upfront and resolved, nothing will move. Transformation Cell officers were not aligned on a number of issues but most of the issues were resolved after discussions.

Epidemic Defects

Whenever a defect occurs in 20 per cent or more of the population of a particular component, assembly or sub-assembly of the 12,000 HP locomotive over any rolling period of 36 months within the maintenance period, the Government will notify the same to the JV company, and such defect or deficiency will be classified as an Epidemic Defect. The company shall take actions and measures to rectify the same and submit the rectification plan to the Government.

Price 'P' of the Locomotive

The price to be bid by the prospective bidders while submitting their financial offers will be the price of 35 indigenous locomotives to be manufactured at Madhepura in the third year of supply. This price is referred as 'P' for ease of understanding.

This price is escalated by a factor of 1.1(110%) to arrive at the price of 5 imported locomotives (this will be 1.1P) to be supplied by the JV company within the first 2 years.

The price of 60 locomotives that will be supplied by the JV company in the 4th year of supply will be 97 per cent of the price P and we may be defined as 'P1'. Thus, the Price for the 5th year of supply will be 97 per cent of P1. This process will continue till the 11th year of supply of locomotives. There will therefore be a 26 per cent reduction in the price of locomotive in the 11th year of supply.

If Railways exercises the option to buy additional 200 locomotives after 11 years, the price will be 90 per cent of the Price of 11th year of supply.

Maintenance Fee for 13 Years

To ensure that all the prospective bidders consider the same opex, we decided to fix the maintenance fee for all the 13 years starting from a maintenance fee of:
- 1.25 per cent of p for the 1st and 2nd years of the maintenance;
- 3.25 per cent of the price of the locomotive for the relevant year for the 3rd, 4th, and 5th year of supply;
- 4.75 per cent of the price of the locomotive for the 6th year of supply;
- 3.25 per cent of the price of the locomotive for the 7th, 8th, 9th, 10th and 11th year of supply;
- 8.25 per cent of the price of the locomotive for the 12th year of supply; and
- 3.25 per cent of the price of the locomotive for the 13th year of supply

This ensured discovery of the least 'Total Cost of Ownership' for the project. Whosoever had bid the lowest P was therefore the successful bidder.

Madhepura Factory

The Madhepura Factory was incorporated as Madhepura Electric Locomotive Private Limited (MELPL) – a JV of Alstom France and Ministry of Railways, under the Company Act 2013.

It has a debt equity ratio of 70:30. Railways equity is 26 per cent and that of Alstom 74 per cent. Railways 26 per cent equity has been limited to ₹100 crore of a total investment of ₹1,300 crore, equity being around ₹390 crore.

Career Progression in Group 'A' services

1. Junior Scale (Assistant Secretary);
2. Senior Scale (Assistant Secretary, Senior Scale) – 4 years of service Divisional Officer;
3. Junior Administrative Grade (Dy Secretary) – 6 to 9 years of service Branch Officer;
4. Selection Grade (Director) – 13 years of service with the Branch Office;
5. Senior Administrative Grade (Joint Secretary) – 18 to 20 years of service HOD, ADRM, CWM, DRM (28 years plus);
6. Higher Administrative Grade (Additional Secretary) – 30 to 33 years of service PHOD, Principal ED, AGM;
7. Higher Administrative Grade plus (Special Secretary) – 35 years plus GMs, Additional Members, DG NAIR, RDSO;
8. Apex Grade (full Secretary) – 36 years plus Members, CRB.

> **What Is One Megawatt of Power?**
>
> A megawatt (MW) is a unit of measuring power that is equivalent to one million watts. As a rule of thumb, one MW of coal-based power plant can supply electricity to around 650 homes.
>
> An average Television (TV) is of 100 to 150 watts capacity. 1,000 watts is called as one kilowatt (KW), and 1,000 KW is 1 MW.
>
> Madhepura locomotive is of 9 MW (12,000 Horsepower) capacity

Emotional Intelligence EQi 2.0 Critically Analysed

Self-Regard

When I took over as DRM Dhanbad on East Central Railway on October 14, 2011, the safety track record of the Division was quite dismal. Overall health of the Division was not very satisfactory. The freight loading had been stagnant for few years. CRB had briefed me before my being relieved from Railway Board. In fact, I was briefed by various Executive Directors and senior officers of the Railway Board prior to my departure for Dhanbad that a number of infrastructure works were pending completion, and therefore the asset reliability was not satisfactory. This was leading to poor safety performance.

Within a span of three months of my taking charge of the Division, three serious rail accidents took place, all due to poor maintenance of the assets. There was a case of fire in the Doon Express wherein nine passengers had lost their lives. The situation was pathetic.

In early December 2011, I had told all my Branch Officers that I would like to empower all the employees to stop a train if they noticed anything unusual while train was running in front of them at any of the stations. Not only that, I would also like to give them spot award of ₹1,000, as a token of my appreciation every time they stopped a train to avert an accident. They could get as many awards of ₹1,000, as many times they would detect an unsafe event in a running train.

There was an immediate reaction against this. I was told that there would be serious disruption to train running. The arguments were that even for a flimsy reason the staff would stop trains and ask for the spot award of ₹1,000. The situation might go out of control. There could be genuine error of judgement and all the staff were not well trained in rolling stock practices. Performance of the Division was already compromised and such empowerment would further aggravate the situation.

By now I had visited the whole Division a few times and I had my assessment that unless I made safety every one's responsibility, with complete empowerment, it would not be possible to see a cultural change. There was a need to change the mindset. Safety needed to be the highest priority of everyone in the Division. The empowerment was therefore made, and the system of spot award announced.

Within 15 days we saw trains being stopped. We were feeling happy that the staff had been taking right decisions to identify correct reasons to stop trains. It was a major relief. A case of hot axle in a freight train, if it had gone unnoticed, would have caused serious dislocation to traffic by causing a major accident. It was detected by the train passing staff before the ghat section. It was a loaded train going towards Gaya. Gradually the spot award gained support even from staff. Every staff was very serious in taking a decision to stop a train, unlike what was initially expected that untrained staff would detain trains due to errors of judgement.

Over a two-year period, this empowerment paid rich dividends. Out of about 860 awards sanctioned on this account, not even one award was given for stopping a train without a genuine reason.

Everyone in the Division started realising that this was one big change that improved the safety record of the Division as all staff and supervisors became ambassadors of safety. It became a mass movement. The mindset of the people changed.

The Division got the overall safety shield from the GM for being the best performing Division of the Zone in the following year, that is, 2012-13.

I assign this decision to the sub-scale 'Self-regard' due to my inner strength and conviction that the mindset to become safety conscious cannot be achieved unless everyone in the field, irrespective of the hierarchy, felt on similar lines. And for taking this decision, no one else could contribute. There was a general feeling was that it would jeopardise the Division's performance. And therefore, I had to be all alone in taking this decision. It was out of my self-confidence, after seeing the ground realities and the spate of accidents. I was to be accountable for this decision. It paid rich dividends.

Self-Actualisation

On October 18, 2017, a day before Deepavali, major reform initiatives were approved by the full Board and issued by the Transformation Cell at 8 p.m. There was euphoria amongst all GMs, DRMs and other field officers across Indian Railways as no one had ever imagined that such a wide-ranging empowerment and delegation (both financial and administrative) of powers would be made to the field units. This had not been experienced in the past 30–35 years of our service. The following day was Deepavali.

At 11 p.m. on October 18 (the same day), the Financial Commissioner (FC) rung me up and asked me to keep the letter conveying 'empowerment delegations of powers' in abeyance till it was further examined afresh by the Finance Department. He had been briefed by the Finance Officers in the field against such large-scale delegations. The examination was to be done after the Deepavali celebrations. He wanted everything communicated at 8 p.m. to be put on hold. Within three hours, the reforms were to be reversed. The whole night I was thinking that this organisation needed a big 'change of mindset' if the situation was to improve.

The next morning (that is, on October 19) at 8 a.m. the FC again called me to keep the letter in abeyance, if not withdrawn. He further requested me that both the officers of Transformation Cell (who were signatories to the letter) must go to office and issue a letter jointly withdrawing the previous day's letter. It was simply intriguing to me. But I kept my cool and heard the FC without making any commitment. Within the next 15 minutes, Sanjeeb Kumar, my Executive Director (Accounts) Transformation Cell, informed me that the Additional Member Finance (AM/F) also wanted him to go to the office and issue a letter withdrawing the previous day's communication. At this stage I told him not to do any such thing till I told him so.

Around 9 a.m., I called up Ashwini Lohani, CRB, and informed him that I wanted to meet him urgently. He instantly asked me to come to his residence. As soon as I reached, I got a call from AM/F asking me to withdraw the letter.

I briefed the CRB and told him that if this decision was reversed, the Transformation Cell should also be wound up. The change that we were aspiring could not be managed under such humiliating circumstances. We needed to make a hard decision. And right then.

In fact, I suggested that he should decide and convey firmly that this would not be tolerated. The CRB agreed with me completely and conveyed the same to the FC. By 10 a.m. on the day of Deepavali, the issue was settled, and it was decided that the empowerment and delegation that has been conveyed would stay firm. After settling the issue, I went back home.

From that day onwards, the Transformation journey continued, and we never looked back. Amazing works of unprecedented dimension were carried out by Transformation Cell during the next three-and-a-half years that I headed the Cell.

I assign this decision to the sub-scale 'Self-Actualisation' as by the time such bold decisions were taken, I had spent ten months as head of Transformation Cell, and I had realised that unless I engaged in such personally relevant and meaningful goals, my continuing with Transformation Cell would serve no purpose. If I could not contribute to improving service delivery by simplifying processes and reducing layers of decision making by empowering the field units, I needed to recommend dissolution of the Cell. In any case, Railways were facing adverse public reactions. Any change in decision making would demoralise the team and defeat the big initiative.

Emotional Self Awareness

On an eventful day, one of the staff of Loco Shed Kanpur, Sitaram Shukla, died while performing shunting operations inside the Shed. As a matter of fact, the circumstances were quite suspect. There were hush-hush talks of suicide. He had strained family relations. I did not pay heed to any of these things. For me, it was an accident of a staff on duty. A staff agitation followed. The Shed had a staff strength of about 1,100. This agitation took a wild turn, and all staff went on a dharna (sit-in) to block mainline rail traffic in front of the Area Control Office in the Juhi Goods Yard of Kanpur. The whole train movement on the Delhi–Howrah route came to a grinding halt.

Whenever a staff dies while on duty, ex-gratia is paid immediately.

I reached the Loco Shed at 5.30 a.m. as soon as I came to know about the incident. It was summer season.

By 11 a.m., we paid ex-gratia of ₹15,000 to his wife while the body of the deceased was still in the Railway Hospital. The Railway Hospital completed all the paper formalities and sent the dead body to the Civil Hospital Kanpur by 12 noon.

In the meantime, M.N. Chopra, the DRM Allahabad, called me over phone to inform me about the dharna in Juhi Goods Yard. The Shed's staff were alleged to be involved in this agitation. I was informed that more than 1,000 men were squatting and blocking rail movement. Some outsiders had also gathered there. The Railways residential colony was nearby.

Since the body of Sita Ram Shukla had been sent for post-mortem, I decided to go to the place of agitation. I decided not to take any police force or any escort whatsoever with me. I had just my driver Aijaz Ahemad, and Rakesh Srivastava, my Supervisor.

As soon I reached Juhi Goods Yard, sloganeering started: *'Rail Prashashan Murdabad, Inqilab Zindabad'* (death to rail administration and long live revolution). It did not bother me.

Civil police were already there in large numbers, along with the DSP leading the force. The DSP asked me about the action to be taken. I asked him to wait and not do anything. I could not have asked the DSP to use force as the people blocking the rail movement were predominantly my own staff and were supposed to give output every day in the electric loco shed.

Any police action would have resulted in injuries to the staff and registering of a police case, which would have been to the detriment of the peace and industrial relations within the Shed's ecosystem. The staff who were so dear to me would have faced the wrath of the police, as well as other disciplinary actions. The Shed's environment which had been so cordial all through, would never be the same again. It would also have been the end of my stay at this place as it would become impossible for me to command the same respect and response any further. I would have sought transfer on my own. These feelings were at the back of my mind.

In the meantime, I was able to identify some of my staff. A few driver's line boxes were lying there. I asked Aijaz and Rakesh to make a raised platform using the driver's line boxes to enable me to address the crowd. So boxes were kept one over the other to make a raised platform and I climbed on top of them to address the people. The DSP was standing by my side, quietly.

I requested all the people to come closer so that I could brief them about the incident, the actions already taken and the actions that I proposed to take over next 15-20 days. The sloganeering stopped. People were willing to listen to me. I informed everyone in a humble tone that what had happened was tragic and sad, but I wanted to assure all of them that best possible actions would be taken to set an example for others to follow in such tragic incidents. Kanpur Shed had been a shining example of performance in Indian Railways and rated as the best Shed. It was therefore incumbent upon all of us to maintain that pride. We should not give any chance to dent that image.

I gave the assurance of a job to the ward of the deceased, house to the family and all payments within 15-20 days. This was what the staff wanted the administration to commit. Some of the staff had been apprehensive. The case could as well be considered as suicide. In case of suicide, the case would get dealt with differently for compensation and all other benefits.

As soon as I committed to the compassionate appointment, it struck a connect with the crowd and made an impact. I then requested all the staff to go back to the Shed and complete the day's work. I also told them that no action would be taken if the pending work was completed before they left in the evening after duty at 5 p.m.

The crowd slowly started leaving the track and within 10–15 minutes they allowed train movement to continue.

I then went to the post-mortem house to ensure quick release of the body of Sitaram Shukla.

I assign this decision to the sub-scale 'Emotional Self-Awareness' as I was able to understand the emotions of the staff engaged in the dharna. I was convinced of myself since I had worked for a long time at that place with the highest degree of integrity, ethics and probity in public life. I had always walked the talk, and therefore I was able to connect with the agitating staff and be understood by them. My words meant my gentleman's commitment. Carrying an escort never crossed my mind as I had done no harm to the people and therefore there was no reason why someone would harm me. And therefore, I went alone.

Emotional Self Expression

There was a flash strike by Guards in the Gomoh lobby (lobby is a place where Guards are allotted trains to work, as per roster). This led to disruption of train movement from 11 p.m. to 2 a.m. The strike was called due to non-payment of arrears of employees for a long time and one of my officers had behaved rudely with the Guards over phone. This was resolved by promising that the cause of strike would be resolved as soon as possible. The concerned officer who had an altercation with the Guards was asked to apologise on the day of the strike itself. Thereafter train movement resumed.

The following day, about 40 Guards came in a procession to my office. This happened to be a Saturday. All of them were seated in a conference room and each of them was allowed to put his point of view in a respectful manner. Once everyone had spoken, I told them that while the reason for resentment was genuine, no one had the authority to disrupt train operations and stop train movement on such a matter. It was also communicated to them that if such an event happened in the future, strong disciplinary action would be taken, which might include break in service. However, I told them that no disciplinary action was being taken simply because the demand for payment of arrears was justified. I also assured that every possible action would be taken to arrange payment of arrears to the employees of about ₹40 crore, pending for a few years.

The matter was settled, and money was arranged after completing the paperwork.

I assign this incident to the sub-scale 'Emotional Self Expression' as I was able to verbally communicate that what was legitimately due for the staff, would be given by the administration. But what they had done was against any acceptable behaviour and would be dealt with sternly in the future. This was done as I had always kept my words. It was well-received by the guards. Despite pressure from the Headquarters, I did not take action against the staff as their grievance was genuine and the behaviour of my officer was not in keeping with the sentiments of the staff. My officer had to apologise. This helped in resolving the matter.

Assertiveness

A presentation was made to Shri Sadananda Gowda and Shri Manoj Sinha, the two Ministers of State for Railways, in September 2014 on one of the biggest Make-in-India and Public Private Partnership (PPP) projects of setting up a factory to manufacture the world's most powerful electric locomotives at Madhepura, Bihar. Full Board was also present during the presentation.

This project had been languishing for more than six years; and on some count or the other the project had got stalled. PPP was however a high priority of the Modi Government.

At the start of the presentation itself, after giving the background of the project, I humbly submitted that if the intention of the Railways was to run freight trains like bullock carts at 22 to 23 kmph, the Madhepura project was not required. This was definitely a bitter truth but was told upfront. The top bureaucracy of Railways and the Ministers understood the message.

I was simply driving a point home that unless we took it seriously, the project would not move forward, and we would be wasting huge resources on the project.

Some Board Members in fact had a smile on their face as what I mentioned was a harsh reality. The project was given a go ahead and from then onwards we did not look back. The project was awarded to Alstom France on November on 30, 2015.

I assign this action to the sub-scale 'Assertiveness' as I openly communicated my feelings and beliefs that there was a need to look for a new technology keeping in view the situation in the Railways. Speed of freight trains were really low But all this was mentioned in a context, as the Ministers needed to understand the hard facts. Nothing could have been a better place than in front of the full Board. It was not offensive as Members of the Board agreed and supported the arguments.

Independence

A bomb blast took place near Parasnath (around 25 km from Dhanbad) on the Howrah–Delhi route during my tenure as DRM Dhanbad.

Bomb blasts were generally the handywork of Maoist Communist Centre (MCC). I, along with my team of Divisional officers and the Superintendent of Police Dhanbad, went to the site of bomb blast at 3 a.m., breaking all the protocols and the precedence wherein any site of the bomb blast was approached only after sunrise. This was an age-old practice. We however left for the site in the middle of night.

When we started from Dhanbad by an ART, and were on way to Parasnath, some gunshots were heard. Everyone believed that Maoists had started firing on ART. There was a panic inside the coach in which we were travelling.

Everyone had been apprehensive about my decision to go to the site in the dead of night. I wanted to ensure faster restoration, and also break the age-old practice. I kept my cool and asked SP Dhanbad to get in touch with his team on the ground near Parasnath and Gomoh to understand about movement of the Maoists. The train had stopped in the midst of the jungle.

After about ten minutes, it became clear that a detonator, which would have been kept on the rail track, had burst due to the movement of our train engine over it. This would have been kept by the Guard of the preceding train to warn the driver of the next approaching train. This is the safety protocol followed on Railways.

I saw the mood of the staff and the officers travelling by ART changing. There was a sense of relief and comfort amongst all present.

There was a risk in going to the site at night, but then the benefit was to restore the traffic quickly and change the mindset. As soon as we reached the site, SP Dhanbad gave the clearance and the staff started repairing the broken track. We were able to restore normalcy by 8 a.m.

It was an amazing experience for all the staff and officers. They were very upbeat as they had restored the traffic in such a short time. It would have otherwise taken at least four to five hours more.

I assign this action to the sub-scale 'Independence' as this decision did not gel with the precedence of handling such cases. It was self-directed. I could not have been guided by the emotions of others as it was to beak the age-old tradition. But I had to be at the forefront of this change. I therefore decided to go to the site myself. My personal relations with DG Police Jharkhand enabled me to have SP Dhanbad accompany me to the site by ART for faster police clearance at site, otherwise the purpose of going to the site before sunrise would have been defeated. This was also needed to enthuse the team to break the tradition. It became a talk of the Division that first time ever SP of a city accompanied the ART to reach a bomb blast site.

Interpersonal Relations

Ashwini Lohani, as CRB, had huge a trust in me, and therefore he would approve many decisions and policy changes even on WhatsApp when he was on inspection in the field. There were occasions when he would want policy changes to be made and policy directives issued in one day while he would be in the field. Such decisions used to be ratified on file later, after his arrival in the office.

Similarly, I had a mutually satisfying relationship with A.K. Mital, CRB, who would go with my decisions, despite sometimes being a little unsure. One such decision was the production of electric locos at DLW Varanasi. DLW was a dedicated factory for manufacture of diesel locomotives and therefore starting of manufacture of electric locomotives at DLW was seen as an industrial relations problem. Moreover, this was the constituency of the Prime Minister of India. On the strength of my logic and assurance that I would personally take care due to the sensitivity of the issue, Mital agreed with my proposal to manufacture just two electric locomotives in January 2017.

Today, DLW is manufacturing only electric locos. Both these Chairmen had trust in me and we enjoyed good interpersonal relations. This had impact on the pace and quality of decisions.

I assign this decision to the sub-scale 'Interpersonal Relations' as, obviously, such relations allow you to scale up the decision making. I was lucky to have known the two Chairmen for a long time. Lohani was my next-door neighbour for a long time and therefore certain level of trust already existed. As regards A.K. Mital, he was my concerned Member more than two years earlier, and I had worked with him very closely for six months. Both these things helped.

Empathy

One Master Craftsman, Badri Nath Dutta, of Carriage and Wagon department at Dhanbad, died on January 31, 2013, the day of his retirement on superannuation. He had attained the age of 60 years already on 9 January. There were talks that he was under serious stress since none of his children were able to get settled with any job or regular business. Keeping in view the circumstances, I decided to appoint his son on compassionate grounds. There was no rule prohibiting such an appointment. The mood of the Personnel Department was ambivalent for such an appointment as he had already reached 60 years of his age. Manoj Kumar, my Head of Personnel Department, was quite positive, but needed speaking orders on file. He was quite clear that we would not be in breach of any rule. But such a thing had not been done earlier, or we were not aware of any precedence. I appointed his son Gopal Kumar Dutta as Trains Clerk, on April 1, 2013.

Ashutosh Chaurasia was the Assistant Engineer posted at Gomoh station and was responsible for the track maintenance. He met with an accident in the section while he was on an inspection of the track in Dhanbad-Koderma section when his Push Trolley was hit by a locomotive. We shifted him from site to Dhanbad and got him admitted to Mission Hospital, Durgapur by depositing ₹5 lakh required by the hospital as an advance. This money was paid by the Officers Club on my advice. He had been badly injured in the accident and had fractured his knee.

This was done to save his limb and life. He underwent radical surgery at the hospital. The Club was a private affair of the Divisional officers. The money could not be reimbursed to the Club quickly. Officers were feeling a little unhappy about the decision that DRM had used their Club's money for the treatment of Ashutosh. Following the official procedure at the time of the incident to get sanction for this treatment would have led to serious delays in treatment and would have been posed risk to Ashutosh's life. The Club's money was reimbursed 6–7 months later, but we were able to save the life of a young officer who was so loyal and devoted to his duty that he tried his best, even in face of an imminent danger to his life, to extricate the Push Trolley from the track to avert an accident.

Son of Sitaram Shukla, who died while performing duty in Kanpur Shed, was appointed despite the fact that his claim for appointment to Group C was found fake due to fabricated certificate for tenth standard. Had this not been done, there would have been double jeopardy for the family because an improper certificate would have led to the arrest of the son. I went out of my way to convince the Welfare Department to process a fresh for an appointment in the lowest possible category – Group D.

I assign these decisions to the sub-scale 'Empathy' as I was able to put myself in their shoes and then realise what kind of emotions would the next-of-kin of the deceased be undergoing while trying to manage the trauma of the tragedy. The remote possibility of suicide in the case of Sitaram Shukla and B.N. Dutta, which was being talked about, was also in the background. I wanted to let the families of the two employees have all the possible help that is normally rendered by the administration under 'death on duty' as a demonstration of compassion on my part. This would result in a smooth flow of settlement and a closure to the tragedy.

Social Responsibility

A school bus was arranged for the wards of the employee from Staff Benefit Fund for commuting between Gajhandi and Koderma. Hearing aids and laptops were given to the girl-children of railway employees.

Study centres were opened for preparing the wards of railway employees for competitive examination. Free books were made available at these centres.

In one of the fire accidents (Doon Express), seven passengers lost their lives. This was jointly witnessed and recorded by the officials of the State Government of Jharkhand and the Railways. Seven officials had signed that joint statement.

However, on discovering that two more people had succumbed in the fire tragedy in the ill-fated Doon Express, a team was constituted to confidentially visit the hometowns of the claimants. Based on their reports, ex-gratia of ₹5 lakh was paid to each of the two families. They would have otherwise suffered by not getting the ex-gratia immediately and getting into prolonged litigation. They would have gone to Railway Claims Tribunal to seek their claim, which might have taken years together.

I assign these decisions to the sub-scale 'Social Responsibility', as welfare of the next-of-kin of the deceased was uppermost in my mind to resolve the matter. They would have suffered double jeopardy if this had not been done. Body bags were filled in my presence. What was haunting me was that maybe we were not able to identify more casualties due to the extent and magnitude of the fire, and therefore were not able to identify the other two deaths. Not finding a solution would have generated lot of guilt within myself. I was therefore genuinely working out an out-of-the-box solution. It was also a question of serving a larger 'public faith' in the government machinery. We needed to go beyond the constraints. The very fact that everyone had signed on a joint note was not to be seen as something cast in stone if new facts came to my notice. I therefore worked for the greater good of the society. The solution worked out well.

Problem Solving

There was a flash strike at the Barwadih and Barkakana crew booking lobbies as one e locomotive Driver was taken hostage by Maoists and was made to climb the locomotive roof in Central Industrial Chord section and asked to remove the metallised carbon strip from the pantograph. This happened at night.

No Driver was prepared to work trains during the night without police escort thereafter. The matter was reported to DGP Railways and DGP Jharkhand over phone and followed up by a personal letter. This letter was pasted at all the 12 lobbies of the Division to convey my concern for the staff. The matter was resolved and the culprits apprehended after two days.

The response received from the DGP Railways was also brought to the notice of all the Drivers through the lobbies. The letter was pasted on all the crew lobbies. An extremely sensitive matter was thus resolved satisfactorily.

I assign these actions to the sub-scale 'Problem Solving'. The emotions of the Drivers were very high as one of their colleagues had been made hostage in the dead of the night while performing his legitimate duty under most challenging circumstances. It was the mental alertness of the Driver that the pantograph was lowered by him before climbing the roof of the locomotive. It would have been fatal to his life if he had got electric shock of 25 KV. I therefore needed to go beyond filing a normal FIR. I spoke to the Chief Secretary, the DGP and DGP Railways to register my profound concern with the State machinery responsible for dealing with law-and-order problems. Not only that, I decided to make the official communication public as nothing could have been confidential. It was a matter of safety of my most crucial set of staff, responsible for running trains. This helped in conveying my feelings to my own staff and sensitising everyone in the State Government. It helped to resolve the issue. Within two days the culprits were apprehended. This was also conveyed to all concerned through notice in lobbies. We were able to solve an emotive issue of the safety of driving staff.

Reality Test

During a visit to Japan in December 2010 for finalisation of the scope of Special Terms of Economic Partnership (STEP), linked to the soft loan by JICA for the Western DFC, negotiations were held for 3½ days without reaching an agreement. On the fourth and final day of our stay at Japan, at about 10 p.m., the Japanese side agreed not only for supplying 9,000 HP locomotives for Western DFC, but also for undertaking their comprehensive maintenance, and setting up a Maintenance Depot at Rewari, Haryana. We were a delegation of four officers and the negotiations pertaining to other items on the agenda like signalling, railway track and electrification, had concluded. The project pertaining to 9,000 HP locomotive was the biggest of the total deal. If such an agreement had not been reached, the project would not have brought dividends of new technology in a comprehensive manner. Ultimately, we succeeded.

When the Transformation Cell was constituted, I was asked to shift from Rail Bhawan to Pragati Maidan for operationalising the Cell. But I persuaded the CRB and convinced him that staying within the proximity of the Railway Board complex would be vital for the success of the initiative. Finally, I got a new Transformation Office constructed at an estimated cost of ₹1.2 crore. I was sure that no transformation journey could be navigated without being in proximity of the decision-making body – the Railway Board Members. This was finally agreed to, and the Transformation Cell delivered on large number of reform processes, something which had not happened in 40 years of Railways history.

I assign these decisions to the sub-scale 'Reality Test' as it was the very objective in my understanding of the technology that we were looking for. This was to serve Railways for the next generation, and therefore a long-term hand holding by the technology provider was a must. This was also to ensure management of risk in the most appropriate manner. As regards setting up office in Rail Bhawan, I was able to visualise the need for a high level of interactions between the Board Members and the officers of the Cell. This would not have been possible without being in proximity. There was no personal bias, rather it was for the success of the initiatives.

Impulse Control

There was unprecedented rain in Kanpur which led to complete flooding of the Kanpur Shed, including submerging of an Underfloor Wheel Lathe, a machinery and equipment which was very vital for the working of the Shed. The reason for the flooding was not cleaning the drain running by the side of the Shed. The Medical Department was supposed to do this work, and therefore the doctors were responsible.

Once this news reached Northern Railway HQ at New Delhi, there was quite a bit of pressure to fix the responsibility for this catastrophe. But I decided to seek cooperation from everybody to reach normalcy quickly in the Shed. I also decided to spend ten days in a row at the site of the Underfloor Wheel Lathe to quickly bring the important machine back to work.

Despite serious pressure from all concerned, I decided not to blame anybody as my view was that such unprecedented rains were primarily an act of God.

I assign this a sub-scale 'Impulse Control' as it would have been easier to ward off the pressure from Headquarters and assign blame to the people responsible for the unprecedented situation and make my own life comfortable. But I decided to seek cooperation from the doctors and bear the pressure. Doctors knew that they were responsible for the problem. Their commitment increased many folds to do their job and clean the drain even faster and be more loyal to Railways in the future. Allocating blame would have resulted in spoiling the relations for a very long time. Whatever damage was to happen had happened and I had plans to mitigate it by simply employing the resources of the Shed and rectify the machine. This was seen as magnanimity by the Shed.

Flexibility

The work of RRI was pending for ten years at Dhanbad. The plans and drawings were not getting finalised. There was no agreement as to how the yard should be re-modelled. I made more than a hundred visits to the yard to accommodate everyone's point of view and move forward, while remaining focused on the ultimate outcome, which was to improved safety. Everyone's wish-list was accommodated, and the work was completed in April 2013.

I assign this to the sub-scale 'Flexibility' as many times during our visits to the Dhanbad yard, we had to re-do the plans which were agreed upon on earlier days. This generated positive orientation about the over-delayed RRI, as most suggestions were accommodated. If this had not been done, the negative atmosphere created around RRI would have continued, and I too would have passed my tenure without any long-term inputs to improve safety.

Stress Tolerance

The GM's Special Train got derailed while we were returning after an Annual Inspection of a section which had not been inspected for 13 years. Annual Inspection is considered a big event. Even after the derailment, I maintained my cool, only to ensure that the success of the day's inspection should not be lost sight due to the mishap of a derailment at the last moment when we were about to reach Dhanbad and enjoy the Club evening. Investigations and corrective actions were taken the next day, after the Headquarters inspection team had left Dhanbad.

Similarly, on the day of fire on the Doon Express, which was the first day of Parliament working, on November 22, 2011, we decided not only to restore the traffic but also to pay ex-gratia to the passengers quickly, while they were still travelling to their destination and were in the train.

I assign this to the sub-scale 'Stress Tolerance' as both situations were unprecedented and would have led to demoralising the whole team which would have been to the detriment of the Division. Bearing the stress, motivating the team to do better, and converting the tragedy into a virtue would make people remember the event in a much more positive manner. This allowed people to work with more focus and deliver higher results. I always believed that staff would work better if they were given a more congenial environment. The safety record of the Division improved more than anyone ever thought it could.

This helped in faster restoration of the traffic after the Doon Express fire tragedy. As regards Annual Inspection, I took the blame of the derailment on myself, as head of the Division, and therefore the Club event was well managed where families were involved and the focus remained on the inspection, which had been well conducted. It reduced the stress on the Branch Officers. The Division did its highest loading in 2011-12. All this, however, did not reduce the concern that the officers were feeling about the incident, on their own.

Optimism

A total of 400 ideas came before the due date while organising the Parivartan Sangoshthi. I was sure that some of these ideas could be taken to the next level of reforms, and therefore made 12 groups of GMs. The ideas received earlier were given to all the 12 groups, the groups were made heterogenous, and no one knew in advance about the composition of the group. There was an unprecedented alignment of the views. The two most important decisions of the re-organisation of eight services into one service – Indian Railway Management Service – and constituting Board Members based on functions, with the CRB designated as CRB & CEO, were taken by the group. These decisions were later ratified by the full Board in the meeting held at Pravasi Bhartiya Kendra itself. This was subsequently approved by the Cabinet.

I assign this to the sub-scale 'Optimism' as I had a firm belief that right-thinking people, if collected under one roof and allowed to express themselves freely in a congenial atmosphere, would be able to reach positive outcomes.

Acknowledgements

The idea of writing a book germinated in October 2018 after a chance meeting with Rajeshwar Upadhyaya, the master trainer of Emotional Intelligence (EQi) in India, in my office at Rail Bhawan. He suggested to me that I should write a detailed account of my professional journey in the Railways. My journey of writing this book started with that. I wrote about a couple of key projects and passed the output to Rajeshwar. He gave me comprehensive feedback on each aspect of my experiences. That was very vital in motivating me to write further. It finally turned out that the narrative could easily be published as a book. I therefore owe this book to Rajeshwar.

Various assignments that I handled in the Railways were unique and quite interesting. This was my intrinsic motivating force to do well in the organisation.

Veda Thakur was my efficiency multiplier. She was my Senior Principal Private Secretary. She had tremendous capacity to transcribe directly on the desktop with ease and enthusiasm. This work used to be done after the official business was over. In my entire career, rarely did I have a private secretary with such dexterity. I would like to convey my heartfelt thanks to Veda for her help.

Jyoti Dutta, a brilliant English teacher in Kolkata, read the entire manuscript several times and had several Zoom meetings with me to understand the book in detail. She suggested a few changes, and I agreed with her. I thank her for this help.

B.K. Singh, Chief Engineer, East Central Railway and Ved Prakash, Group General Manager (Operation) DFCCIL, who worked with me in the Dhanbad Division, provided all the pictures and intricate details of the yester years whenever I needed them. I would like to thank both of them. Without their support it would not have been possible to complete this book.

Israr Ahmad and Romit Roy were my immediate support to collate the pictures. This has allowed me to suitably present the antecedents to the reader.

Dr Phil Zerrillo, the Deputy Dean ISB, introduced me to Dr Saumya Sindhwani, Professor at ISB, who in turn introduced me to

Acknowledgements

Mr Surendra Ghai of Sterling Publishers, for doing the most important part – publishing the book. I would like to thank Phil and Saumya.

Sanjiv Sarin, an exceptionally brilliant editor, edited the book with a finesse that I cannot express in words. He had an eye for smallest detail. I simply accepted all his suggestions – some of them were vital. Sanjiv displayed amazing patience and the highest level of professional competence. From the core of my heart, I thank him for his untiring efforts in bringing out this book.

Nothing could have happened without Mr Surendra Ghai, CMD, Sterling Publishers. He invited me to his place a few times and discussed the entire scheme of publication. I thank Mr Ghai for his hospitality and consideration to publish this book.

My mother and father, who unfortunately passed away in May 2021, were a continuous source of inspiration and were eagerly waiting to see this book published. Their desire will be fulfilled while they are not there. God's wish!

I would like to thank my parents-in-laws, my brothers and sisters, brothers-in-laws, and sister-in-law without whose support I would not have been able to traverse this journey, that I cherish so deeply.

Finally, Dr Suchitra, my wife, who was not only an ocean of inspiration while I was writing this book, but is the entire reason for my success in the Railways. She facilitated whatever I achieved in my entire career. Neither did she ever interfere in my professional work, nor did she expect any assistance on the domestic front, even though she was an extremely busy, senior professional, working in Guru Gobind Singh Indraprastha University, Delhi. I have a special debt to her which I can never repay.

My son was an invisible driver (like Saraswati, the legendary river at Sangam, Prayag) in my professional journey of the last two decades. He was extremely decent as a child, as an adolescent and as a young professional. His only demand as a child used to be 'show me a locomotive/simulator' as he had an astronomical fascination for trains. The idea of pursuing a PhD came to mind when I attended his graduation ceremony at Oxford University in 2016. I was amazed to see Guthlac Ceri Klaus Peach, a 72-year-old man, receive his Doctorate Degree at the start of the ceremony. My son kept reminding me to pursue academics after my superannuation. I would like to thank him and bless him all the success in life.

At the end, I would like to thank the entire family of railwaymen and women, my friends, my colleagues, my seniors and my bosses who gave me full freedom and an opportunity to serve the great Indian Railways for over 37 years.